Don't Need No Thought Control

Don't Need No Thought Control

Western Culture in East Germany and the Fall of the Berlin Wall

Gerd Horten

berghahn
NEW YORK·OXFORD
www.berghahnbooks.com

First published in 2020 by
Berghahn Books
www.berghahnbooks.com

© 2020, 2024 Gerd Horten
First paperback edition published in 2024

All rights reserved. Except for the quotation of short passages for the purposes of criticism and review, no part of this book may be reproduced in any form or by any means, electronic or mechanical, including photocopying, recording, or any information storage and retrieval system now known or to be invented, without written permission of the publisher.

Library of Congress Cataloging-in-Publication Data

A C.I.P. cataloging record is available from the Library of Congress
Library of Congress Cataloging in Publication Control Number: 2020937152

British Library Cataloguing in Publication Data

A catalogue record for this book is available from the British Library

ISBN 978-1-78920-733-0 hardback
ISBN 978-1-80539-146-3 paperback
ISBN 978-1-80539-557-7 epub
ISBN 978-1-78920-734-7 web pdf

https://doi.org/10.3167/9781789207330

For my parents:
Margaretha and Hubert Hortent

And my siblings:
Adelheid, Manfredt, Inge, Maria, Stephan,
and families

Contents

List of Illustrations   viii

Acknowledgments   x

Introduction. Disempowering a Dictatorship: Media and Consumer Culture in East Germany   1

Chapter 1. Successful Media Campaigns in East Germany in the 1960s and 1970s: The Vietnam War and the 1972 Olympics   19

Chapter 2. Fade Out: Hollywood Movie Imports and the Cultural Surrender of the GDR Film Control in the 1970s and 1980s   54

Chapter 3. The Westernization of East German Television in the 1970s and 1980s   88

Chapter 4. Fighting against All Odds: GDR Popular Music and Youth Radio in an International Context   123

Chapter 5. Western Consumer Culture or Bust: Intershops and East German Consumption Policies in the 1970s and 1980s   160

Epilogue. Out with the Old—in with the New? *Wende, Ostalgie*, and the Serpentine Unification   199

Bibliography   229

Index   251

Illustrations

Figure 1.1. GDR Vietnam Solidarity Committee, 1969   25

Figure 1.2. Anti–Vietnam War demonstration in East Berlin, Unter den Linden, late 1968   29

Figure 1.3. Reception for North Vietnamese representatives in East Berlin, 6 February 1973   33

Figure 1.4. Entry of the East German Olympic team into the Munich Stadium, 26 August 1972   36

Figure 1.5. IOC president Avery Brundage visits Leipzig and other GDR cities in July 1969   38

Figure 1.6. Erich Honecker and the GDR minister of sports Manfred Ewald hosting a reception for East German Olympic athletes   43

Figure 2.1. Capitol Movie Theater in Leipzig, 18 November 1983   58

Figure 2.2. Movie audience in the Capitol Movie Theater in Leipzig, 28 November 1984   64

Figure 2.3. East German film poster for *One Flew Over the Cuckoo's Nest*, which premiered in the GDR in 1978   72

Figure 2.4. Movie theater in Wurzen, East Germany, 1990   77

Figure 3.1. Scene from *Our Dear Fellow Men*   95

Figure 3.2. Scene from *Retired People Are Always Busy*   99

Figure 3.3. Store for radios and televisions in Bad Salzungen, March 1974 — 104

Figure 4.1. The Pudhys performing on GDR television on New Year's Eve in 1984 — 128

Figure 4.2. Roving groups of rock fans in the 1970s and 1980s — 132

Figure 4.3. Graffiti on a GDR bus stop — 137

Figure 4.4. Springsteen concert in East Berlin, July 1988 — 149

Figure 5.1. Queuing shoppers in front of a Leipzig grocery store — 166

Figure 5.2. Customers at bakery counter in Berlin, 7 August 1985 — 170

Figure 5.3. Delikat store in East Berlin in 1969 — 174

Figure 5.4. Intershop in Magdeburg, 1984 — 182

Figure 5.5. HO Store in Berlin, 25 November 1973 — 188

Figure 6.1. "Marxismus to Markismus," 1990 — 202

Figure 6.2. "Ossi," 1990 — 207

Figure 6.3. "Menschen-Mauer" (People-Wall), 1996 — 216

Acknowledgments

Although my professional engagement with East Germany has emerged relatively late in my professional career, it most certainly was spawned by several trips to East Germany in the early 1980s when I was a student at the University of Heidelberg. One weeklong stay in the GDR in the fall of 1982 was particularly memorable because of the in-depth, contradictory, and at times perplexing experiences our group of students made while traveling from city to city in East Germany. On the morning of our first day, for example, a painter working on the outside of our youth hostel called down to us, "Don't believe everything you hear!" Having grown up in West Germany with the stereotypical image of an East German dictatorship firmly implanted in my mind, I was surprised by this statement and the potential risk he was taking. As the week went on, and with limited knowledge of the workings of the GDR society at the time, our official visits, scheduled discussions, and private, spontaneous conversations left me confused and slightly bewildered about this "other Germany." My interest in the former East Germany was rekindled when I returned to the reunited Germany and Berlin on a regular basis many years later. I wondered what had actually been going on behind the scenes of the confusing façade that I encountered during the latter stages of the GDR and if I could I make some sense of the contradictory experiences I had observed so many years earlier.

Since I have focused on media history and cultural studies over the course of my professional career, the direction of my study emerged rather quickly once I embarked on the first serious research trip roughly ten years ago. During the intervening years, I have been the beneficiary of much direct support and helpful advice. On an institutional level, I want to thank Concordia University for several summer research grants, which allowed me to undertake the archival research for this book. Likewise, I owe a great amount of debt to our excellent library staff, who have supplied me with hundreds of books, articles, and hard-to-find sources and resources over the years. On my numerous research trips, I encountered equally knowledgeable and helpful librarians and archivists. First and foremost my thanks go to the staff of the Bundesarchiv Berlin-Lichterfelde, who were always welcoming and extremely supportive. Their colleagues at the Bundesarchiv Koblenz were just as professional and helpful. The other important archives and institutes where staff and archivists provided very valuable assistance were the following: Bundesarchiv-Filmarchiv (Berlin), Deutsches Rundfunkarchiv Babelsberg, Bibliothek der Hochschule für Film und Fernsehen "Konrad Wolf" (Berlin), Ministerium für Auswärtige Angelengenheiten der DDR (Berlin), Bundesbeauftragter für die Unterlagen des Staatssicherheitsdienstes der ehemaligen DDR (Berlin), and Friedrich-Ebert Stiftung Bonn—Archiv der sozialen Demokratie. Finally, I want to express my gratitude to two American archives, which hosted me for weeklong stays: the National Archives at College Park, Maryland, and the Archives at the University of Illinois, Urbana-Champaign.

Many fellow historians and researchers were of invaluable help as this project took shape. Principal among these were the reviewers for published articles that appeared in *German Studies Review* and *German History*, respectively, as well as many fellow presenters and commentators at a number of German Studies Association conferences over the last several years. And the three reviewers of the book manuscript deserve an enormous amount of credit for pointing out both the strengths and weaknesses of my project, as well as for providing me with extremely constructive commentaries and suggestions for improving and clarifying my core arguments. Every step along the way, my study was fine-tuned as new nuances and connections emerged. I would also be remiss if I did not single out Chris Chappell at Berghahn Books for his wise counsel and excellent guidance throughout the review process.

On a more personal level, I want to thank my wife Anette and our children for their support and patience as I pursued this project over the past ten years. Anette, in particular, deserves much credit for editing successive drafts of chapters and for providing reliably constructive feedback as this manuscript emerged over the years. Finally, my deep and lasting gratitude also goes to my parents as well as my siblings and their families in Germany, who hosted and spoiled me over the weekends of my many research trips. It is to them that I dedicate this book.

INTRODUCTION
Disempowering a Dictatorship
Media and Consumer Culture in East Germany

This book focuses on an intriguing paradox of East German society and the overall dynamics of the cultural Cold War. On the one hand, the German Democratic Republic (GDR) was a totalitarian regime that attempted to impose a monopoly as well as strict control over its media and culture and frequently asserted these ambitions with brutal efficiency and a complete disregard for the resulting casualties. On the other hand, especially in the 1970s and 1980s, the regime led by the Socialist Unity Party of Germany (Sozialistische Einheitspartei Deutschlands [SED]) condoned an ever-greater influx of especially Western popular and consumer culture that directly contradicted and undermined its own vision of a new and unique socialist culture. This paradox created a remarkably hybrid international popular culture in East Germany, especially during the late socialist era. In addition to its own unique cultural expressions, imports and influences from the West stood side by side with Soviet and Eastern European media and consumer products, all of which daily vied for the attention of the East German public. This diverse popular culture and "consumer socialism" stands in stark contrast to the popular notion of a closed-off, provincial socialist GDR state where all the power rested in the hands of the party elite.[1]

Even when it came to its own media, the SED leadership was never able to impose a tight political control or a strict homogeneity among official East German media expressions. What is often referred to as the "politically staged public sphere" (politisch inszenierte Öffentlichkeit) of the East German dictatorship developed cracks and frequently had to bend to overwhelming popular demand or the irrepressible intrusion of an internationally mediated culture. As in all of Europe, East and West, the GDR regime could not escape an unmistakable and seemingly unstoppable trend toward entertainment programming in the postwar decades—nor the erosive commercializing effects of this cultural trajectory. Likewise, in the spirit of engagement with the world at large and its own propagated openness to a variety of political perspectives, East German officials tolerated a tightly controlled satirical magazine, slightly varying editorial perspectives of newspapers, annual events like the international Leipzig Book Fair, as well as the introduction of video and computer games in the 1970s and 1980s. In addition, despite the fear of Stasi surveillance and recriminations, ordinary East Germans smuggled, duplicated, and hand-copied prohibited or hard-to-get books, albums, and other cultural products. Because of the variety of media sources and cultural expressions, East Germans became experts at reading between the lines, perennially skeptical of both Eastern and Western political news and adroit at forming their own opinions as well as individualized cultural preferences within the confines of a circumscribed surveillance state.[2]

As this introduction indicates, my book squarely sides with historians who have emphasized the limits of the totalitarian East German regime, while not overlooking the dictatorial practices and aspirations of the SED leadership throughout the existence of its socialist state. As Konrad Jarausch has emphasized, "The GDR [was] a contradictory system of both repression and every-day normalcy." Despite the steady expansion of the Stasi network of informants as well as the expulsion of political opponents and cultural critics, for example, there remained both direct and indirect ways for the East German population to talk and push back against the attempts by the SED regime to dictate and impose its exclusive political, economic, and cultural priorities. And East Germans pushed back in diverse ways, both large and small, from submitting complaints through the officially sanctioned petition process and participating in oppositional subcultures to shopping or exchanging currency on the black market and many more. As Andrew Port has aptly put it, despite the highly controlled GDR public sphere there was a surprising and widespread willingness to voice criticism in East Germany despite the intimidation and terror of Stasi surveillance: "There was no deafening silence of the lambs; in fact, many bleated quite vigorously." The East German people thus had limited influence and agency in their society—and not just in 1953 or the last few years before the fall of the Berlin Wall.[3]

Eigen-Sinn—translated as "gumption" or "a dogged and creative self-reliance"—and *Meckerkultur*—a culture of constant grumbling and dissatisfaction—were well-known and distinct aspects of East German society and could at times work as useful safety valves for the GDR regime. But individualized low-level dissent could also swell into a chorus of loud semi-public criticisms, which did get the attention of the SED leadership and repeatedly forced it into accommodations and course directions. Significantly aided by broader political, economic, and international developments, this constant pressure and criticism by the East German people produced limited but cumulatively significant results, which usually materialized not immediately and abruptly, but influenced their society and culture more like the proverbial bending of the arc of history. At best most East Germans only extended reluctant loyalty to their government, tolerating its political dominance and patronizing control rather than embracing it. And this grumbling acceptance implied a certain bargain. Sensitive to popular opinion and the potential for large-scale protests like the 1953 uprising, East German politicians knew that the stability of their regime was dependent on meeting the basic needs of the population and demonstrating gradual progress in the standard of living for ordinary people. The numerous crises these negotiations and protests provoked allowed East Germans—together with broader international developments—to steadily alter the course of East German history and change the nature of the socialist society and culture in ways that were subtle, but ultimately defining. Therefore, this constant churning of popular disinterest, dissonance, or—more rarely—outright dissent on the part of GDR citizens and groups produced long-term results that significantly contributed to the steady crumbling of the Berlin Wall and the eventual collapse of the East German regime.[4]

This book focuses on one specific arena of this larger bargain and a set of central questions: How did the popular demand for and increasing influence of Western mass media and consumer culture in the 1970s and 1980s contribute to the fall of the Berlin Wall? And equally significant, why did the East German government not just condone but increasingly embrace and showcase Western culture over its own socialist expressions in the late 1970s and 1980s? Clearly, allowing more Western cultural influences and consumer products into the GDR was not what the East German political elite desired or envisioned, since it directly challenged its own rule as well as cultural vision and often reflected poorly on East Germany in the always present comparison with its archenemy, the West German government (Federal Republic of Germany [FRG]).[5]

Meeting the demand for Western culture and consumer products on the part of the East German public was one of the key concessions that the SED leadership felt it had to make. In fact, negotiating Western media and consumer culture in East Germany is a prime example of the continuous accommodations between the East German leadership and its population. However, especially in the 1980s the GDR government no longer just condoned but frequently embraced and privileged Western media and consumer culture over its own socialist alternatives. This was done in a desperate attempt to preserve audiences for its media outlets to be sure and placate an ever-increasing popular demand. But just as important, these Western imports frequently secured financial resources needed to fund the continuation of Erich Honecker's consumer socialism. In fact, as this study argues, it was the dynamic and intricate interplay between popular demands, economic and fiscal crises, and the inexorable influences of Western media and consumer culture that cumulatively had a decisive impact on disempowering the GDR dictatorship during the late 1970s and 1980s and the eventual fall of the Berlin Wall.

Grudging accommodation was a common feature on the part of the majority of the GDR population, but it also reflected one of the main governing strategies of the GDR leadership. For the SED party officials, this accommodation most commonly came about as the result of popular pressure, against the increase of prices or the preference for Western films, for example, which was filtered up through the East German surveillance network. These course directions were made reluctantly by the GDR government, usually when no other options seemed available. It was generally a forced accommodation of spurts, stops, and reversals, carried out in an inconsistent manner. It should also be clear that this was a very uneven and asymmetrical relationship, in which the state always held the overwhelming power and did not meet the population halfway. But with an eye toward the unrest in Poland and other Eastern European countries in the 1970s and 1980s, the SED leaders certainly understood that their power had limits and that a certain quid pro quo with the people was necessary, especially when it came to meeting the basic needs of the population and securing a steadily increasing standard of living. As Erich Honecker frequently stated during the economic crises of the late 1970s and 1980s, the mood of the people had to remain as positive as possible, which meant that significant reductions in consumer goods or subsidies had to be avoided because of the potential for large-scale protests or an uncontrollable popular backlash.[6]

In fact, this policy of steady and often reluctant accommodations by the GDR leadership became far more explicit and binding when Honecker replaced Walter Ulbricht as the general secretary of the SED in 1971 and took control of the Politburo in East Germany. The focus of his new initiative, "the policy of social and economic unity"—often shortened to the "Main Task"—was to increase consumer goods as well as to improve the standard of living of the GDR population. In 1973, as part and parcel of this new beginning and as a sign of increased openness and more direct competition with the West, Honecker and his advisors also lifted the prohibition against watching West German television. In 1974 the Politburo allowed East Germans with access to Western currency entry to Intershops; up until 1973, these East German luxury stores had been reserved for visitors and guests of the GDR. All of this amounted to a new departure toward consumer socialism, developed in the heyday of East Germany's newfound confidence after the international recognition of the country had been achieved in the wake of the Vietnam War, détente, and the implementation of *Ostpolitik*. Introduced in the early 1970s, Honecker's "Main Task" was a policy filled with hope and built on the assumption that East Germany's economy would further improve, that its government would stabilize, and that the GDR would establish itself as a normal country, an accepted socialist neighbor to Western countries and a sovereign actor in the international sphere.[7]

As a myriad of studies have highlighted, Honecker's vision did not come to pass. One of the central reasons for its failure was that East Germany was caught in an increasingly vicious cycle of indebtedness and economic crisis mode by the late 1970s already. To be sure, the SED government reaped some immediate successes in the early to mid-1970s, achieving greater political stability and slightly more acceptance by its own population in the few short years after the implementation of the "Main Task" policies. Yet the advances were purchased through loans from Western creditors, which increased as the 1970s progressed. Honecker refused to reverse course, despite the dire warnings of his economic advisors. By the early 1980s, East Germany's debt had spiraled out of control, driven by the grand bargain that Honecker had struck with the East German population in the early 1970s. But the GDR economy was unable to sustain it for very long, especially as the oil shocks of this era and the global recession began to take their toll on the East German economy as well. While one might have been able to find a respectable GDR economist who genuinely believed that East Germany could outcompete the capitalist FRG economically in the late 1960s, it would have been impossible to find such a brave soul a decade later. Honecker's priority for consumption and the expansion of social policies over production and technological innovation, implemented in the 1970s and stubbornly defended in the 1980s, ultimately reduced the long-term opportunities for the next generation and sharply limited the economic prospects for the future development of the GDR by the mid- to late 1980s.[8]

However, it should be clear that there was no single factor or single development that caused a historical event such as the fall of the Berlin Wall. Numerous developments contributed to it. The GDR was a weak country from the start, a "rump state" as some historians have referred to it, which despite its eventual recognition by the international community always remained subservient to and dependent on the Soviet Union. Moreover, because of its close proximity to its powerful West German neighbor, East Germany was locked in an unenviable and asymmetrical daily political, economic, and cultural Cold War battle. There is also no doubt that the economic central planning at the heart of the communist enterprise handicapped and significantly weakened East Germany just as it did the other countries in Eastern Europe. In addition, the political leadership of the Socialist Unity Party was frequently aloof and became more disconnected from the population as time went on, and the top-down political approach of governing allowed for no significant chances for meaningful reforms or reversals. Finally, the East German regime always lacked real legitimacy and was only grudgingly tolerated by its people. The leadership's hold on power was tenuous and needed to be shored up by terror and intimidation as well as a generous welfare state and increasingly rising living standards. When this bargain was no longer feasible by the late 1980s, increasing segments of the East German population balked and took to the streets. The audacious mass protests in the last years of the 1980s, which were supported by the churches as well as other oppositional groups, further weakened the hold of the GDR regime on power and emboldened a greater number of GDR citizens to voice their demands for significant reforms more vocally in the "peaceful revolution" of 1989.[9]

This book will put the cultural reasons for the crumbling of the Berlin Wall center stage. Certainly, numerous individual studies have shown that the pervasive influence of Western culture and the daily consumer temptations from West Germany in particular contributed to the weakening of the East German state. This study integrates this diverse scholarship into a broader framework and an overall synthesis. The first monograph of its kind, it analyzes the major East German mass media as well as the GDR consumer culture side by side in a comprehensive and comparative manner. It surveys the political and cultural journey of the GDR under the Honecker administration (1971–89), paying particularly close attention to the dynamic interplay between the popular demands, intensifying economic crises, and cultural policy decisions by the SED leadership during the last two decades of East Germany's existence. What emerges rather clearly is that the East German mass culture was primarily driven not by the preferred vision and priorities of the SED government, but rather by the unrelenting pressure of the majority of the East German people as well as international developments beyond the control of the East German government. The main argument of this book is that the popular demand for and influence of Western media and consumer culture forced the SED leadership into a series of grudging and fateful accommodations that were intended to ensure its survival in the late 1970s and especially during the 1980s. Instead their combined cultural impact further weakened the East German government's political legitimacy as well as its economic stability and cumulatively became one of the root causes for the GDR's ultimate demise in the late 1980s.

Since this study focuses primarily on the last two decades of the GDR and highlights developments related to popular culture, it is also important to recognize a partial generational slant inherent in this analysis. While all GDR citizens were affected by the cultural influences and changes, much of the ensuing discussion applies most directly to those referred to as the third generation of East Germany, generally those born in the 1960s and early 1970s, who were supposed to carry the socialist torch into the twenty-first century. As many scholars have highlighted, this generation had little interest in taking over this leadership role. Instead, they are frequently characterized as "the distanced generation" (die distanzierte Generation) or "the unintegrated generation" (Generation der Nicht-Mehr-Eingestiegenen). They were quite different from the first and second generation in the GDR. The first or "founder generation" (Aufbaugeneration) were the true believers, many of them born in the late 1920s and early 1930s, who built socialist East Germany and stayed in the 1950s when there was still an easy way to leave. The second generation, referred to as the "integrated generation" (integrierte Generation), "born into the GDR" in the 1940s and early 1950s, largely followed the lead of their elders, despite the setbacks of the building of the Berlin Wall in 1961 and the disappointment of the violent dismantling of reform efforts such as the Prague Spring in the late 1960s. For those born in the 1960s and early 1970s, by contrast, the appeal of socialism and their willingness to integrate themselves had dwindled significantly. They were more likely to embrace Western culture more thoroughly as well as to resist the regime in both subtle and sometimes overt ways than the previous two generations.[10]

The reluctant embrace of Western-style consumption and media developments discussed above was not unique to the GDR socialist government. The leadership in every Eastern European country, including the Soviet Union, adopted and adapted to the dominant modes of Western-style consumer society and the overpowering impact of rapidly expanding media models and technologies during the late socialist phase, especially from the 1960s toward the end of the communist era in Europe. Moreover, the national responses to the dual processes of expanding consumption and mediatization in Eastern Bloc countries created diverse and hybrid media and consumer cultures, each of which was uniquely embedded in its national context. Likewise, the tacit agreement or social contract between national socialist governments and their populations, which promised greater access to consumer goods, higher living standards, and enjoyment of Western media, became—to varying degrees—a hallmark of all Eastern Bloc countries in the decades of the late socialist era. This implied bargain is reflected in developments all across Eastern Europe since the 1960s, from the steady expansion of Western-style department stores in communist countries to the emphasis on "goulash communism" in Hungary and the consumer-focused policy adjustments in the Czechoslovakia after the crushing of the Prague Spring in 1968. The Westernizing trends and cultural adaptations of the media in the Soviet Union during the last few decades prior to 1990 reflect a similar trajectory. All of them highlight the powerful influences of modern media and consumer cultures and especially the inexorable pull that the "Imaginary West" had on the respective populations. Every socialist government was painfully aware of the inherent ideological contradictions involved in these cultural and consumerist negotiations as well as the potential ideological and political damage they inflicted. But simply denying access to such attractive influences or remaining irresponsive to the popular desires and demands they created was not an option for any government in Eastern Europe.[11]

While a comprehensive and systematic transnational analysis of the many similarities and differences of Eastern European countries is well beyond the scope of this study, what becomes very apparent through a selective comparative perspective is that no Eastern Bloc country experienced these influences and their seductive attractiveness more powerfully than the East German leadership and its population. Because of the shared language, culture, and history with West Germany as well as its unique geographical location, the GDR could never escape the head-to-head rivalry and direct encounter with the capitalist media and consumer culture. Despite its high living standard compared to its Eastern

European neighbors, the comparison that mattered to its population was the material culture, economic standards, and cultural trends in the FRG. This daily exposure heightened the significance and impact Western influences had in the GDR and made this competition all the more urgent and ultimately dire.

The series of adjustments and accommodations analyzed in this study highlight the difficult choices and dilemmas that the SED leadership faced in terms of responding to the Western media and consumer culture. To be sure, this never led to a wholesale takeover of GDR culture by Western influences, but the consequences were systemic and deeply troubling nevertheless. In response to the constant churning of consumerist and media demand and fearing public dissent and perhaps even large-scale unrest in the late 1970s and the 1980s, the GDR government eventually negotiated itself into a corner and significantly reduced its control through a series of disempowering accommodations by the mid- to late 1980s. In the process of allowing ever more Western cultural and consumer products into East Germany, the SED leadership ultimately forfeited the cultural vision for its popular media and consumer culture.

Just as important, by the early to mid-1980s GDR officials no longer simply condoned Western imports and influences, but actively began to privilege and showcase capitalist cultural expressions and products over its own GDR counterparts in a desperate search for public approval, ratings, or economic resources. For example, GDR film officials loosened their restrictions against certain Western film imports in the 1980s because they knew that these imports, especially Hollywood blockbuster films, would attract larger audiences and produce much-needed revenue for its struggling film industry. Likewise, East German television planners were well aware that imported Western films and TV adaptations slated for GDR television would find wide approval among its population and drive up ratings. In a similar vein, SED cultural planners could be certain that allowing a Western rock band to appear in concert on East German soil bought a significant, though temporary, portion of goodwill from its alienated youth. Finally, those in charge of trade and commerce in the GDR understood only too well that East Germans were willing to spend far more on imported Western consumer goods and would part with their safely guarded Western currency to attain these highly desired products, which added desperately needed hard currency to the East German coffers.

As this comparative analysis highlights, this compensatory, and to a large degree economically motivated, importation of Western media and consumer culture escalated in the 1980s, when increased ratings and public approval as well as economic gain and profits, rather than ideological priority or vision, drove the decision-making process of the East German leadership. The ultimate political and economic failure of the SED regime was closely intertwined with its failures in the areas of popular culture and consumption, then, and eventually led to the widespread adoption, adaptation, and embrace of Western influences, products, and models. And while this enormous shift from an ideologically based media and consumer strategy in the late 1960s and early 1970s to a predominantly popularity- and profit-based approach in the late 1970s and 1980s reflected a broad trend in all Eastern Bloc countries, it will be up to broad-based syntheses of specific Eastern European countries to ascertain whether the argument advanced in this book applies to them with the same dynamic force and to the same degree.

***

The opening chapter ("Successful Media Campaigns in East Germany in the 1960s and 1970s: The Vietnam War and the 1972 Olympics") sets the stage for the main part of the book. It is important to remember that Erich Honecker started his tenure at the helm of the SED government in 1971 with a lot of wind at his back. This chapter focuses on the promising early period of the Honecker era and highlights two of the most successful developments of the early 1970s: the GDR's prominent role in the anti–Vietnam War activities of the late 1960s and early 1970s and its spectacular successes at the 1972 and 1976 Olympics. Both of these international achievements and their accompanying media campaigns significantly enhanced the status and legitimacy of East Germany both abroad and at home by the mid-1970s.

The succeeding chapters of this book focus on the fairly sudden shift from the guarded optimism of the early 1970s to the sudden and quickly deteriorating public mood in the GDR in the late 1970s and analyze this transformation through the lens of the cultural policies and developments in East Germany from the mid-1970s to the late 1980s. In these comparative chapters, the analysis focuses on the major mass cultural arenas in East Germany: film, television, youth radio and popular music, as well as consumer culture. In all of these areas, East German political and cultural officials began the 1970s still hopeful that the goal of establishing an independent and culturally vibrant socialist alternative that compared favorably with that of the capitalist West could be accomplished. Buoyed by the political tailwinds of the early to mid-1970s, which included America's loss in Vietnam as well as political and economic crises in both the United States and West Germany, they envisioned a robust GDR society and culture that could hold its own in the ideological and cultural competition with the West. By the late 1980s, this vision was lying in shambles. Plagued by an aging and increasingly inefficient economic and technological infrastructure as well as strong political headwinds, SED policy makers had to make one painful accommodation after another. And each step of the way, they had to concede a bit more of their cultural home turf to the relentless drive of the Western media and consumer culture as well as the reach of ever more powerful international influences.

Chapter 2 ("Fade Out: Hollywood Movie Imports and the Cultural Surrender of the GDR Film Control in the 1970s and 1980s") focuses on the importation of American feature films in the GDR in the 1970s and 1980s and the cultural, economic, and political repercussions that arose in their wake. Roughly ten US films were imported to the GDR every year. This chapter explores which American movies were chosen for import and how they were advertised and received, as well as analyzes their influence on the overall cultural policies of the GDR. What becomes apparent rather quickly is that ideological priorities were receding into the background by the late 1970s and early 1980s. Instead the key questions in the selection process became focused on their potential to deliver much-needed revenue for the struggling East German film industry. Throughout the 1980s, GDR cultural officials reluctantly undertook one accommodation after another, which ultimately left its film policy a bundle of contradictions. Left with no alternatives, the SED leadership lost control over its film policy and programs during the 1980s and culturally capitulated to the combined forces of East German popular demands, economic pressures, and political fears, as well as the relentless expansion of a Western, especially Hollywood-dominated, international film culture.

After its rise to media dominance in the 1960s, television was seen as the primary and most vital of all media by the East German political and cultural officials. Its cultural and political significance was unchallenged and far superseded that of the film industry, as chapter 3 argues ("The Westernization of East German Television in the 1970s and 1980s"). Even before the prohibition against West German television viewing was officially lifted in 1973, GDR officials constantly calibrated their own broadcasts as well as their TV strategy along the lines of the programming and initiatives of its West German rival. In the 1970s especially, East German cultural planners and TV producers premiered several new family series, which proved to be very popular with their general TV audiences. Yet despite such innovations, the outcome for the GDR television industry was similar to the movie sector: ultimately, East Germany's television planners lost control over the industry due to relentless viewer demands, increasingly tight economic budgets, and international developments beyond their control.

As chapter 4 ("Fighting against All Odds: GDR Popular Music and Youth Radio in an International Context") shows, East German youth radio and, closely related to it, popular music were particularly exposed to the continuous confrontation with the West because of the quickly multiplying Western options that East Germans had at their fingertips. With a turn of the dial, they could tune in to Cold War broadcasting stations like Voice of America, Radio Free Europe, or the popular Berlin-based Radio in the American Sector (RIAS). By the late 1970s and especially in the mid-1980s, private, commercial Western radio stations added their channels to the already plentiful mix that penetrated deep into East Germany. The other major strand of this chapter focuses on the diverse impact of popular music and its related subcultures in the GDR. Rock, pop, and punk music forever altered the cultural life in the GDR as well as the identity formations of a large number of East German youth. As this chapter emphasizes, GDR officials in charge of popular music and youth radio were faced not only with Western competition and the unyielding demands of their youth, but also with the structural transformations of an international media environment against which their initiatives and responses ultimately proved ineffective.

Consumer culture and consumption were highly politicized in the former East Germany, just like sports and popular culture. Chapter 5 ("Western Consumer Culture or Bust: Intershops and East German Consumption Policies in the 1970s and 1980s") turns its attention to this critical area of the contest between the socialist East and the capitalist West. The SED party leadership was painfully aware of the constant comparisons in the marketplace and the public debate that they engendered. It was not a theoretical debate, but a perennial part of everyday life and conversations. It mattered greatly which products one could buy and which ones were out of reach. Likewise it mattered greatly how products tasted, looked, or felt because it was a daily reflection of the economic and political system that had produced them. At the heart of this lure for Western consumer products were Intershops, the hard-currency stores where those with Western money could fulfill their long-delayed consumer desires among a cornucopia of imported products. Intershops are a good barometer of the economic and political developments of East Germany as well as the consumerist aspirations of the government and its citizens in the last two decades of the GDR. They also reflect the desperate degree to which the SED leadership would go in order to buy legitimacy from a perennially disgruntled population. Just as importantly, against the best economic advice, the SED's accommodations to meet East Germans' rising consumer expectations led to continuous overspending, which mortgaged East Germany's future and further divided an already stratified and deeply demoralized East German population. The ensuing consumer policy, which the East German government pursued in the late 1970s and 1980s, was politically and economically ruinous, and it was one of the root causes for the repeated economic crises during these two decades as well as the ultimate demise of the GDR in 1989.

When East Germans finally came face-to-face with the Western mass media and consumer culture as well as the political and economic realities that accompanied them after the fall of the Berlin Wall, they soon realized that the West was not as golden as they had imagined it to be. The epilogue, entitled "Out with the Old—in with the New? *Wende, Ostalgie*, and the Serpentine Unification," analyzes some of the most significant changes, transformations, and adjustments that occurred in the cultural and consumer landscapes of the former East Germany from 1990 through the early twenty-first century. For many East German citizens, the early euphoria and consumerist buying frenzy receded rather quickly when the security of the socialist welfare state was stripped away and as their lives were turned upside down with the arrival of a capitalist market economy. In addition, the jubilant celebrations and the chant "We are one people!" (Wir sind ein Volk!) faded into history as the welcome of East Germans in the reunified republic soured. In fact, Germans on either side of the collapsed Wall soon referred to each other as *Ossis* and *Wessis*, terms that emphasized demarcation rather than unification. The return of a more somber public mood in the 1990s and early 2000s included the emergence of *Ostalgie*, a nostalgic desire to return to the familiar, material landscape of the socialist lifestyle and a shared past in the eastern regions of Germany. As many West Germans were wondering if the price of reunification was too high, the majority of East Germans struggled to adjust to the disorienting and life-altering transformations of the post-socialist period and resented what they saw as their second-class citizenship in the new Berlin Republic. All of these turbulent post-1989 twists and turns are reminders that German unification followed an unexpectedly serpentine path and that the often invoked "inner unity" of Germany still remains a work in progress.

Notes

1. On the diverse and often contradictory media culture in East Germany, see, for example, Franziska Kuschel, *Schwarzhörer, Schwarzseher und heimlische Leser: Die DDR und die Westmedien* (Göttingen: Wallstein Verlag, 2016); Wolfgang Mühl-Benninghaus, *Unterhaltung als Eigensinn: Eine ostdeutsche Mediengeschichte* (Frankfurt and New York: Campus Verlag, 2012); Stefan Zahlmann, ed., *Wie im Westen, nur anders: Medien in der DDR* (Berlin: Panama Verlag, 2010); Michael Meyen and Anke Fiedler, eds., *Die Grenze im Kopf: Journalisten in der DDR* (Berlin: Panama Verlag, 2010); Michael Meyen, *Einschalten, Umschalten, Ausschalten? Das Fernsehen im DDR-Alltag* (Leipzig: Leipziger Universitätsverlag, 2003); Kurt R. Hesse, *Westmedien in der DDR. Nutzung, Image und Auswirkungen bundesrepublikanischen Hörfunks und Fernsehens* (Cologne: Böhlau Verlag, 1988); and Simone Barck, Christoph Classen, and Thomas Heimann, "The Fettered Media," in *Dictatorship as Experience: Towards a Socio-Cultural History of the GDR*, ed. Konrad Jarausch (New York and Oxford: Berghahn Books, 1999), 213–39.

    Hubertus Knabe, *Der Diskrete Charme der DDR: Stasi und Westmedien* (Berlin: Propyläen, 2001), and Historische Kommission der ARD, ed., *Die Ideologiepolizei: Die rundfunkbezogenen Aktivitäten des Ministeriums für Staatssicherheit der ehemaligen DDR in der DDR sowie in der Bundesrepublik Deutschland* (Frankfurt am Main: Redaktion ARD Jahrbuch im Deutschen Rundfunkarchiv, 2008), among other works, highlight the surveillance and propaganda imperatives of the GDR state very effectively.

    For other intriguing studies on everyday GDR culture, see among others David F. Crew, ed., *Consuming Germany in the Cold War* (Oxford and New York: Berg, 2003); Judd Stitziel, *Fashioning Socialism: Clothing, Politics, and Consumer Culture in East Germany* (New York and Oxford: Berghahn Books, 2005); Katherine Pence and Paul Betts, eds., *Socialist Modern: East German Everyday Culture and Politics* (Ann Arbor: University of Michigan Press, 2008); Eli Rubin, *Synthetic Socialism: Plastics and Dictatorship in the German Democratic Republic* (Chapel Hill: North Carolina Press, 2008); and Esther von Richthofen, *Bringing Culture to the Masses: Control, Compromise and Participation in the GDR* (New York and Oxford: Berghahn Books, 2009).

2. In addition to Meyen's study *Einschalten, Umschalten, Ausschalten?*, which highlights East Germans' skeptical attitude toward both East and West German political news sources, see also the various articles in Zahlmann's anthology *Wie im Westen, nur anders*: Stefan Zahlmann, "Medien in der DDR: Medienproduktion und Medienrezeption als kulturelle Praktiken," 9–34; Michael Meyen and Anke Fiedler, "Totalitäre Vernichtung der politischen Öffentlichkeit? Tageszeitungen und Kommunikationsstrukturen in der DDR," 35–59; Sylvia Klötzer, "Im Rahmen des Unmöglichen: 'Konkrete Sat-

ire' im *Eulenspiegel*," 60–78; Patricia F. Zeckert, "DDR-Leser im Schlaraffenland: Westliteratur, Buchmesse und alternative Medienkultur," 96–118; Knut Hickethier, "Das Fernsehen der DDR," 119–30; Klaus Arnold, "Musikbox mit Volkserziehungsauftrag: Radio in der DDR 1," 307–25; Boris Kretzinger, "Pac-Man vs. Hase und Wolf: Computer- und Videospiele in der DDR," 378–384; and Christoph Classen, "DDR-Medien im Spannungsfeld von Gesellschaft und Politik," 385–407. For an example of the illegal copying of prohibited literature, see Thomas Rusch's interview with Stefan Zahlmann, "'Ich war kein Oppositioneller. Ich war Kopierer,'" 86–95. For a particularly insightful discussion of the commercializing impact of an international media culture, finally, see Edward Larkey's study, *Rotes Rockradio: Populäre Musik und die Kommerzialisierung des DDR-Rundfunks* (Berlin: LIT-Verlag, 2007).
3. Primary among the historians who have challenged the view of the GDR as first and foremost "the second German dictatorship" are Mary Fulbrook, Konrad Jarausch, Martin Sabrow, Thomas Lindenberger, Alf Lüdtke, Ina Merkel, and Andrew Port. For the quotes, see Konrad Jarausch, "Beyond the National Narrative: Implications of Reunification for Recent German History," in "Contemporary History as Transatlantic Project: The German Problem, 1960–2000," supplement, *Historical Social Research/Historische Sozialforschung* 24 (2012): 340; and Andrew I. Port, introduction to *Becoming East German: Socialist Structures and Sensibilities after Hitler*, ed. Mary Fulbrook and Andrew I. Port (New York and Oxford: Berghahn Books, 2013), 16. For other works analyzing the limits of the GDR dictatorship, see Alf Lüdtke and Peter Becker, eds., *Akten. Eingaben. Schaufenster. Die DDR und Ihre Texte: Erkundungen zu Herrschaft und Alltag* (Berlin: Akademie-Verlag, 1997); Jarausch, *Dictatorship as Experience*; Thomas Lindenberger, ed., *Herrschaft und Eigensinn in der Diktatur: Studien zur Gesellschaftsgeschichte der DDR* (Cologne: Böhlau Verlag, 1999); Ina Merkel, *Utopie und Bedürfnis: Die Geschichte der Konsumkultur in der DDR* (Cologne: Böhlau Verlag, 1999); Mary Fulbrook, *The People's State: East German Society from Hitler to Honecker* (New Haven and London: Yale University Press, 2005); Andrew I. Port, *Conflict and Stability in the German Democratic Republic* (Cambridge and New York: Cambridge University Press, 2007); and Martin Sabrow, ed., *Erinnerungsorte der DDR* (Munich: C. H. Beck, 2009).
4. The term *Eigen-Sinn* originates with Alf Lüdtke; see especially his article "'Helden der Arbeit'—Mühen beim Arbeiten. Zur missmutigen Loyalität von Industriearbeitern in der DDR," in *Sozialgeschichte der DDR*, ed. Hartmut Kaeble, Jürgen Kocka, and Hartmut Zwahr (Stuttgart: Klett-Cotta, 1994), 188–213. The translation here is from Eli Rubin, "The Trabant: Consumption, Eigen-Sinn, and Movement," *History Workshop Journal* 68, no. 3 (2009): 28.

In the introduction to his edited volume, Christoph Kleßmann talks about a "tacit social contract between the SED government and the East German people": *The Divided Past: Rewriting Post-War German History* (Oxford and New York: Berg, 2001), 14–15; see also Thomas Lindenberger's essay in the same volume: "Everyday History: New Approaches to the History of Post-War Germanies," 43–67.

For other authors highlighting these contrarian activities of the GDR population, see Konrad H. Jarausch, "Care and Coercion: The GDR as Welfare Dictatorship," and Burghard Ciesla and Patrice C. Poutrus, "Food Supply in a Planned Economy: SED Nutrition Policy between Crisis Response and Popular Needs," both in Jarausch, *Dictatorship as Experience*, 47–69 and 143–62, respectively; Merkel, *Utopie und Bedürfnis*; Philipp Heldmann, *Herrschaft, Wirtschaft, Anoraks: Konsumpolitik in der DDR der Sechzigerjahre* (Göttingen: Vandenhoeck & Ruprecht, 2004); Stitziel, *Fashioning Socialism*; Fulbrook, *The People's State*, introduction; as well as Christoph Boyer, "Stabilisation of Power through Social and Consumer Policy in the GDR," in *Totalitarian and Authoritarian Regimes in Europe: Legacies and Lessons from the Twentieth Century*, ed. Jerzy W. Borejsza and Klaus Zimmer (New York and Oxford: Berghahn Books, 2006), 209–27.

5. For an insightful discussion highlighting Honecker's unwillingness to cut social services or increase prices, see Andreas Malycha, *Die SED in der Ära Hecker: Machtstrukturen, Entscheidungsmechanismen und Konfliktfelder in der Staatspartei 1971 bis 1989* (Oldenburg: De Gruyter, 2014), especially part 4, "Der 'Konsumsozialismus der Honecker-Ära'"; and Alexander Burdumy, "Reconsidering the Role of the Welfare State within the German Democratic Republic's Political System," *Journal of Contemporary History* 48, no. 4 (2013): 872–89. See also von Richthofen, *Bringing Culture to the Masses*, and Mark Landsman, *Dictatorship and Demand: The Politics of Consumerism in East Germany* (Cambridge, MA, and London: Harvard University Press, 2005), on the central role of culture and consumption for the policies of the SED regime.

6. Malycha sums up Honecker's credo with the following quote: "When the people work, they also need to be able to afford things. Decisive cutbacks cannot occur because it will only lead to unpredictable disruptions." Malycha, *Die SED in der Ära Honecker*, 245–46. The compensatory nature of the GDR social policies is also discussed in Alexander Burmundy, *Sozialpolitik und Repression in der DDR: Ost-Berlin, 1971–1989* (Essen: Klartext Verlag, 2013). On the growth of oppositional groups in the 1970s, see Christoph Kleßmann, "Die Opposition in der DDR vom Beginn der Ära Honecker bis zur polnischen Revolution 1980/81," in Enquette-Kommission, *Möglichkeiten und Formen abweichenden und widerständigen Verhaltens und oppositionellen Handels, die friedliche Revolution im Herbst 1989, die Wiedervereinigung Deutschlands und das Fortwirken von Strukturen und Mechanismen der Diktatur* (Frankfurt am Main: Suhrkamp Verlag, 1995), 1080–1109.

7. See Gert-Joachim Glaeßner, ed., *Die DDR in der Ära Honecker: Politik–Kultur–Gesellschaft* (Opladen: Westdeutscher Verlag, 1988); Malycha, *Die SED in der Ära Honecker*; and Stefan Wolle, *Die heile Welt der Diktatur: Alltag und Herrschaft in der DDR, 1971–1989*, 3rd ed. (Berlin: Ch. Links Ver-

lag, 2009). The more upbeat and positive public mood in the early 1970s is discussed in Mary Fulbrook, *Anatomy of a Dictatorship: Inside the GDR, 1949–1989* (Oxford and New York: Oxford University Press, 1998), chapter 5, and reflected by the surveys discussed in Heinz Niemann, *Meinungsumfragen in der DDR: Die geheimen Berichte des Instituts für Meinungsforschung an das Politbüro der SED* (Cologne: Bund-Verlag, 1993), parts 4 and 5.

8. One of the best and most succinct analyses of the GDR economy is provided by André Steiner, *The Plans That Failed: An Economic History of the GDR* (New York and Oxford: Berghahn Books, 2010). Steiner discusses the positive outlook and optimistic internal assessment in the late 1960s on pp. 122–23; on the 1970s, see chapter 5. See also Hartmut Berghoff and Uta Andrea Balbier, eds., *The East German Economy, 1945–2010: Falling Behind or Catching Up?* (New York: German Historical Institute and Cambridge University Press, 2013), especially part 3.

9. For studies that address the causes for the fall of the Berlin Wall, see among others Jonathan Grix, *The Role of the Masses in the Collapse of the GDR* (London and New York: Macmillan, 2000); Klaus-Dietmar Henke, Peter Steinbach, and Johannes Tuchel, eds., *Widerstand und Opposition in der DDR* (Cologne, Weimar, and Vienna: Böhlau Verlag, 1999); Achilleas Megas, *Soviet Foreign Policy towards East Germany* (London: Springer, 2015); Oliver Bange and Gottfried Niedhart, eds., *Helsinki 1975 and the Transformation of Europe* (New York and Oxford: Berghahn Books, 2008); Steiner, *The Plans That Failed*; Wolle, *Die heile Welt der Diktatur*; and Patrick Major, *Behind the Berlin Wall: East Germany and the Frontiers of Power* (Oxford and New York: Oxford University Press, 2010).

10. For great insights into this generational divide in the GDR, see the excellent anthology of essays edited by Annegret Schüle, Thomas Ahbe, and Rainer Gries, *Die DDR aus generationengeschichtlicher Perspektive: Eine Inventur* (Leipzig: Leipziger Universitätsverlag, 2006). For a good overview of the generational breakdown in the GDR and its terminology, see especially two articles in this collection: Bernd Lindner, "Die Generation der Unberatenen: Zur Generationsfolge in der DDR und ihren strukturellen Konsequenzen für die Nachwendezeit," 93–112, and Karin Bock, "Politische Sozialisationsprozesse in Drei-Generationen-Familien aus Ostdeutschland," 377–98; Bock uses the term "Nicht-Mehr-Integrierte" for those born in the late 1960s and early 1970s. In his article "Alltägliche Mediennutzung in der DDR: Rezeption und Wertschätzung der Ost- und West-Medien in unterschiedlichen Kohorten," 247–70, Michael Meyen demonstrates the changed attitude of the third generation toward the use of Western media very convincingly. In addition, see Mary Fulbrook's focus on the founder generation in this same anthology: "Generationen und Kohorte in der DDR: Protagonisten und Widersacher des DDR-Systems aus der Perspektive biographischer Daten," 113–30. Her extensive study focusing on a generational approach toward German history in the twentieth century, *Dissonant Lives: Generations and Violence*

through the German Dictatorships (Oxford and New York: Oxford University Press, 2011), adds further breadth as well as depth to this overall analysis.

11. For just a few excellent analyses of these developments, see Paulina Bren and Mary Neuberger, eds., *Communism Unwrapped: Consumption in Cold War Eastern Europe* (New York: Oxford University Press, 2012). Of particular interest here are the introduction by the editors as well as Paulina Bren's article on post-1968 Czechoslovakia, "Tuzex and the Hustler: Living It Up in Czechoslovakia," 27–48; Patrick Hyder Patterson's discussion of the expansion of department stores, "Risky Business: What Was Really Being Sold in the Department Stores of Socialist Eastern Europe?," 116–39; and the article by Tamas Dombos and Lena Pellandini-Simanyi on consumption in late socialist Hungary: "Kids, Cars, or Cashews? Debating and Remembering Consumption in Socialist Hungary," 325–350. See also Paulina Bren's book, *The Greengrocer and His TV: The Culture of Communism after the 1968 Prague Spring* (Ithaca and London: Cornell University Press, 2010). Another outstanding set of articles is compiled in the anthology edited by David Crowley and Susan E. Reid, *Pleasures in Socialism: Leisure and Luxury in the Eastern Bloc* (Evanston, IL: Northwestern University Press, 2010), as well as in the collection of essays edited by Annette Vowinckel, Marcus M. Payk, and Thomas Lindenberger, *Cold War Cultures: Perspectives on Eastern and Western European Societies* (New York and Oxford: Berghahn Books, 2012). For the development of the Soviet media and culture, see Kristin Roth-Ey's excellent study *Moscow Prime Time: How the Soviet Union Built the Media Empire That Lost the Cultural Cold War* (Ithaca and London: Cornell University Press, 2011), as well as Alexei Yurchak's influential book, *Everything Was Forever, Until It Was No More: The Last Soviet Generation* (Princeton and Oxford: Princeton University Press, 2005); the term "Imaginary West" is borrowed from his study (chapter 6).

CHAPTER 1

Successful Media Campaigns in East Germany in the 1960s and 1970s

The Vietnam War and the 1972 Olympics

The Vietnam War provided the East German government with a golden opportunity. No functionary of the Socialist Unity Party of Germany (Sozialistische Einheitspartei Deutschlands [SED]) could have dreamed up a better script for the country's Cold War propaganda. It had all of the ingredients and characters for a gripping and winning formula: an aggressive capitalist American intruder, who became all the more menacing as the war went on; the evil West German ally, who was assisting the imperialist bully and became implicated in its destructive actions; a socialist Vietnamese underdog, who much of the world and your own population eventually supported; and a benevolent Soviet neighbor, who supplied and aided the Vietnamese victim at the same time as it was seeking to bring all sides to the negotiating table. Even the ongoing conflict between the two great communist powers, China and the Soviet Union, which intensified during the second half of the 1960s, could not spoil this powerful narrative. While the GDR followed the lead of the Soviet Union and worked in close collaboration with its Eastern Bloc allies, the propaganda value of the Vietnam War was all too good to be true, and most certainly too good to pass up.[1]

Best of all, unlike the campaign of the building of the Berlin Wall, which was allegedly constructed in 1961 to protect the East German population, or the campaign surrounding the invasion of Czechoslovakia in 1968, which was justified as brotherly assistance for a neighbor facing an alleged threat of a "counterrevolution," this Vietnam War narrative did not have to be invented nor stubbornly defended against the better knowledge of an ever-skeptical East German population. On this issue, the SED leadership would ultimately be vindicated for its early condemnation of the war and joined by an ever-widening number of Western media and publics as well. Not surprisingly, then, its anti–Vietnam War stance and numerous Vietnam solidarity campaigns were the centerpieces of its critique of the capitalist system and often functioned as a key linchpin in its media campaigns against the West in the late 1960s and early 1970s. And the longer the war lasted, the more convincing this narrative became.[2]

Even American officials had to concede that they had handed the East German government an important strategic victory. As a secret public opinion survey by the United States Information Agency (USIA) highlighted, the Vietnam War proved to be a trump card for the GDR propaganda war with East German audiences: "The East German regime's propaganda drumfire and its 'solidarity' meetings on VN [Vietnam] doubtless [sic] have had some impact, fostering the belief that the US is a colonialist and imperialist power bent on squashing a legitimate national liberation movement in SE Asia." Equally important, it gave the SED regime a significant boost in its standing with its own population, as the American survey emphasized: "While East Germans are constitutionally skeptical of regime propaganda on all issues, the official line may have more credibility on VN than all other issues. One of the main counteracting sources of information for East Germans, western TV, has not been notably effective in presenting the US case."[3] And this assessment was reported in 1966, well before the American war effort deteriorated and in advance of increasing reports of US war crimes in Vietnam, which would create strong worldwide opposition and provide even more fuel for the East German media campaigns.[4]

As the Vietnam War was escalating, East Germany was simultaneously gearing up for its competition against the West in the sports arena, foremost the Olympic Games of the 1970s. For East Germany, sports was one of the highlights in its unceasing competition with its West German rival and the capitalist system as a whole. This henpecked state—overshadowed by the West Germany's economic power, lorded over by the USSR, and largely ignored by the United States—was not going to be denied in the sports arena. For much of its existence, the GDR was playing defense, responding and reacting to political developments but rarely able to initiate and control them. Things looked very different in the athletic arena, however. Here the rules of politics had only limited application, and the East German government learned to play its cards deftly. It stayed on the offensive for much of the 1950s and 1960s, forcing the Federal Republic to play defense for a change, eager to transform its athletic prowess into a pathway to international recognition as well as a reflection of the superiority of the socialist ideology and system. West Germany might host the 1972 Olympics and gain the accompanying international recognition, for example, but East Germany was going to trump it in the athletic arenas. As Manfred Ewald, East Germany's minister of sports, put it, "They build the arenas, we take the medals."[5]

And win they would—not just the East German athletes, but the Olympic teams from the Soviet Union as well. The 1968 Olympics were the last Olympic Games when the teams from the West were still able to hold their own against the increasingly overpowering communist competitors. In 1968, the United States won the medal count against the Soviet Union for the last time, while the two independent German teams tied. At the 1972 Munich Olympics, the Soviet Union won the race for medals ahead of the United States, while East Germany scored third place ahead of West Germany. Driven by its urgent need for political legitimization through sports, the GDR in particular established an ever more scientific and rigorous athletic selection and preparation process. Combined with draconian exercise schedules and an aggressive, state-controlled doping program, GDR sports reached ever-greater heights in athletic and especially Olympic competitions. By 1976, East Germany (with a population of eighteen million) placed second in the medal count, right behind the Soviet Union and ahead of both the United States and West Germany.[6]

Despite ongoing obstacles and challenges, then, the GDR anti–Vietnam War campaigns and its athletic rise as a sports superpower bode well for Honecker's East Germany in the early 1970s and reflected the country's emergence as a respected member of the world community. Combined, these developments and the accompanying media campaigns significantly elevated East Germany's international status as well as boosted the internal stability of the GDR in the early to mid-1970s in particular.

The Vietnam Media Campaign: Exposing the True Intentions of the American and West German Enemies

One of the great advantages of the Vietnam War for East Berlin was that the escalating conflict merged so easily with the main propaganda themes of East Germany's Cold War rhetoric. One of the central ones was that the United States was an imperialist power bent on economic exploitation as well as world conquest and committed to subduing liberation movements in the developing world.[7] Not surprisingly, the GDR blasted the United States for its aggressive actions in Vietnam with the onset of the war, as reflected in the coverage of *Neues Deutschland*, East Germany's main party newspaper. As early as August 1964, the newspaper accused the United States of a "war of aggression" in connection with the Gulf of Tonkin crisis and argued that President Johnson was purposefully provoking a war in Vietnam. When the American Congress passed the Gulf of Tonkin Resolution, the GDR vigorously condemned the early bombing campaigns against North Vietnam, highlighted the worldwide protests against the US actions, and solidly placed itself on the side of the North Vietnamese people in the conflict.[8] As might be expected, these harsh attacks against the US-led war increased after 1965 as the American ground war intensified and the bombing raids escalated, coinciding with heightened international criticism of the conflict and intensifying solidarity campaigns and demonstrations in East Germany.

Even as détente policies were gathering speed in the late 1960s, the Vietnam War provided an easy target for steady media campaigns against "barbaric Americans" and ongoing criticism against ruthless US attacks. The GDR interpreted the US military campaigns in Vietnam and the eventual invasions of Cambodia and Laos as part of a worldwide campaign of aggression and as a blatant attempt to halt communism's historic march toward victory. Articles like those entitled "Adventurous Plans of the Pentagon" or "Poison War against Women and Children in South Vietnam" ran continuously in the East German media throughout the late 1960s and beyond. Likewise, East Germany eagerly followed the growing financial and economic difficulties that the United States encountered in its pursuit of the war and increasingly merged coverage of America's international aggression with its domestic ills and racial turmoil. Finally, it was of incalculable value to the GDR government that few of these stories had to be manufactured or manipulated and that more and more Western, and especially West German, media were seconding the East German point of view by the late 1960s and especially in the early 1970s.[9]

The unrivaled strength of the Vietnam War narrative from an East German perspective was that the SED leadership could attack its two main Cold War enemies simultaneously: it easily lent itself for attacks against the imperialist motives of the United States, yet it was equally easy to implicate West Germany in this narrative. By March 1966, *Neues*

Deutschland escalated its rhetoric against the United States and referred to a war of destruction (Vernichtungskrieg) in Vietnam. And as East German journalists saw it, West Germany was providing both political and military support for the US campaigns. As one article put it, "Even the bourgeois press has to concede: Bonn is providing bombs for the dirty war in Vietnam! This naked fact exposes that all the talk about 'humanitarian aid' is cynical double-talk." The GDR media focused on the escalation of the war, the use of poison gas, and the increasing protests in both East and West in 1966. Meanwhile East Germany portrayed itself as the true "German peace state," offering support and assistance to the innocent workers and farmers of the Democratic Republic of Vietnam (DRV).[10]

Another continuous thread in the verbal assault against the West German neighbor was the persistent innuendos hinting at the participation of German troops in Vietnam. As early as June of 1965, East Germany was reporting that the West German army (Bundeswehr) was preparing military missions in Vietnam. In addition to the financial and military aid that the FRG was already providing, *Neues Deutschland* argued that the Bonn government was just waiting for the "appropriate moment" when West German soldiers would become engaged in the war. By March of 1966, the paper was referring to detailed studies by West Germany's armed forces that allegedly advocated for the use of its troops in the Vietnam War campaigns. The cited study recommended active West German military participation in order to consolidate the alliance with the United States.[11] The fact that no such West German troops ever materialized and that the Bonn government consistently rejected American requests for German boots on the ground did not dissuade the ongoing use of these allegations.

The fact of the matter was that the East German government was well informed about the extent of the West German support for South Vietnam as well as its relations with the United States. In a detailed internal report from April 1966, for example, SED officials highlighted especially the economic and humanitarian aid that the Bonn government was providing the South Vietnamese government and analyzed the potential economic advantages that West Germany was reaping because of the increased American war economy. The report conceded that the direct benefits of the war for West Germany were rather minor. There was no "Vietnam-boom"—nothing equivalent to the "Korea-boom" that the West German economy allegedly experienced in connection with the war in the early 1950s. Much of the support for South Vietnam, moreover, had come in the form of deliveries of food and medical supplies or by providing civilian internships to South Vietnamese students and trainees. In an almost disappointed tone, the GDR officials had to admit in their report that "there were no West German investments worth mentioning in South Vietnam." Overall the analysis concluded that while the German economic interests in the war were rather negligible, "the West German government viewed its support to South Vietnam as moral assistance for the United States with the hope of shifting the balance of the international system in favor of the imperialist forces."[12]

Nevertheless, the central Vietnam narrative in the GDR that condemned West Germany as a militaristic accomplice of the United States allowed for numerous variations and explorations, and it was woven deeply into the East German propaganda tapestry of the late 1960s and early 1970s. It provided an easy segue way for the overarching argument that the capitalist countries were embarked on a neo-imperialist campaign with global ambitions. Vietnam was just the latest example in a number of military campaigns that defined this capitalist strategy. But, as one GDR historian argued, it took on a special role because it was the most flagrant example of this neo-imperialist campaign and represented the "most horrific colonial warfare in human history." Simultaneously, it was seen as one piece in America's Cold War "strategy of roll-back," through which it was trying to thwart the blossoming of recently liberated, socialist states in regions ripe for freedom and self-determination. Southeast Asia, together with Latin America and Africa, was viewed as the latest and third front in this concerted global US-led strategy.[13]

What is of course noticeable here is how closely these arguments overlapped with the emerging critiques against the Vietnam War both in Western Europe and the United States. As the war dragged on, growing segments of populations in Western countries no longer viewed America through the lens of World War II liberator and protector of democracy and freedom. The war slowly but surely eroded this attractive image and put even the staunchest defenders of the United States on the defensive. After the repeated and brutal bombing raids, after My Lai and the invasion of Cambodia, after the use of napalm and other poison gases, who in their right mind would want to defend this raging giant seemingly bent on mindless destruction? By 1969, this shift in Western and world opinion was widespread and epidemic, and well-known in Washington. A secret 1969 USIA public opinion survey captured this emerging global consensus well: "The results of the survey research provide a rather bleak picture," the report conceded. In all regions of the globe, with the sole exception of some countries in South Asia such as

Thailand, Malaysia, and the Philippines, majorities in most countries of the world wanted the United States to end the war in Vietnam and pull out its troops. The most compelling arguments for this call for withdrawal were that the war was seen as brutal and illegitimate, that the Saigon government was viewed as corrupt and ineffective, and as the study put it, because "the 'David-and Goliath' image grew as the struggle wore on."[14]

However, the East German government reserved its most biting comments and criticisms for its West German adversary. It emphasized the fact that the Bonn government, even its widely respected chancellor Willy Brandt, was a most compliant ally supportive of America's Vietnam War. Interpreting this acquiescence as steady support for the US policies, East Berlin ascribed West Germany a particularly significant role in the overall neo-imperialist capitalist global strategy and liked to refer to the "special alliance" (Sonderbündnis) between Washington and Bonn. As Horst Rennhack put it in his government-sponsored analysis, the "special alliance of the West German and American imperialism [represented] not only the longest and strongest, but also the most aggres-

Figure 1.1. GDR Vietnam Solidarity Committee, 1969. Exhibits like this one were displayed in numerous East German cities in order to generate support for the government's antiwar campaigns. (Courtesy of BStU Archiv; MfS-ZAIG-Fo-1361-0026.)

sive union of economic and political interests." As he argued, the FRG quietly overlooked even the most egregious violations of basic human rights and international laws in Vietnam and effectively had become the co-conspirator of the United States in what he referred to as "a ruthless genocide."[15]

West German politicians were very aware that they were vulnerable to what became known as the "guilt-by-association" argument (Mitschuld), but they felt that they had little leeway to blunt these cutting attacks. They believed that the country owed a great debt to the United States for its past assistance and knew that it continued to rely on American protection more urgently than any other Western European country. In addition, the Brandt government was very cognizant that it needed US backing if it wanted its *Ostpolitik* to have any chance of success. In short, because of its unique military and geostrategic location as well as its own foreign relations initiatives that needed US backing, West Germany was trapped, forced to stand side-by-side with an ever more unpopular America in a conflict the world and its own population increasingly despised.[16]

Not surprisingly, this notion of West Germany as an accomplice and most trusted ally in Vietnam remained a core element in East Germany's Cold War battle and seamlessly continued a key theme advanced by the SED government since the late 1940s. By the late 1960s, articles insinuating the shipment of West German poison gas to Vietnam, Bonn's willingness "to pay for the US war without reservation," as well as the overall imperialist plans of the FRG all cemented and elaborated on the "guilt-by-association argument"—a charge that became increasingly difficult to refute.[17]

East Berlin's politicians and media frequently returned to these accusations. By the summer of 1967, in articles such as "In Hitler's Tracks," *Neues Deutschland* compared the "pacification attempts by South Vietnam and the United States to the early phase of Hitler's conquest." A couple of weeks later it published a similar attack under the heading "The Nazi Cross on the US Dollar." This latter article argued that the foreign relations of the United States in Vietnam were littered with atrocious war crimes and found their domestic equivalent in the ruthless exploitation and suppression of the Black minorities within its own borders. In all of this, the continued and steady West German monetary support was of critical importance and deeply implicated the Bonn government, as the writers emphasized.[18]

Importantly, this fear of the resurgence of fascism as well as of once again failing the test of history ran like a red thread through all of the

West German protest movements and the antiwar campaigns as well. As early as 1966 the leading FRG student organization (Sozialistischer Deutscher Studentenbund [SDS]) began to refer to the "American genocide in Vietnam" and drew direct connections between the US atrocities committed in Vietnam and those carried out by the Nazis during World War II. A poster distributed by the West German SDS in 1966 asked the poignant question: "How much longer will we allow murder to be committed in our names?" As the American bombing campaigns kept rolling over North Vietnam again and again, the events reminded Germans of their own ruined cities and inevitably aroused sympathy for the innocent North Vietnamese victims caught up in the inevitable slaughter.[19] Moreover, the compelling rationale of the antiwar protests was not to once again condone atrocities and war crimes but instead to answer the call implied in the popular German protest slogan "He who keeps quiet agrees."[20]

In West Germany, the Tet Offensive and the revelations of the atrocities at My Lai and other locations reported in 1969 caused a significant revision in media coverage, but they were also deeply embedded in the domestic struggles of the FRG. Not only did the ideological differences of the West German print media become more pronounced, but more journalists were moving toward critical or even outright oppositional reporting of the Vietnam War starting in 1969. A final trope of reporting, which gained more currency in the latter stage of the war, was the indirect and inadvertent blurring of Nazi war crimes and American atrocities in Vietnam. The reports of the use of chemical warfare by the United States, the barbaric bombing campaigns, and the mass killings of innocent civilians by American GIs merged with the domestic discourse of German World War II war crimes.[21] In East and West Germany, the war in Vietnam was increasingly viewed as unjustifiable, immoral, and reprehensible by the late 1960s and early 1970s, giving ever more sustenance to the concerted GDR antiwar campaigns.

Reaping the Political Rewards through International Antiwar Campaigns

The manifold activities of the GDR Vietnam Committee were accompanied by a flurry of international antiwar politics on the part of East Germany's broader Solidarity Committee, which led to significant conferences both inside and outside of the country. Particularly vital in terms of international cooperation and recognition was the increasing participation of the GDR in antiwar conferences held in Western European countries. Most significant among these were the annual Vietnam Conferences in Stockholm, which first convened in 1966 and eventually gained broad-based international recognition and were later attended by national governmental representatives as well. East Germany sent its first delegation in 1967 and gradually gained the respect of the fellow attendees. In 1970, the GDR Vietnam Committee was invited to join the Executive Committee of the Stockholm Vietnam Conference in recognition of its numerous contributions to the international antiwar campaigns. Aside from monetary and other donations, the GDR documentaries about the Vietnam War as well as its scientific studies that proved the use of biological and chemical warfare in Vietnam were seen as the most influential contributions.[22]

In terms of the media campaigns, one venture in particular added to the prestige of the GDR in the international anti–Vietnam War movement: the powerful documentaries made by Studio H&S, named after the two documentary filmmakers Walter Heynowski and Gerhard Scheumann. During the heyday of its influence between the mid-1960s and the late 1970s, this legendary team focused most of its films on biting critiques against Western imperialism, especially the war in Vietnam, as well as attacks against West Germany. While the documentaries were primarily made for domestic consumption, many were purchased by news and TV organizations outside the Eastern Bloc and viewed in different parts of Western Europe and the developing world.[23]

The two most renowned early anti-imperialist and antiwar documentaries were *The Laughing Man: Confessions of a Murderer* (*Der lachende Mann: Bekenntnisse eines Mörders*), which aired in 1966, and *Pilots in Pajamas* (*Piloten im Pyjama*), released in 1968. The first focused on a German foreign legionnaire, an ex-soldier of the Wehrmacht from World War II, who had continued his murderous trade in the name of anticommunism under the guise of Western imperialism in different parts of the developing world. *Pilots in Pajamas*, by contrast, focused directly on the United States and the Vietnam War. It consisted of interviews with ten American pilots who had been shot down in attacks over North Vietnam. It was not their murderous intent but rather their ordinary nature that was the focal point of the four-part series. Important in a German context, like the Nazi defendants in the post–World War II Nuremberg Trials, their default answer to the question of their motivation was that they had simply followed orders when attacking targets in the DRV.[24]

Figure 1.2. Anti–Vietnam War demonstration in East Berlin, Unter den Linden, late 1968. (Courtesy of BStU Archiv; MfS-OTS-Fo-0055-Bild-0002.)

East Germany also became especially involved in consecutive conferences that focused on the US war crimes in Indochina. After the initial ones held in Stockholm, two later ones were hosted by NATO countries—Norway and Denmark—a point that was not lost on the SED officials. At the conference held in Oslo in June 1971, the GDR delegation distributed a powerful report on the use of herbicides by the United States in Vietnam. The report detailed in scientific yet accessible language the use of various herbicides (Agent Orange, Agent Blue, and Agent White) and described the companies involved in the manufacture and distribution of the herbicides. It targeted powerful American corporations such as Dow Chemical but also implicated segments of the West German BASF Company. The internal conference report emphasized that the GDR delegation came well prepared for the deliberations and that its contributions were widely praised by the participants.[25]

Although none of these international activities led to long-term political alliances, there is little doubt that these policies and antiwar efforts on the part of the GDR garnered a great amount of respect for the country and established it as a fellow leader in antiwar circles. And as the movement against the war grew and as it attracted increasing numbers of politicians especially to the Stockholm Vietnam Conferences in the early 1970s, East Germany could delight both in the remarkable victory of the Vietnamese people against overwhelming odds as well as the increasing recognition that its own contributions yielded. It established itself as an anti-imperialist champion in the eyes of many Third World countries and raised its status among many Western European nations as well.[26] Despite all of its horrors and tragedies, the Vietnam War presented a long-term political advantage for the SED government.

At least as significant as the international recognition was the grudging but increasing support by the East German population. The official solidarity campaigns with North Vietnam began early in East Germany and well before the American invasion. In the early 1950s, the two countries established diplomatic relations, and East Germany soon began supporting the DRV with economic and humanitarian aid. By 1957, East Germany was already the third-largest provider of aid, behind China and the Soviet Union. In the early 1960s, East Germany was also one of the first countries to recognize the South Vietnamese Liberation Front (FNL) and supported the rebel group with military aid.[27] In July 1965, during the commemoration of the eleventh anniversary of the Geneva Accords that ended the French Indochina War in 1954, the GDR government announced the creation of the Vietnam Committee (Vietnam Ausschuss). This committee was established as part of the larger Afro-Asian Solidarity Committee (Afro-Asiatische Solidaritätskomitee), which had been created in 1963 and which would be renamed the Solidarity Committee of the GDR (Solidaritätskomitee der DDR) in early 1973. The Vietnam Committee was the main hub of the anti–Vietnam War efforts in the GDR throughout the 1960s and the 1970s, which coordinated the numerous government campaigns and aligned them with the overall foreign relations policies of the SED government and those of the Eastern Bloc countries.[28]

To be sure, it is no easy task to assess the true degree of public support for the Vietnam solidarity campaigns that were rolled out over the next decade and more. As many historians have attested, it is always difficult to get a reliable read on the public opinion in the GDR. Even when statistics and public opinion reports are available, they are fraught with potential pitfalls and complications. While East Germans were frequently surprisingly frank in their complaints and disagreements, everyone understood that there were limits to the grumbling that the state tolerated and penalties attached to excessive noncooperation and outright opposition. East Germans knew to be circumspect in voicing their true opinions for fear of jeopardizing their career opportunities or just the chance of receiving a new apartment or other favors from state officials. "Double-talk" was the name of the game and an essential element of living within the confines of the East German dictatorship.[29]

Despite this caveat, the main trend lines of the popular support for the Vietnam solidarity campaigns do emerge from documentary evidence. They show that the East German public was uncooperative or resistant to most official campaigns in the early years of the war in the mid-1960s. Like much of the rest of the world, the sentiment began to change in the late 1960s, however, as many East Germans became incensed by the war and were willing to do more to support the North Vietnamese people. This public antiwar mood and support for the solidarity campaigns reached their peak in the early 1970s, especially in 1972 and 1973, when the relentless US bombing raids and the eventual withdrawal of American troops further heightened support for the North Vietnamese underdog. The certainty of a DRV victory against South Vietnam assured high interest until 1975, when it began to fade despite the best efforts of the GDR government to keep the memory relevant and alive. In general, then, the Vietnam solidarity and media campaigns were quite successful overall and possibly unique in the history of the GDR in terms of the large-scale public support it engendered. As Hermann Schwiesau, a longtime leading official in the East German foreign office and GDR ambassador to several countries, recalled after the fall of the Berlin Wall, "This was a unique solidarity campaign in GDR history in terms of its breadth, longevity, and volume. . . . The willingness to donate on the part of the GDR population surpassed all previous campaigns."[30]

Based on the reports of the Ministry for State Security (Ministerium für Staatssicherheit [MfS or Stasi]), this support was rather halting in the initial years of the war. Across the GDR, the official calls for solidarity donations were largely rebuffed or went unanswered, especially between 1964 and 1966. A Stasi official in Leipzig reported this broad negative sentiment in his district in August of 1966: "The missing sense of solidarity with and disinterest toward the Vietnamese people is predominant based on the unofficial reactions of all population groups—even among some comrades."[31] Frequently such rejections were justified with comments by East Germans that they did not want to unnecessarily prolong the war or simply that Vietnam was none of their business. At the same time, some requests for blood donations also revealed racist resentment, such as not wanting to provide "the yellow race with white blood." And when the Warsaw Pact countries met in Bucharest in July 1966 and leaders opened the door to possibly sending military volunteers to Vietnam, the GDR public response was especially loud and unanimous in opposition to such an initiative.[32]

As might be expected, reports of negative responses remained part of the mix for the duration of the war, yet there was a palpable sense that the public support was increasing toward the end of the decade. By 1970, Stasi officials were reporting a greater willingness to donate time and money to the solidarity campaigns, as well as increased and more vocal opposition to the war. In fact, at times positive reports came in the form of criticisms, as in the case of one collective that had produced motorcycles through overtime and as a direct donation to the DRV; yet they stood uncollected in the parking lot and were rusting away. By early 1973, one district official reflected the changing mood of the population at the official end of the war: "The first reports after the signing of the end of the Vietnam War make it clear that the public is following these events with great interest and that they are welcomed unanimously."[33]

In addition, the monthly reports from the districts corroborated the notion that the GDR public had become far more involved in the solidarity campaigns by the early 1970s. Reports from Dresden, for example, highlighted a growing willingness to participate in the donation campaigns and referred to "thousands of new acts of solidarity and donation campaigns." As one report from February 1973 summed up the situation, "The ever-widening solidarity movement is especially evident because many workers are willing to donate 1 to 5 percent of their yearly bonus and an ever-larger number have increased their monthly solidarity donations."[34] The same was true for Leipzig, where a majority of the population strongly condemned the renewed US bombing raids in 1972 and where a large number of local solidarity campaigns were underway in late 1972 and 1973.[35]

These reports also correspond with the overall increase in public donations over the decade between 1966 and 1975. The yearly public donations amounted to roughly 16 million Ostmarks (Mark der DDR) in 1966 and more than doubled by 1968. They reached a new peak in 1973, with more than 48 million, and almost doubled again by 1975 to a total

Figure 1.3. Reception for North Vietnamese representatives in East Berlin, 6 February 1973. (Courtesy of Bundesarchiv Koblenz; Bild 183-MO228-427.)

of 83 million Ostmarks. Even though these donations always made up only a small portion (around 20 percent) of the overall government aid provided to North Vietnam, they are notable for their size as well as the increases over the years.[36] In addition to the ongoing monetary donations, the East German population also contributed over 10,000 bikes, 400 trucks, over 800 motorcycles, more than 4,000 sewing machines, as well as educational, vocational, and medical supplies and equipment over the course of this long war between 1965 and 1975.[37]

By early 1973, GDR officials working in the Solidarity Committee of the GDR felt decidedly more upbeat about the response to their solidarity and media campaigns than they had at the beginning of the war. Especially after the agreement to end the war in Vietnam was signed in January 1973, they noted an especially "lively echo" among the East

German population and "an even wider expansion of the solidarity movement." After listing all the various past and present campaigns on behalf of the Vietnamese people, the committee also resolved to bring ten thousand North Vietnamese to the GDR by the end of the decade in order to help with the education and training of the population, as well as the rebuilding of the country after the devastating war.[38]

Mobilizing for the 1972 Munich Olympics

Similar to the Vietnam War, the preparations for the 1972 Olympics very quickly converged into a flashpoint in the East-West competition and the head-to-head rivalry between the FRG and the GDR in particular. It was the first Olympics held on German ground since the infamous 1936 Games, and West Germany planned to use this event to showcase the new, peaceful side of its postwar nation, while the GDR government was determined to highlight what it saw as the political parallels between the two German Olympics. Piggybacking on the Vietnam narrative, the East German leadership argued that the FRG still maintained many of the fascist, imperialist legacies of the Nazi regime, even though it was trying to hide them behind the façade of the "Happy Munich Games." In addition, the two Germanys had been battling each other over the participation in the Olympic Games ever since the end of World War II. Initially, West Germany had upstaged its rival in this competition; it was allowed to participate and represent the German nation in the 1952 Olympics. After objections and international wrangling, both countries were made to compete in the 1956 Olympics as a combined team under a neutral flag, while medals by either country's athletes were celebrated by playing Ludwig Beethoven's *Ode to Joy*. This compromise held roughly ten years and governed both Olympics in the early 1960s.[39]

In 1965, the International Olympic Committee (IOC) added one further twist to the already suspenseful and convoluted German Olympic drama. In the fall of that year, IOC president Avery Brundage confidentially informed his friend and FRG National Olympic Committee president Willi Daume that the IOC would welcome a bid by West Germany for the 1972 Olympics. What was becoming apparent in the fall of 1965 was that Moscow might be the only viable European candidate for the 1972 Games, a notion that did not sit well with the West-dominated IOC and its American president. Daume had floated the idea of a Berlin Games in the early 1960s, but the IOC feared too many complications from such a decision and instead suggested Munich when presented with the surprising offer. With tacit IOC blessing and the rapid approval of the Munich city council, the Bavarian legislature, and the Bonn Parliament, Munich quickly readied its bid in time for the decisive IOC meeting in Rome in April 1966.[40]

Given the genesis of the Munich bid, it was no surprise that Munich emerged as winner of the IOC selection process in the spring of 1966. The West German republic rejoiced in the decision, viewing it as a validation of Germany's rise as a democratic and economically powerful country ready to be readmitted into the world community. Yet nagging questions remained, especially in terms of the FRG's treatment of East Germany. How would the West German host welcome and treat the East German athletes, especially since its politics (Hallstein Doctrine) demanded that West Germany alone represented the German nation and that it keep the GDR diplomatically isolated? How would West Germany handle the delicate issues of East German statehood, then, and the long-standing feuds surrounding the GDR flag, emblems, and anthem? In a letter from December 1966, Avery Brundage informed Daume that the "question of East Germany's participation" had come up at a recent Executive Board meeting of the IOC in late 1966, and he told Daume very clearly which way the wind was blowing: "It will not be surprising if they [the East Germans] are granted the right to use their own flag and emblem after 1968, and I hope you will be prepared to handle this contingency."[41]

Daume might well have been ready for this contingency and probably had seen it coming for a while, but he seemed to have kept it to himself. When the IOC finally established its new policy concerning two separate and fully independent German teams in its August 1968 Mexico meeting, West German politicians, however, were caught by surprise, especially since the vote was forty-four to four in favor of a separate and fully sovereign GDR team with its own flag and anthem for the 1972 Olympics. The confusion was understandable because when the West German government had signed off on the Munich bid in March 1966, it had insisted that the 1972 Games would be held "on the basis of the regulations of the IOC presently in force," meaning no separate, independent GDR Olympic team. However, in November 1967, the Munich Organizing Committee had agreed "that the Olympic Games will be organized in the spirit of the Olympic Rules of the International Olympic Committee *prevailing at that time* [emphasis added]."[42] And since Olympics were hosted by cities and not countries, the response by the Munich Committee was decisive. This meant that the GDR was going to compete in the 1972 Olympics as a fully sovereign and fully recognized

Figure 1.4. Entry of the East German Olympic team into the Munich Stadium, 26 August 1972. (Courtesy of Bundesarchiv Koblenz; Bild 183-L0827-207.)

country on West German soil. The unbridgeable gap between the Hallstein Doctrine, which dictated that East Germany remain internationally isolated, and the opportunity to host the 1972 Olympics had finally been exposed. As a result, the West German government had to accept the reality of an equal East German sports nation competing in Munich.

In East Germany, the Olympic decisions of the late 1960s created just as much political furor as in West Germany. Even before the IOC had officially selected Munich as the host for the 1972 Olympics, the GDR Sports Association (Deutscher Turn- und Sportbund [DTSB]) and the East German government had readied their political response to the anticipated selection in March of 1966. They viewed it as part of an ongoing campaign of "West German imperialism that was going to exploit the preparation of the Olympic Games as a political and ideological offensive in order to increase the prestige of the FRG." As the GDR saw it, the Munich Games would no doubt highlight similar goals as the ones pursued by Nazi Germany with the 1936 Berlin Olympics.[43] Even before Munich was officially chosen, then, some of the major themes of the GDR media campaigns against the Games were already well established.

When the IOC finally recognized East Germany as a full and equal competitor for the 1972 Olympics in its October 1968 meeting, the GDR redoubled its efforts for ideological sports warfare in Munich. In internal memos, the Munich Olympics were referred to as the "Fateful Munich Games" (Schicksalsspiele München), highlighting the greater significance that the competitions acquired for German-German politics. No effort was going to be spared to achieve the overarching goals of the Munich Games: to increase East Germany's medal count and win additional international recognition for the GDR. But most important was the singular goal of beating the West German team on its own soil.[44] By late 1968, the stage was thus set for the 1972 Olympics, and the two German sides were beginning to mobilize their forces for the athletic battles ahead.

There were many fronts in the battle between the two Germanys both leading up to and running parallel to the 1972 Olympics. One strategically important one was the IOC, especially its powerful president, Avery Brundage. By the late 1960s, he was a seasoned international sports official. Elected IOC president in 1952, Brundage was already in his late seventies in the mid-1960s, and the 1972 Olympics would be his last Games. For the most part, the West German National Olympic Committee (NOC), especially its president and longtime friend Willi Daume, had Brundage's ear, but international politics were changing swiftly in the 1960s. In addition, Brundage insisted at least publicly on an apolitical or politically neutral stance on the part of the IOC in order to stay true to the original spirit of the Olympic idea, which was to foster a friendly and welcoming forum for all athletes and nations. In order to gain more leverage with the IOC, the East German government worked assiduously to gain Brundage's trust and goodwill in the 1960s. The front man in this public relations campaign was the president of the East German NOC, Heinz Schöbel, who after repeated Russian lobbying finally joined the IOC in 1966.[45]

Although all national representatives pampered the IOC president and wined and dined him and his IOC colleagues on visits to their countries, Schöbel and the East German government were particularly relentless and apparent in their ingratiating campaign to win over Brundage's heart and mind. The opening salvo of the media campaign was a book on the history of the Olympic Games published by Schöbel in 1965, which presented a mirror image of Brundage's nostalgic view of the Olympic movement, for which Brundage agreed to write the preface. Schöbel followed this up with an uncritical and glowing biography of the IOC president in 1968, titled *The Four Dimensions of Avery Brundage*. All the pictures, which took up three-quarters of the book, were supplied by the director of the Brundage Foundation, while the captions were written by its longtime secretary. To make sure that he got everything right—and to Brundage's liking—Schöbel was in frequent contact with the IOC president and sent him the manuscript for corrections and input prior to publication. He was able to present Brundage with the published biography at the IOC meeting in Mexico in October 1968—the same meeting where the IOC voted for the full Olympic recognition of the GDR.[46]

Less than a year later, Schöbel and the GDR government landed another coup in this public relations campaign to win over the IOC president and gain increased international recognition. In preparation for the twentieth anniversary celebrations of the GDR in late 1969, Brundage accepted an invitation to visit the country in July of that year and received the full red-carpet treatment. On a five-day visit, he was treated to the best East Germany had to offer. Among other events, Brundage attended the fifth German Gymnastics and Sports Festival in Leipzig for two days as the government's and Schöbel's special guest of honor. These competitions were meant to reflect East Germany's emphasis on broad-based physical education and fitness as well as to highlight the GDR's commitment to amateurism, an ideal that firmly undergirded the traditional Olympic idea and that was near and dear to Brundage's heart.[47]

Figure 1.5. IOC president Avery Brundage (*left*) visits Leipzig and other GDR cities in July 1969, hosted by East German NOC president Heinz Schöbel (*third from left*). (Courtesy of University of Illinois at Urbana-Champaign Archives.)

On the second front of the mobilization campaign for the Munich Games, the preparation of the GDR athletes and sports machinery, the focus was different from the professed commitment to amateurism. Contrary to the broad-based support for sport that was presented to Brundage on his visit to the GDR, East Germany had in fact committed itself to a very targeted and Olympia-focused sports strategy just a few months earlier. In a watershed decision in April 1969, the GDR sports association decided to focus its limited resources on elite sports, especially on those disciplines that would most likely increase the medal count in the 1972 as well as successive Olympics. In order to do so, the GDR sports world was separated into two broad categories. Sport I included all those disciplines that were easiest to fund and especially medal-rich (like swimming or track-and-field competitions) as well as areas where the GDR already had a solid foundation, such as gymnastics. Sport II captured those athletic areas that demanded a lot of resources (like team sports or alpine skiing); they were going to be reduced in funding or were discontinued at the elite level altogether. The decision to fund only medal-rich sports, which would increase the point count in the 1972 Olympics and help the GDR beat the FRG and other Western countries, dictated the future of East German sport, with the blessing of the GDR political leadership. As an internal memo put it bluntly, "The goal for the Olympic Games is to consolidate the GDR performance from 1968 and to achieve a ranking [in points as well as medals] ahead of the FRG."[48] Even though West Germany might outshine the GDR in politics and economics, the East German government was increasingly confident that it could burnish its image through the battles in the sport arenas.

Parallel to this complete takeover of sports by the state and relentless focus on medal-rich sports, the GDR also embarked on what Grit Hartmann has called a "radical reorientation of sports medicine in preparation for the Munich Games." In this respect, a new kind of research institute for sports medicine was established in Leipzig (Forschungsinstitut für Körperkultur und Sport [FKS]) in early 1969, which would fundamentally alter the training and preparation of GDR athletes. Everything in an athlete's life would now be researched and studied medically in order to optimize the performance, endurance, and strength of GDR elite competitors. In preparation for the Munich Games, political schooling and a hardening of the ideological commitment were also part of the selection process, since nothing was more embarrassing than having athletes from East Germany request political asylum abroad, the dreaded *Republikflucht*. And finally, this new research incorporated the infamous and government-supported experimentation with performance-enhancing drugs, which became part and parcel of the GDR preparation for athletic and Olympic competitions.[49]

In addition to the two initiatives already discussed, the charm offensive on Brundage and the radical reorientation of GDR elite sports in the late 1960s, the East German government also fought its pre-Munich battles on a third front: it launched persistent media campaigns against West Germany and the Munich host city, the overall goal of which was to counter West German political gains and to protest any and all infractions of the IOC rules and the Olympic protocol.[50] One successful GDR campaign, for example, targeted the two American radio stations Radio Liberty and Radio Free Europe, both of which were based in Munich. For decades they had broadcast Western news and pop music across Eastern Bloc countries in a concerted effort to puncture and disrupt communist media dominance. The two stations had long been the focus of Cold War animosity, since the GDR and other Eastern European governments saw them as vehicles of Cold War aggression and Western propaganda, while the West viewed them as effective tools for disseminating information across the Iron Curtain and part of the cultural opening of the Eastern Bloc. After repeated criticisms by the East German NOC and a personal appeal by Daume to the presidents of the two stations, an Olympic peace deal was brokered. The stations stopped broadcasting for the duration of the Olympic Games in order to avoid ongoing ideological wrangling and political skirmishes.[51]

Just to be clear, though, while West Germany was rolling out the welcome mat as the host of the 1972 Olympics, its government also made sure that it was not going to be torched by the East German athletic teams. In order to counter the GDR initiatives, the FRG undertook a major reorganization as part of its Olympic preparation with a focus on elite sport as well. The West German parliament took up the issue in March 1969 and passed a law that supported the increased funding and further professionalization of elite sport. In early 1969, it created a special committee that was to oversee the preparation of the West German athletes and teams for the 1972 Olympics. Rather tellingly, government funding for elite sport doubled from slightly over 11 million Deutschmarks in 1969 to roughly 23.5 million by 1972. After all, West Germany had already been defeated by the East German Olympic team at the 1968 Olympics. Despite the lighthearted and playful tone it projected with its Olympic designs and activities, West Germany was no stranger to "the class struggle in the sports arenas," and it planned to be ready for the athletic confrontations to come.[52]

When the athletic competitions got underway in late August of 1972, then, the two German states and their athletic teams arrived well-prepared. Based on the increased funding and intensified focus on elite sports, both teams were able to significantly increase their medal count in comparison with the 1968 Olympics. In fact, in no small measure spurred by their athletic Cold War rivalry, the two Germanys were the two most improved nations among all Olympic competitors. The host country improved its medal count from twenty-six in 1968 to forty in 1972. West Germany especially excelled in track-and-field competitions as well as in water sports such as swimming, canoeing and rowing. In terms of the national rankings, the FRG achieved a fourth-place finish in the Munich medal count.[53]

By far the most improved team at the 1972 Olympic Games, however, was East Germany. Even though the athletes of the host country performed well in Munich, the East German teams beat them in the medal count in each discipline as well as the overall point count. In fact, the GDR competitors more than doubled their medals in the 1972 Olympics compared to four years earlier: they won sixty-six medals in 1972, twenty of them gold. Half of those medals were won in track-and-field and swimming. As East German sports officials had predicted, the West German orchestra had better practice the GDR anthem, because it was going to be played frequently in Munich. In the national rankings, the GDR moved to third place in 1972, right behind the first-placed USSR and the overall runner-up, the team from the United States.[54]

In order to ensure that its Olympic successes were properly recognized and celebrated by its own population, the East German government also developed an elaborate, long-term strategy for the media coverage of the Munich Games. To be sure, most countries consume international sports coverage with a decisive national bias, but in terms of detail and precision the GDR took this one step further. Fully aware that West Germany held the upper hand in financial and technological resources in this area of the ideological battle, East Germany utilized its limited resources strategically and wisely. While the FRG as the host nation broadcast all Olympic competitions live, which created a kind of oversaturation after a few days, the GDR channeled its limited resources to targeted competitions in which its teams excelled, as well as select and limited prime-time slots when most East German traditionally watched television. Specifically, SED officials responsible for GDR television coverage decided to utilize the prime-time slot from 7:45 to 8:30 p.m. as their core daily viewing bloc to cover the Olympic Games. On specific days and evenings as well as weekends, which promised to be especially medal-rich for the East German team, GDR television officials reserved additional prime-time blocs. Alternatively, TV officials scheduled music programs or other shows that could easily be interrupted for short, targeted live coverage of ongoing Olympic competitions highlighting East German athletes and GDR medal wins.[55]

As it turned out, this limited, but strategically targeted TV coverage was well received by the vast majority of GDR television viewers. Since East German television was limited to two channels, oversaturation or tuning out viewers not interested in sports was a real concern. Surveys conducted during and after the Munich Olympics confirmed that roughly 70 percent of the East German viewers were very satisfied with the TV coverage of the Olympic Games. These same surveys confirmed that more East Germans were turning on their sets especially during the core prime-time slots reserved for Olympic coverage: the average ratings for the 7:45–8:30 p.m. slot, for example, increased from its usual 32 percent rating to an average of 40 percent of TV households during the two weeks of the Olympic Games; on specific evenings viewership even increased close to or above 50 percent. These were indeed stellar ratings for GDR television, as the more detailed discussions in chapter 3 will emphasize. As might be expected, East German viewers also intermittently scanned or watched the Olympic coverage on FRG television, as was common practice by then, and some East Germans naturally complained that GDR television was late in highlighting some of the competitions, even some GDR wins. Other viewers were also annoyed by some heavily politicized commentaries on GDR TV or the less polished and at times stiff interviewing habits of their own reporters. In general, however, the SED leadership rightly considered the TV coverage of the Olympic Games a success, which was reflected in the overwhelmingly positive viewer letters they received as well.[56]

Similar to the domestic celebrations and accolades, East Germany also gained a tremendous amount of international recognition because of the stellar performance of its athletes at the Munich Olympics. While *Neues Deutschland* as well as other GDR media elatedly celebrated the performance of its team and cited it as a clear reflection of the superiority of socialism over capitalism, the international media took note of the increased status and prestige of the GDR as well. "Honecker's sports officials arrived in Munich ready to settle their accounts with West Germany and prove themselves to the West. They have certainly accomplished that!," an Austrian newspaper commented in one of its summary articles of the 1972 Olympic Games. The *Baltimore Sun* congratulated both German teams by rightly pointing out that their combined successes

Figure 1.6. Erich Honecker (*middle*) and the GDR minister of sports Manfred Ewald (*left*) hosting a reception for East German Olympic athletes. (Courtesy of Bundesarchiv Koblenz, Bild L1027/41H.)

placed "the German nation" ahead of the United States and the Soviet Union in first place of the international medal competition. The newspaper especially singled out the new self-confidence of East Germany, which in addition "was able to send its team to Munich without the fear of desertions." In general, the media coverage reflected high praises for the GDR team and, by association, enhanced respect for the East German government.[57]

While the Munich Games represented a very important stepping-stone for East Germany, it is noteworthy that the GDR athletic team was able to further improve upon its successes four years later in the Montreal Olympics. The East German athletes were able to increase their medal count once again, from sixty-six in 1972 to ninety in 1976. In fact, in a stunning upset, the GDR placed second in the national rankings at the 1976 Games—behind the Soviet Union but ahead of the United States. Within less than a decade, East Germany had become a sports superpower. The head of East German sports affairs, Manfred Ewald, celebrated the two weeks of the Montreal Olympics as the time when the GDR became even further known to millions of spectators around the world. Because of the dominant performances of the Soviet and East German teams, a Canadian newspaper quipped that the 1976 Games should be renamed the "Karl-Marx-Games." Even the conservative West German newspaper *Frankfurter Allgemeine Zeitung* agreed that these athletic victories added further recognition for the East German state: "The days of Montreal are the days when the GDR is placed on the world map for millions of people."[58]

Conclusion

The East German international sports diplomacy with its focus on Olympic gold clearly paid off in the 1970s. Parallel to significant international political developments, these athletic successes were instrumental in garnering international prestige and polishing the tarnished image of the communist "rump-state." It buoyed the spirits of the East German population, added political legitimacy to the SED government, and showcased a successful socialist country that was willing and able to compete with the FRG and the West. More than that, it projected an image of a competitive or perhaps even superior political model, since East Germany demonstrated that it could not just compete with, but in fact beat the Western teams when it really put its mind to it.

These international athletic successes were a great boon to the East German state, as they provided continuous fodder for its media campaigns. East Germany accomplished in the sports world what was frequently denied to it in the political realm. While it often remained rather marginalized in international politics and largely ignored by the United States and other Western powers, in Olympic competitions the GDR was important—a true contender and a power with which they had to reckon. Here it could defeat its West German archenemy and even the most powerful imperialist nation of them all, the United States of America, to the delight of its officials and its often distrustful population. Like its opposition to the Vietnam War, which garnered genuine support and at times enthusiasm, Olympic gold added to the legitimacy of the East German state and consolidated the GDR government in the early to mid-1970s.

Ongoing political crosscurrents notwithstanding, the activities and media campaigns surrounding the Vietnam War similarly represented a significant net plus for the East German government in its Cold War battle against the West. First, it provided the SED leadership with significant support for its long-held claim that the United States was a capitalist octopus set on strangling nascent socialist regimes and stretching its imperialist tentacles into the far corners of the globe. Likewise, the antiwar rhetoric opened up numerous venues to implicate the West German capitalist adversary and to put the Bonn government on the defensive. Second, it allowed the GDR to join and at times lead a burgeoning international opposition against the Vietnam War, which included not just the usual communist allies but found particularly receptive audiences in the developing world as well. Finally, the antiwar campaign bolstered the credibility and support of the government with its own people. Unlike most officially run media campaigns, the opposition to the Vietnam War was eventually backed by the majority of the East German population and reduced its disaffection from the SED leadership.

In addition, despite the well-placed fears that *Ostpolitik* might lead to the convergence of the GDR and FRG as well as undermine the SED government, its impact initially proved both energizing and stabilizing for the East German leadership.[59] Similar to the GDR's anti–Vietnam War campaigns, *Ostpolitik* was well received by the global community. Combined, these two policy initiates helped the GDR to achieve one of the primary goals it had pursued for the past twenty years. Rather quickly, the GDR was swept up in a wave of international recognition, which enabled it to establish diplomatic relations with numerous countries, including Western powers like Great Britain, France, and the United States; all three were finalized during the course of 1974. Equally important, East Germany, together with its West German counterpart, was officially admitted to the United Nations in 1973, where they both quickly became members of many of the UN's subsidiary organizations. And finally, East Berlin was able to expand its activist, anti-imperialist international reputation with two related events in the early 1970s. In 1972, civil rights activist Angela Davis was greeted by tens of thousands of adoring East German fans after her release from US prison on her visit to the GDR. As Dorothee Wierling highlights, the GDR's solidarity campaign on Davis's behalf and the World Youth Festival of 1973 were two moments when significant segments of East German youth genuinely connected with and supported SED government's mobilizing campaigns—creating a political and cultural synergy that was rare in the life of the GDR.[60]

As several historians have reminded us, within the life span of East Germany there were always periods when the GDR was more stable and when the compromise of "passive conformity and leaving politics to the party" was more widely accepted. As Mary Fulbrook argues, "This compromise was, very nearly, achieved—perhaps for the space of two or three years in the early to mid-1970s, let us say 1972–75." Marc-Dietrich Ohse concurs and even goes so far as calling the early 1970s the "golden years" of the GDR. In his recollections, Christoph Dieckmann similarly refers to 1973 as the time of "the closest relationship between the government and the [East German] youth."[61]

While the population never accepted the SED government as fully legitimate, the reasons for the increased identification with the GDR during these years were manifold: the strengthening of the party apparatus and the Stasi, to be sure, but also rising living standards and greater cultural openness as well as an enhanced international status and expanded travel within the Eastern Bloc. East Germany's stellar performance at the 1972 Munich Olympics and the successful anti–Vietnam War media campaigns were particularly significant in this context, and both increased the GDR's international recognition as well as a greater acquiescence on the part of the East German population from the early to mid-1970s.[62]

Notes

1. For good overviews of the international history of the Vietnam War, see Mark Atwood Lawrence, *The Vietnam War: A Concise International History* (Oxford and New York: Oxford University Press, 2008) as well as two collections of essays: Lloyd C. Gardner and Ted Gittinger, eds., *International Perspectives on Vietnam* (College Station: Texas A&M University Press, 2000); and Andreas W. Daum, Lloyd C. Gardner, and Wilfried Mausbach, eds., *America, the Vietnam War, and the World: Comparative and International Perspectives* (Washington, DC, and Cambridge: Cambridge University Press, 2003). The Soviet Union's policies toward Vietnam are discussed in Ilya V. Gaiduk, *The Soviet Union and the Vietnam War* (Chicago: Ivan R. Dee, 1996); and Jonathan Haslam, *Russia's Cold War: From the October Revolution to the Fall of the Wall* (New Haven and London: Yale University Press, 2011), chapters 8 and 9.
2. On the Berlin Wall, see, for example, Patrick Major, *Behind the Berlin Wall: East Germany and the Frontiers of Power* (Oxford and New York: Oxford University Press, 2010), chapters 5 and 6. On the supposed "counterrevolutionary threat" of the Prague Spring, see Manfred Wilke, "Ulbricht, East Germany, and the Prague Spring," in *The Prague Spring and the Warsaw Pact Invasion of Czechoslovakia in 1968*, ed. Günter Bischof, Stefan Karner, and Peter Ruggenthaler (Plymouth, UK: Lexington Books, 2010), 341–70.
3. See "Vietnam and World Opinion: Analysis and Recommendations," August 1966; National Archives [hereafter NA] RG 306, USIA, Office of Research; folder "Special Reports, 1964–1982."

4. It is somewhat surprising how little the Vietnam War, specifically the consistent and forceful opposition of the East German government to the war, has been incorporated into the overall historical scholarship of the GDR in the late 1960s and 1970s. The two notable exceptions are Günter Wernicke, *"Solidarität hilft siegen!" Zur Solidaritätsbewegung mit Vietnam in beiden deutschen Staaten: Mitte der 60er bis Anfang der 70er Jahre*, Hefte zur DDR-Geschichte 72 (Berlin, 2001); and Nguyen van Huong, "Die Politik der DDR gegenüber Vietnam und den Vertragsarbeitern aus Vietnam sowie die Situation der Vietnamesen in Deutschland heute," in *Materialien der Enquete-Kommission "Überwindung der Folgen der SED-Diktatur im Prozess der deutschen Einheit,"* ed. Deutscher Bundestag, vol. 8, 2 (Baden-Baden: Nomos Verlagsgesellschaft, 1995), 1301–63. Even fine and generally well-received studies have largely overlooked this topic. See, for example, Hermann Wentker, *Aussenpolitik in engen Grenzen: Die DDR im internationalen System, 1949–1989* (Munich: R. Oldenbourg Verlag, 2007); or Marc-Dietrich Ohse, *Jugend nach dem Mauerbau: Anpassung, Protest und Eigensinn (DDR 1961–1974)* (Berlin: Ch. Links Verlag, 2003). For an excellent addition to the broader topic of GDR foreign relations, however, see Quinn Slobodian, ed., *Comrades of Color: East Germany in the Cold War* (New York and London: Berghahn Books, 2015).
5. Grit Hartmann, *Goldkinder: Die DDR im Spiegel ihres Spitzensports* (Leipzig: Forum Verlag Leipzig, 1997), 74; chapter 3 focuses on the preparation for the 1972 Olympics. Equally insightful and important as Hartmann's study is Uta Andrea Balbier's book, *Kalter Krieg auf der Aschenbahn: Der deutsch-deutsche Sport, 1952–1972. Eine politische Geschichte* (Paderborn: Ferdinand Schöningh, 2007), chapters 4 and 5; and especially also Kay Schiller and Christopher Young's excellent study, *The 1972 Munich Olympics and the Making of Modern Germany* (Berkeley and Los Angeles: University of California Press, 2010).
6. For medal tables of the respective Olympics, see James Riordan, *Sports, Politics and Communism* (Manchester and New York: Manchester University Press, 1991), 139–40; and Gunter Holzweissig, *Diplomatie im Trainingsanzug: Sport als politisches Instrument der DDR in den innerdeutschen und internationalen Beziehungen* (Munich and Vienna: R. Oldenbourg Verlag, 1981), 188–90. Willi Ph. Knecht, *Das Medaillenkollektiv: Fakten, Dokumente und Kommentare zum Sport in der DDR* (Berlin: Verlag Gebr. Holzapfel, 1978), 111–13, provides the exact points in the German-German Olympic competition between 1968 and 1976; by the 1976 Summer Olympics in Montreal, East Germany had more than twice as many points (638) as the FRG (282).
7. Despite this overall hostile stance and rhetoric, there were also multiple attempts by the GDR to engage with the United States during this time period: see, for example, Christian M. Ostermann, "Die USA und die DDR," in *Die DDR und der Westen: Transnationale Beziehungen, 1949–1989*, ed. Ulrich Pfeil (Berlin: Ch. Links Verlag, 2001), 165–83; as well as Dorothee

Wierling, "Amerikabilder in der DDR," and Philip Matthes, "David and Goliath: Der Anerkennungslobbyismus der DDR in den USA von 1964 bis 1974," in *Umworbener Klassenfeind: Das Verhältnis der DDR zu den USA*, ed. Uta A. Balbier and Christiane Rösch (Berlin: Ch. Links Verlag, 2006), 32–38 and 40–58, respectively.

8. "USA-Bomben auf Vietnam," *Neues Deutschland* [hereafter *ND*], 6 August 1964, cover page. Side-by-side articles on US atrocities and GDR solidarity campaigns early on became a standard feature of this reporting style: see articles "USA geben Urheberrolle zu" and "DDR an der Seite Vietnams," *ND*, 8 August 1964, cover page. Both articles were bracketed by the heading "Weltweite Protestwelle gegen die amerikanische Aggression."
9. For an overall GDR assessment of the US international policies in connection with Vietnam, see "Ziele und Auswirkungen der Aggression der USA in Indochina," June 1965–May 1970, Abteilung USA des Ministeriums für Auswärtige Angelengenheiten der DDR [hereafter MfAA], C 506/74. The two mentioned articles were published in *ND*, 20 July 1968 and 13 August 1968, respectively. As an example of the increasing equation of America's domestic and international policies, see "Panzer und Hubschrauber jagen Neger," *ND*, 27 July 1967; and "Vietnam-Killer wüten in Detroit," *ND*, 28 July 1967.
10. The quote is from "Amerikaner führen Vernichtungskrieg in Südvietnam," *ND*, 8 March 1966. The use of poison gases is discussed in the front-page article on 11 March 1966. For a typical portrayal of East Germany as the peaceful of the two German states, see front-page article, 13 March 1966.
11. "Bunderwehreinsatz in Südvietnam wird vorbereitet," *ND*, 19 June 1965; and "Sensationelle Studie über die Beteiligung der Bundeswehr an USA-Aggression in Vietnam," *ND*, 19 March 1966.
12. "Das ökonomische Engagement der BRD im Zusammenhang mit der USA-Aggression in Südvietnam," 2 April 1966, MfAA, A 18325.
13. Horst Rennhack, *BRD-Imperialismus: Komplice der USA-Agressoren in Indochina* (Berlin: Staatsverlag der Deutschen Demokratischen Republik, 1973), 9–24; the quotes are on pp. 9 and 15.
14. "Current Climate of Foreign Opinion on Viet-Nam," 21 April 1969, NA, RG 306, Records of the U.S. Information Agency, Office of Research, folder "Special Reports, 1964–1982."
15. Rennhack, *BRD-Imperialismus*, chapter 2; the quote is on p. 27.
16. For a discussion of the "guilt-by-association" argument and dispute, see Alexandra Friedrich, "Awakenings: The Impact of the Vietnam War on West German–American Relations in the late 1960s" (PhD dissertation, Temple University, 2000), chapters 3 and 4. On the broader tensions created by the war, see also Wolfram F. Hanrieder, *Germany, America, Europe: Forty Years of German Foreign Policy* (New Haven and London: Yale University Press, 1989), chapter 9. On Brandt's strong misgivings about the war, see Peter Merseburger, *Willy Brandt, 1913–1992: Visionär und Realist* (Munich: Deutsche Verlags-Anstalt, 2006), 554–63.

17. See articles in *ND*: "FNL brandmarkt Mitschuld Bonns," 1 September 1966; "Bonn will weiterhin rückhaltslos für den USA-Krieg zahlen," 6 January 1968; and "Ein System und seine Methoden," 9 January 1971.
18. "Auf Hitler's Spuren," *ND*, 27 July 1967; and "Das Hakenkreuz auf dem Dollar," *ND*, 6 August 1967.
19. Nick Thomas, *Protest Movements in 1960s West Germany: A Social History of Dissent and Democracy* (Oxford and New York: Berg, 2003), chapter 4; the quote is on p. 73.
20. Wilfried Mausbach, "Auschwitz and Vietnam: West German Protest against America's War during the 1960s," in *America, the Vietnam War, and the World*, ed. Daum, Gardner, and Mausbach; the quotes are from p. 286.
21. This trend is well reflected in Anita Eichholz, *Der Vietnamkrieg im SPIEGEL: Eine inhaltsanalytische Untersuchung* (Berlin: Verlag Volker Spiess, 1979), 74–86, 164–69. On this overall shift in attitudes toward the war, see also Joachim Arendt, *Johnson, Vietnam, und der Westen: Transatlantische Beziehungen, 1963–1969* (Munich: Olzog Verlag, 1994); and Gerd Horten, "The Mediatization of War: A Comparison of the American and German Media Coverage of the Vietnam and Iraq Wars," *American Journalism: A Journal of Media History* 28, no. 4 (Fall 2011): 29–54.
22. Wernicke, *"Solidarität hilft siegen!,"* 19, 54. At a 1969 conference in East Berlin, for example, the forty-seven foreign participants came from eighteen different countries. Of the five from the West, two each came from Italy and Great Britain and one from Belgium. "Bericht über die Woche wissenschaftlicher Tagungen und Kolloquien," 6 March 1969, SAPMO-BArch, DZ 8/139.
23. For good overviews of these films and the Studio H&S, see Rüdiger Steinmetz, "Heynowski & Scheumann: The GDR's Leading Documentary Team," *Historical Journal of Film, Radio and Television* 24, no. 3 (2004): 365–79; and Nora Alter, *Projecting History: German Nonfiction Cinema, 1967–2000* (Ann Arbor: University of Michigan Press, 2002), chapter 1.
24. Steinmetz, "Heynowski & Scheumann," 370–74. On the reception of the films in Western Europe, see also Mogens Rukov, "Respekt vor der Autorität der Tatsachen: Zur Rezeption der H&S-Filme in Westeuropa," in *Dokument und Kunst: Vietnam bei H&S. Eine Werkstatt-Ein Thema-Elf Jahre-Dreizehn Filme* (Berlin: Akademie der Künste der Deutschen Demokratischen Republik, 1977), 37–40. These and other documentaries focused on the Vietnam War and American atrocities were also a central focal point of the well-known annual International Documentary Film Festival in Leipzig in the late 1960s and early 1970s; see Victor Grossman, "Sauerstoff im stickigen Leipzig: Eindrücke eines US-Amerikaners von der Internationalen Dokumentarfilmwoche in Leipzig," in *Umworbener Klassenfeind*, ed. Balbier and Rösch, 180–91.
25. Gerhard Grümmer, "Herbizide in Vietnam (Teil 1)," published in *Wissenschaft und Fortschritt* 20, no. 3 (1970), SAMPO-BArch, DZ 8/106. For the report on the 1971 conference, see "Information über die 2. Sitzung der Internatio-

nalen Kommission zur Untersuchung amerikanischer Kriegsverbrechen in Indochina (Oslo, 20.–24. Juni 1971)," SAPMO-BArch, DZ 8/129.

26. For the GDR's raised status in Africa in the 1970s, see Gareth M. Winrow, *The Foreign Policy of the GDR in Africa* (Cambridge: Cambridge University Press, 1990), chapter 3. In her essay "Die Westpolitik der DDR zwischen internationaler Aufwertung und ideologischer Offensive (1966–1989)," Marianne Howarth argues that the immediate years after 1973 represented for the SED "[eine] Phase [der] Blütezeit ihrer Diplomatie und ihrer auswärtigen Politik"; in *Die DDR und der Westen*, ed. Pfeil, 89.

27. Van Huong, "Die Politik der DDR gegenüber Vietnam und den Vertragsarbeitern aus Vietnam," 1304–11.

28. Wernicke, "*Solidarität hilft siegen!,*" 14.

29. Andrew Port, *Conflict and Stability in the German Democratic Republic* (Cambridge and New York: Cambridge University Press, 2007), chapter 5; Major, *Behind the Berlin Wall*, chapter 6; and Ohse, *Jugend nach dem Mauerbau*, 287–95.

30. Siegfried Bock, Ingrid Muth, and Hermann Schwiesau, eds., *DDR-Aussenpolitik im Rückspiegel: Diplomaten im Gespräch* (Münster: LIT Verlag, 2004), 287.

31. For the Leipzig report, see Bundesbeauftragter für die Unterlagen des Staatssicherheitsdienstes der ehemaligen Deutschen Demokratischen Republik [hereafter BStU], BVfS Leipzig, AKG 00312/02, 29 August 1966. For the Berlin report, see BStU, MfS, BV Berlin, AKG 441, 10 August 1967.

32. Comments like these, especially the one about not wanting to prolong the war, were frequent among those who did not participate in the solidarity campaigns. The racist rejections seem far less frequent by comparison. For an example, though, see BStU, BVfS Leipzig, AKG 00313/01, 18 January 1967.

33. For the complaint, see BStU Chemnitz, AKG 8255, 8 January 1970. See also BStU, MfS, BV Berlin, Abteilung VIII, 363, 11 May 1972; or BStU, MfS, SED-KL 2079, 10 May 1972. The quote is from BStU Chemnitz, AKG 8849, 29 January 1973.

34. SAPMO-BArch, DY 30/2211 (Büro Erich Honecker). The quotes are from the monthly reports from Dresden from 8 January 1972 and 27 February 1973, respectively.

35. SAPMO-BArch, DY 30/2260; see reports from 2 June 1972 and 1 October 1973.

36. Van Huong, "Die Politik der DDR gegenüber Vietnam," 1312–14.

37. "Faktenmaterial über die Vietnam-Solidarität der DDR-Bevölkerung," 25 April 1973; and memo to Kurt Krüger, Vietnam Committee, 15 August 1974, both in SAPMO-BArch, DZ 8/123.

38. The quote is from the report "Faktenmaterial über die Vietnam-Solidarität der DDR-Bevölkerung," 25 April 1973, and the projection from a report from 15 August 1974; both in SAMPO-BArch, DZ 8/123.

39. Martin H. Geyer, "On the Road to a German 'Postnationalism'? Athletic Competition between the Two German States in the Era of Konrad Adenauer," *German Politics and Society* 25, no. 2 (2007): 147–50; and Hartmann, *Goldkinder*, 38–45. On the intense political nature of this competition, see especially Balbier, *Kalter Krieg auf der Aschenbahn*; as well as Tobias Blasius, *Olympische Bewegung, Kalter Krieg und Deutschlandpolitik, 1949–1972* (Frankfurt am Main: Peter Lang Verlag, 2001).
40. The confidential conversation between Brundage and Daume is discussed in a memo to the West German Secretary of the Interior, 19 November 1965, Bundesarchiv Koblenz (hereafter BAK), Bundeskanzleramt, B 136/5566. For a broader discussion of the Munich bid for the 1972 Olympics, see Blasius, *Olympische Bewegung, Kalter Krieg und Deutschlandpolitik, 1949–1972*, 291–99.
41. Letter by Avery Brundage to Willi Daume, 7 December 1966, Archives of the University of Illinois, Urbana-Champaign (hereafter UCIC), Brundage Collection, Box 56. Brundage's politics in connection with the Cold War and the Olympic movement are discussed in Allen Guttmann, *The Games Must Go On: Avery Brundage and the Olympic Movement* (New York: Columbia University Press, 1984), chapter 9.
42. The surprise of the FRG government is captured in a memo to the Chancellor, 14 October 1968. The differing statements of the FRG government and the Munich Organizing Committee are quoted in a report titled "Gesamtdeutsche Belange bei der Organization und Durchführung der Olympischen Spiele 1972," 14 August 1969; both documents are from BAK, Bundeskanzleramt, B 136/5565.
43. See memorandum titled "Über die Bewerbung der Stadt München für die Olympischen Sommerspiele 1972," 16 March 1966, SAPMO-BArch, DR 510/132.
44. Hartmann, *Goldkinder*, chapter 3. For an excellent analysis of the 1972 Games especially from a West German perspective, see Schiller and Young, *The 1972 Munich Olympics and the Making of Modern Germany*.
45. Guttmann, *The Games Must Go On*; the German-German relationship is discussed in chapter 9, "The Olympic Games and the Cold War." This approach also borrowed from earlier Soviet campaigns: see Jennifer Parks, "Verbal Gymnastics: Sports, Bureaucracy, and the Soviet Union Entrance into the Olympic Games, 1946–1952," in *East Plays West: Sport and the Cold War*, ed. Stephen Wagg and David L. Andrews (London and New York: Routledge, 2007), 27–44.
46. On the 1965 book by Schöbel, see his letter to Brundage from 4 August 1966, UCIC, Brundage Collection, Box 65. For the biography, see Heinz Schöbel, *The Four Dimensions of Avery Brundage* (Leipzig, 1968). The book was simultaneously published in English and German. It consists of thirty pages of text and ninety pages of images with captions.

47. See Scrapbook 57—Visit to GDR/Leipzig, 23–28 July 1969, UCIC, Brundage Collection, Box 316. On the international significance of the visit, see David Childs, "East Germany: Towards the Twentieth Anniversary," *World Today* 23, no. 10 (October 1969): 445.
48. Hartmann, *Goldkinder*, 75–76; and Balbier, *Kalter Krieg auf der Aschenbahn*, 171–72. The quoted report is cited in Hartmann's study (p. 76). Another excellent discussion of this far-reaching shift is provided by Andreas Ritter, *Wandlungen in der Steuerung des DDR-Hochleistungssports in den 1960er und 1970er Jahren* (Potsdam: Universitätsverlag Potsdam, 2003). For a helpful chart of the administrative structure of GDR sport, see Riordan, *Sports, Politics and Communism*, 67.
49. Hartmann, *Goldkinder*; the Leipzig Institute is discussed on pp. 77–78. The selection, training, and doping procedures are covered in chapters 4–6; Hartmann refers to it as the "pathway into secret research" (140).
50. For an early discussion of the ensuing propaganda campaign, see document "1. Konzeption eines Planes zur Vorbereitung der Olympischen Spiele des Jahres 1972 in Sapporo (Japan) und München bzw. Kiel (Westdeutschland)," 1969, SAPMO-BArch, DR 5/1160.
51. "Erklärung des Präsidiums des Nationalen Olympischen Komitees der Deutschen Demokratischen Republik," 29 March 1972, SAPMO-BArch 510/706. The controversy surrounding the radio stations is one of a number of controversies discussed in this document. See also "Die Olympische Idee vor Missbrauch schützen," *Neues Deutschland*, 14 April 1971, BAK, Bundeskanzleramt, B 136/5565.
52. Balbier, *Kalter Krieg auf der Aschenbahn*, 173–89; the funding is discussed on p. 179.
53. For the medal and point count, see Knecht, *Das Medaillenkollektiv*, 112–15; and Holzweissig, *Diplomatie im Trainingsanzug*, 189.
54. Knecht, *Das Medaillenkollektiv*, 112–15; and Holzweissig, *Diplomatie im Trainingsanzug*, 189.
55. "Entwurf: Die Olympischen Spiele 1972 im Fernsehen der DDR," March 1972, SAPMO-BArch, DR 8/123.
56. The two documents that detail the ratings, surveys, and responses to the TV coverage of the Olympic Games most thoroughly are "Die Sendungen des DDR-Fernsehens von den XX. Olympischen Spielen 1972," 18 September 1972; including Anlage 2—"Aus dem Abschlussbericht der "Zuschauerverbindungen" as well as "Monatsbericht September 1972," which includes a section on "Material der Zuschauerforschung zur Olympia-Berichterstattung—Bewertung des Gesamtprogramms," 21 September 1972. Both of these longer documents are located in SAPMO-BArch, DR 8/506.
57. "Bunte Bilder und die Gründe ihrer Beliebtheit," *Neues Deutschland*, 9 September 1972; "Honeckers Medaillen," *Die Presse*, 13 September 1972; and "The German Nation at the Olympics," *Baltimore Sun*, 13 September 1972.

All of them are part of a collection of media articles captured in "Echo Olympia—Nr. 46/72," BAK, B 185/791.
58. Holzweissig, *Diplomatie im Trainingsanzug*, chapter 5; the quotes are from p. 145.
59. For insightful analyses of *Ostpolitik* and its impact, see M. E. Sarotte, *Dealing with the Devil: East Germany, Détente, & Ostpolitik, 1969–1973* (Chapel Hill and London: University of North Carolina Press, 2001); Carole Fink and Bernd Schaefer, eds., *Ostpolitik, 1969–1974: European and Global Responses* (New York: Cambridge University Press, 2009); and Oliver Bange and Gottfried Niedhart, eds., *Helsinki 1975 and the Transformation of Europe* (New York and Oxford: Berghahn Books, 2008).
60. Wentker, *Aussenpolitik in engen Grenzen*, 391–458; and Howarth, "Die Westpolitik der DDR zwischen internationaler Aufwertung und ideologischer Offensive (1966–1989)," in *Die DDR und der Westen*, ed. Pfeil, 81–92. For the GDR's raised status in Africa in the 1970s, see Winrow, *The Foreign Policy of the GDR in Africa*. The successes of the GDR in the developing world are also discussed in Bock et al., *DDR-Aussenpolitik im Rückspiegel*, especially chapters 3 and 5. On the cultural and political significance of Davis's GDR visit and the World Youth Festival, see Dorothee Wierling, "Der Duft der Angela Davis: Politische Jugendkultur in der DDR der frühen 1970er Jahre," in *German Zeitgeschichte: Konturen eines Forschungsfeldes*, ed. Thomas Lindenberger and Martin Sabrow (Göttingen: Wallstein Verlag, 2016), 265–81.
61. Mary Fulbrook, *Anatomy of a Dictatorship: Inside the GDR, 1949–1989* (Oxford and New York: Oxford University Press, 1998), chapter 5; the quote is on p. 141. For a similar assessment, see also Fulbrook's book *The People's State: East German Society from Hitler to Honecker* (New Haven and London: Yale University Press, 2005), where she refers to the "new self-confidence [of the GDR] of the early 1970s" (32); Ohse, *Jugend nach dem Mauerbau*, p. 281; and Christoph Dieckmann, "Küche, Kammer, Weite Welt: Mythen der Erinnerung," in *Bye Bye Lübben City: Bluesfreaks, Tramps und Hippies in der DDR*, ed. Michael Rauhut and Thomas Kochan (Berlin: Schwarzkopf & Schwarzkopf, 2009), 22.
62. For a discussion of the political and economic factors, see Major, *Behind the Berlin Wall*, chapters 5 and 6; Ohse, *Jugend nach dem Mauerbau*, chapter 5; Jeannette Z. Madarász, *Conflict and Compromise in East Germany, 1971–1989: A Precarious Stability* (New York: Palgrave Macmillan, 2003), chapter 2; and Wentker, *Aussenpolitik in engen* Grenzen, 391–459.

CHAPTER 2

Fade Out
Hollywood Movie Imports and the Cultural Surrender of the GDR Film Control in the 1970s and 1980s

Still riding high on the wave of international recognition and athletic successes of the early 1970s, East Germany celebrated another first in late 1975. In November of that year, the first and only Film Week of the German Democratic Republic (GDR) was held in the United States, hosted by the Museum of Modern Art in New York City. Twenty-one East German films were exhibited to American audiences, many of them for the first time. Six years in the making and coming just one year after the establishment of diplomatic relations between the two countries, the GDR film week was clearly a momentous occasion for East Germany. In addition to chronicling the intermingling with the wealthy elite of New York's high society, GDR embassy officials noted with relief that the events had proceeded smoothly and without interruptions: "None of the conversations contained any critical comments," they emphasized. "Quite to the contrary, everyone voiced praise and recognition for East Germany."[1]

The twenty-one films reflected the stand-out achievements of the East German film industry (Deutsche Film-Aktiengesellschaft [DEFA]) over the past thirty years—with a heavy emphasis on anti-fascist and historical films. Each film was shown twice over the course of the week, and a number of the showings in the movie theater, which held over four hundred people, were sold out. Though the Film Week report bemoaned a rather limited interest on the part of the New York media and criticized some of the technical shortcomings of the films, it was seen as an all-around success. Just as importantly, the hope was that this would yield sales for DEFA films in North America as well as open up new social and economic contacts for the diplomatic staff of the new GDR embassy.[2] The relative elation on the part of the East German officials was quite understandable, since the GDR had been seeking such political and cultural recognition for the past three decades. Viewed from East Berlin, it looked like the continuation of the positive trajectory since the late 1960s and early 1970s, building on the successes of the 1972 Olympics and the wave of international recognition in the following years. It seemed to indicate a new reality of normalized relations and routine international cultural exchanges, which had eluded the country for so long.

Yet trouble had already been brewing for a while, even well before Honecker came to power, and the GDR film sector provides a telling barometer of the increasing difficulties that the country was facing as the 1970s continued. The truth of the matter was that GDR cinema was in crisis. With some notable exceptions, DEFA films were not popular with East German audiences, and the technological shortages were growing as the decade progressed. Worst of all, the Ministry of Culture, like every other sector of the East German economy, was slowly running out of money—unable to finance its costly films while simultaneously maintaining the basic infrastructure, from movie theaters to production facilities.[3]

The difficulties of East Germany to assert its cultural competitiveness did not stop there. When he came to power as the new leader and general secretary of the Socialist Unity Party of Germany (Sozialistische Einheitheitspartei Deutschlands [SED]) in 1971, Erich Honecker had promised the East German population increased living standards and greater availability of consumer goods, part of which included more access to Western cultural products and offerings. One of the most visible signs of this change in policy was the lifting of the ban against viewing West German television. Starting in 1973, East Germans no longer had to hide their daily transgressions and instead were free to watch any available TV channel and show—whether they emanated from the east or west side of the wall. This development had very important repercussions for the GDR film policy as well. With the rapid increase of TV ownership in the late 1960s and early 1970s in East Germany, many viewers increasingly stayed home and watched shows and films in the comfort of their living rooms. As a consequence, overall attendance in movie theaters continued to drop steadily in the early 1970s, as East and West German television became more available to the vast majority of East German audiences. Similar to other countries, movie attendance decreased significantly with the emergence of television in the GDR in the 1960s and 1970s. In 1960, movie attendance in East Germany stood at roughly 240 million visits per year. It was cut in half by 1965 to about 120 million viewers and declined again to 90 million visits by 1970, mainly because of the accelerating television competition. By 1975, it was down to approximately 75 million per year, which represented the plateau for movie visits for the remaining decade and a half.[4]

The other aspect that proved particularly challenging for East German cultural planners was that GDR audiences, especially young people, were expecting recent Western films as part of the yearly movie program. This was not a new development in the 1970s, nor was it unique to East Germany. In fact, this trend extended all across the Eastern Bloc and included the Soviet Union as well. In the GDR, American and other Western films had been imported since the very beginning of the country and were part of the regular movie fare. Yet because of the powerful Western TV competition, this expectation of greater availability of Western films was becoming more urgent and politically more complicated in the 1970s. Unless GDR officials wanted to risk losing additional viewers—as well as the significant revenue that could be reaped from these films—they were well advised to keep a steady dose of Western films mixed in with the overall yearly film programs. Western film imports, therefore, were not just a cultural but increasingly also a financial necessity for the struggling East German cinema in the 1970s and beyond.[5]

This chapter will analyze the complications that arose from these culturally complex and politically explosive developments and focus especially on the importation and impact of American feature films in the GDR in the 1970s and 1980s. It will trace which films were chosen for import and how they were advertised and received, as well as analyze their influence on the overall cultural policies of the GDR. What this analysis reveals is that the GDR's cultural film policy was increasingly driven by economic necessity and overwhelming consumer demands, while ideological concerns took a back seat. In fact, the choices of the SED leadership became fewer and their cultural (and political) influence far more limited by the close of the 1970s. By the early 1980s, GDR film policy was a bundle of contradictions. Left with no alternatives, the SED government lost control over its film policy and programs in the 1980s and culturally capitulated to the combined forces of East German popular demands, economic pressures, and political fears, as well as the relentless expansion of a Western, especially Hollywood-dominated, international film culture.

GDR Cinema in the 1970s and Its Growing Dependence on Western Import Films

Based on their internal reports, GDR officials in the Ministry of Culture (Ministerium für Kultur [MfK]) knew that the East German film sector was in trouble in the 1970s. Several trends were headed in the wrong direction. First of all, East German television alone broadcast a combined five hundred feature films on its two broadcasting channels in 1970 already. On the three West German TV channels, more than four hundred films were available to growing East German audiences that same year as well. Movie attendance had dropped by over ten million between 1966 and 1970 in East Germany, and moviegoing had become youth-dominated by the early 1970s, since two-thirds of all moviegoers were between the ages of fourteen and twenty-five. In terms of movie attendance, this very same transformation occurred in West Germany as well as in other European countries. And these youthful GDR audiences were expecting and choosing entertainment films above all else, with adventure and comedy features leading the way, and largely shunned GDR and socialist films in favor of Western film imports.[6]

There were other deep structural problems in the GDR film sector. The number of DEFA films that cost more to produce than they netted was on the increase. Whereas in 1960 the percentage had been at about 65 percent, for example, by 1965 over 80 percent of films did not even cover their cost; this share had further increased to over 90 percent by the close of the decade. Even more disconcerting was the fact that the vast majority of financially unprofitable films were socialist films, and the viewership especially for those films had further declined. An analysis by the Central Film Administration (Hauptverwaltung Film) from the early 1970s summarized the findings in a disappointed tone: "Here again we have to note that the revenues from socialist films have declined almost twice as fast as the revenues for capitalist films. The additional income from capitalist films was not enough, however, to balance the loss of revenues from socialist films."[7] As this last statement makes apparent, it was indeed the revenue from Western import films that partially financed much of the rest of the GDR film industry, including the production of DEFA films.

The agency issuing this report, the Central Film Administration, was one of the units in the Ministry of Culture. For most of the 1970s and 1980s, the Central Film Administration was led by Johannes Starke and Horst Pehnert; the person in charge of the Ministry of Culture from 1973 to 1989 was Hans-Joachim Hoffmann. The role of the Central Film Administration was to carry out and safeguard the policies of the SED Central Committee (SED Zentralkomitee), which was the governing council of the GDR leadership and set the overall policy guidelines for all aspects of East German life. Since the Central Committee was the overriding body, it also had the ultimate say on which films were acceptable and which ones were to be rejected or censored.[8]

When Erich Honecker took the helm of the Socialist Unity Party (SED) in 1971, he initiated a cultural liberalization as part of his "Main Task" policy initiative. Honecker declared a willingness to adopt a more open-minded policy, even going so far as to proclaim that there would be "no taboos" in the future dialogue between artists and the GDR population. While no one was willing to take his words literally, these policies did initiate a breath of fresh air and removed some of the most onerous and restrictive aspects of the 1965 decision, which had culturally handcuffed many GDR artists and banned a number of their works. And GDR filmmakers were only too eager to embrace Honecker's more lenient and pragmatic approach.[9]

Figure 2.1. Capitol Movie Theater in Leipzig, 18 November 1983—one of the premiere movie theaters in the GDR. (Courtesy of Bundesarchiv Koblenz; Bild 183-1983-1118-020.)

There is no doubt that this relatively liberal cultural climate helped to produce some of the most memorable and popular films in DEFA history. The period became known for films that critically dealt with contemporary GDR issues and the everyday struggles and tensions that East Germans encountered (Alltags- und Gegenwartsfilme). *The Legend of Paul and Paula* (*Die Legende von Paul and Paula*, 1973), *Jacob the Liar* (*Jakob der Lügner*, 1975), and *The New Sorrows of Young W.* (*Die neuen Leiden des Jungen W.*, 1976) were outstanding films of this era. Moreover, some of these DEFA features filled GDR movie theaters, and a select few even appealed to the predominantly young audiences as well.[10] Yet as anyone familiar with the fickle cultural policies of the GDR government knew, it was only a matter of time until the relative openness was followed by the inevitable clampdown. This occurred in the latter half of the 1970s, initiated and driven jointly by the controversial expulsion of the popular singer-songwriter Wolf Biermann in 1976 and the worsening economic situation in East Germany.[11]

In terms of the overall trajectory of East German cinema in the 1970s, however, Honecker's short-lived attempt at more cultural liberalization changed very little. The crux of the problem remained that the vast majority of East German films were commercially unprofitable and that the GDR film industry needed increased subsidies in order to survive. A 1973 report from the accounting section of the Ministry of Culture makes clear that many of these fundamental structural problems persisted: "The cultural demands of our working population cannot be met in many important areas." Moreover, shortages prevailed in all cultural sectors, from the printing of books and records to material for the performing and visual arts, as well as the maintenance of buildings and infrastructure. The report pointed out that funds for cultural activities had decreased from 0.74 percent of GDP twenty years ago to 0.29 percent of GDP in 1973. In terms of the film industry, there was a desperate need for renovated, modern movie theaters as well as modern and competitive equipment for film production, editing, and copying.[12]

And the news only got worse from there. By the mid-1970s and into the latter part of the decade, the GDR film sector found itself facing two fundamentally damning and seemingly inexorable trends. One was that East German audiences generally preferred Western films over their own DEFA productions or socialist imports and were willing to pay more to see them. And the other was that resources for cultural activities, including film, were becoming tighter, which forced unappealing policy decisions. Reports by the Central Film Administration highlight these emerging dynamics. "As in the year 1974, everything points to a nonfulfillment of revenue targets for 1975," one analysis surmised ominously in early 1975. In order to reach the projected revenue, GDR cinema needed to attract 1.5 million additional viewers that year, a target that in light of an overall shrinking movie attendance seemed rather illusory. Yet despite this shortfall, GDR officials were willing to spend ever-greater portions of the budget on Western import films. While imports from capitalist countries took up 10 percent of the film budget in 1965, that percentage had increased to 15 percent by 1970 and was already over 25 percent by 1973.[13] However, it is also apparent that Western imports represented a good investment. In 1975, for example, Western feature films produced nearly half of the overall revenue for the GDR film sector even though they represented less than a third of all movie screenings that year. In addition, Western film imports played before larger crowds, and East Germans were willing to pay higher ticket prices for movies from the capitalist West.[14]

By the late 1970s and early 1980s, this increased cultural and financial dependency was creating all kinds of ideological policy adjustments and accommodations, especially as entertaining American box office hits (Millionenfilme) became increasingly popular and sought after by young East German audiences. In 1978, for example, the GDR censors were hoping to import forty Western films, but these films were becoming more expensive due to increased pricing and new insurance and liability fees. Knowing that East German audiences were unwilling to live without them, GDR officials had no choice but to purchase fewer films (thirty-six instead of the forty planned in 1978). And since money was tight and entertainment films were popular, GDR film reviewers could only bemoan the fact that they were often importing crowd-pleasers and had few funds left for socially critical or aesthetically more important films. Yet those in charge of cinema programming had little room to maneuver, as they conceded, "since our film planning is dependent on important cultural and popularly appealing films from the West."[15]

Like so many other cultural trends, this reliance on foreign films to create much of the box office revenue for socialist cinema was not limited to East Germany. In her analysis of the Soviet film industry, for example, Kristin Roth-Ey highlights how significantly the tastes of movie audiences in the republics of the Soviet Union deviated from the socialist cinematic ideal from the 1960s through the 1980s. While a number of Soviet-produced movies premiered to critical acclaim and several were box office successes, it was more often fantastic love stories like the 1962 hit *Amphibian Man* as well as foreign films rather than uplifting, educational Soviet hero dramas that kept the Russian film industry afloat. As Roth-Ey argues, "It was amphibian men plus strategic infusions of [Brigitte] Bardot and Bollywood that filled Soviet movie houses and dominated the moviegoing experience of Soviet audiences. It was in large part these imported films that bankrolled the industry." Bardot's role as an international French film star and sex idol might speak for itself, but the inclusion of Bollywood is probably more surprising. Yet in the vast central Asian and Caucasus regions of the former Soviet Union, these films had great appeal to audiences and filled theaters more easily than many Western imports. This is another important reminder that in each Eastern Bloc country the mix and unique hybrid nature of the dominant popular culture varied significantly.[16]

As in the Soviet Union, with every passing year the actual GDR film program was further and further removed from the socialist realist film ideal propagated as the official paradigm of the East German workers' and farmers' state. The socialist realist ideal, which was to anchor GDR cinema, was based on uplifting films with positive and sympathetic heroes and a didactic and socially instructive plotline that was informed by and in line with communist party policies. On a practical level, however, it is apparent that this ideal was frequently circumvented even by DEFA filmmakers, especially those who managed to produce topical and socially relevant films.[17] These practical, ideological adjustments were even more apparent when it came to selecting film imports from the West. SED officials argued in 1971 already that "in view of the increasing need for entertainment on the part of our population … it will be necessary to pay this group of films [entertainment films from the West] especially close attention." Considerations of humor, comedy, and especially the desire for relaxation on the part of GDR working classes became a key component of this pragmatic readjustment. As a GDR report from 1975 emphasized, "A film can also meet its socially beneficial function if its entertainment and humor contribute to the rejuvenation of the productivity of the workforce."[18] From the vantage point of the socialist film ideal, this line of reasoning represented a major concession indeed.

These ongoing accommodations related to the GDR film policy accelerated in the late 1970s. An internal youth survey in 1977, conducted by the Institute for Youth Research (Jugendforschungsinstitut), highlighted just how disdainful young audiences had become of DEFA and socialist films. In a previous study from 1973–74, for example, young East Germans had still listed five GDR films (both cinema and TV productions) as the most memorable recent viewing experiences; by 1977, only one GDR film was still in the top-fifteen ranking. In what must have been the low point of the survey for cultural officials in East Germany, its authors reported in an unflinchingly analytic tone, "The trend visible in these results is further emphasized by the fact that 32 percent *would go less frequently* [emphasis in original] if more culturally important films from other socialist countries were part of the film program and 33 percent would go less frequently if more DEFA films were being offered." As if it could get any worse, the study found that prior exposure to DEFA movies actually made young East Germans less likely to watch another East German film.[19] GDR film officials were not just losing their most reliable moviegoing audiences, but their youth in general.

The Importation, Selection, and Impact of Hollywood Films in the 1970s

It is in the context of this changing landscape that Western film imports became ever more important for GDR cinema in the 1970s. Their numbers were actually relatively small. In the 1970s, GDR cinema audiences generally could choose between 135 and 150 new films every year. In any given year, roughly 25 percent of the film program consisted of Western film imports—usually varying between 35 and 40 films per year. Socialist films comprised the vast number of program offerings with about 75 percent, or an average of about 100 films per year—roughly 15 of which were DEFA films. In terms of the Western feature films, the vast number of these movies originated from France (about 10 films per year), the United States (roughly 8 movies per year), and Italy (approximately 5 films every year) during the 1970s. Generally half of all imported features, therefore, came from the United States and France—a fact that was often bemoaned by GDR film selectors but that changed little over the course of the two decades. West Germany, Great Britain, and Japan—in that order—were the second-tier countries for nonsocialist Western film imports (with a yearly average of 2–4 movies).[20]

All East German film imports and exports were handled by a special unit within the Central Film Administration, DEFA Export (DEFA Aussenhandel). From 1973 to 1990 it was led by Helmut Diller. Films imported into East Germany had to be approved by the State Film Licensing Committee (Staatliche Filmabnahmekommission). On the domestic side, DEFA Export collaborated closely with the sole GDR distributing agency (Progress Filmverleih), which was led by Wolfgang Harkenthal from the mid-1970s to the late 1980s and was responsible for the distribution of all films in the GDR. DEFA Export was the only film agency not subsidized by state funds, because it was expected to produce its own revenue as well as profits for the East German film sector.[21]

Up until the early 1970s, Western films were individually requested and sent to East Germany for viewing. When this was proving to be too expensive and cumbersome due to increased demand and new insurance costs by the mid-1970s, a team of SED officials from the Central Film Administration and the GDR film distribution agency were allowed to travel to Western film festivals, where they viewed films and selected packages of Western movies. This process further accelerated after 1976, when Horst Pehnert became the head of the Central Film Administration.[22] In terms of purchasing films for GDR television, East German officials also increasingly accessed the Western markets directly. As in the case of West Germany, the leading film distributor was Leo Kirch, who had established himself as the main liaison between Hollywood and the FRG television industry since the late 1950s; he also began supplying East German television with packages of Western film imports by the late 1970s.[23]

As Rosemary Stott convincingly demonstrates in her study on imported Western feature films into East Germany, GDR cultural officials had very strong preferences—as well as respective dislikes—for specific genres and certain film stars. When it came to American films of the early 1970s, East German film selectors loved the socially critical features of the New Hollywood, which often explored the dark underbelly of American social and political life. In addition, crime and detective stories as well as musicals and comedies were a regular part of the GDR film program, especially if they featured darlings of the East German screen such as Barbra Streisand, Dustin Hoffman, Sidney Poitier, or Jane Fonda. Favorites of the later 1970s also included Jack Nicholson, Shirley MacLaine, and Robert Redford. By contrast, GDR film selectors usually avoided the traditional American western, any science fiction and disaster features, horror and graphic combat films, as well as hard-core pornographic films. The reasoning was to avoid showing what they considered excessively violent, destructive, or sexually explicit films or movies that celebrated American myths or glorified warfare.[24]

As mentioned above, GDR film censors were quite enamored with the films of the New Hollywood, which started to emerge in the late 1960s and began to fade by the mid-1970s in the United States. Since American films were usually imported with a two- to four-year delay in East Germany, the first of these films did not arrive until 1970 and stretched all the way into the late 1970s, thereby defining one core strand of US import films that East German audiences saw during that decade.

Figure 2.2. Movie audience in the Capitol Movie Theater in Leipzig, 28 November 1984. Among other things, the Capitol hosted international film festivals and premiered popular Western import films. (Courtesy of Bundesarchiv Koblenz; Bild 183-1984-1128-026.)

From the standpoint of political ideology and audience resonance, they reflected almost the ideal combination for DEFA Export officials. Many of them were aesthetically challenging and artistically innovative at the same time as they presented a bleak and often devastating critique of the United States and the capitalist system.[25]

One of the first films of the New Hollywood that made it over to East Germany was *In the Heat of the Night* (*In der Hitze der Nacht*) by Norman Jewison, which was in many ways a safe import from an official cultural perspective. It focused on the virulent racism in the American South, featured Sidney Poitier as one of the lead characters, and presented a suspenseful crime story of a wrongly accused African American. Originally released in 1967 in the United States, it premiered in East Germany in September 1970 (with a three-year lease). In the Progress summary accompanying the release of the film, GDR officials expected "a powerful audience response" and advised all exhibitors that "with close observation of the political developments in the United States, the film should be shown in the large movie theaters so that the lease time can be maximized." Based on the film reviews, this race film plus crime story—reviewed under headings such as "Murder and Race Hatred" or "Not Only a Crime Story"—clearly confirmed the widely held view in East Germany that the United States had neither dealt with nor effectively solved its race problem. Corruption, racism, and violence, as the film reviews argued, far too often went hand in hand in the United States and prevented even a semblance of justice and equality.[26]

The decision was equally easy for the DEFA Export selectors in the case of two other American films released in East Germany in 1973: *The Strawberry Statement* and *They Shoot Horses—Don't They?* The latter film was released in January 1973 (US release year in 1969) under the title *Nur Pferden gibt man den Gnadenschuss*. Set at the height of the Great Depression in 1932, the film chronicled the marathon dance competitions popular at that time, where hundreds of desperate couples competed for prize money by dancing for days and even weeks with minimal sleep, to the delight of howling spectators. The GDR press release was enthusiastic in its praise of the film and argued that "the death dance of 1932 is an exemplary movie and showcases the merciless business climate of this [American] society." GDR film critics predominantly echoed this assessment, arguing that the film highlighted the ruthlessness and disregard for human dignity in capitalist societies both in the 1930s and, by extension, during subsequent time periods. With Jane Fonda as an additional attraction, this movie received high marks from GDR film critics around the country.[27]

The Strawberry Statement (*Blutige Erdbeeren*) was released in March 1973 in East Germany, three years after it premiered in the United States. The film was loosely based on a nonfiction book by James Simon Kunen, which focused on the student protests at Columbia University in 1968. The basis for the demonstrations was the revelation that one of Columbia University's institutes had collaborated closely with the US Defense Department. In the movie, a naïve but good-hearted student gets caught up in these protests largely because of his love for one of the women leading the student demonstrators. When she is clubbed during one of the protests, he rushes to her aid, only to be killed in the violent confrontation with the policemen at the scene. Once again, GDR selectors recommended that this film should be released as broadly as possible, especially in university towns, since it "demonstrates the dangers of US imperialism and showcases a disillusioned image of the capitalist system."[28]

On a lighter note, GDR selectors generally made sure that the yearly program included at least one American musical or comedy.[29] When *Funny Girl* came along, therefore, which had been a huge box office hit in the United States and which featured the irrepressible Barbra Streisand in the lead role, the GDR selectors jumped on it very quickly. Released in the United States in 1968, it premiered in East German theaters by May 1970, which was a record time for importing US films into the GDR. There was no political aspect to this film, as the DEFA Export officials acknowledged, but they judged the musical numbers to be of "a high artistic caliber" and, of course, Barbra Streisand stole the show. "Because of these advantages the film deserves a spot in our cinema program," they commented pragmatically, "and [*Funny Girl*] will help close the gap in the area of musical entertainment films [in the yearly program]." As expected, the film reviews heaped praise on Streisand for her portrayal of the historical Fanny Brice, who danced her way from rags to riches as one of the Ziegfeld Follies in the early twentieth century, and lauded the masterful film direction by William Wyler.[30]

A slightly more unusual case in terms of musicals was *West Side Story*. When it was released in East Germany in May 1973, the musical was more film history than a new release; it premiered in the United States in 1961 and just a year later in West Germany. Based on the available evidence, it seems that DEFA Export officials made this choice in the early 1970s because of three interrelated factors. One was that this was a world-famous musical that had not been shown in East Germany, and with the X. Weltfestspiele (World Youth Festival) scheduled for the summer of 1973, it seemed like a good addition to the cinema program. Second, the official Progress commentary emphasized that the gang violence at the heart of the story and the slum setting were fitting illustrations of the "hopeless and desperate situation" that many young people experienced under the capitalist system. Finally, based on West German news reports, it was also very likely that GDR selectors tried to pre-empt a new musical series that was going to premiere in the fall of 1973 on a FRG television channel; the first scheduled musical in the eight-part series was *West Side Story*.[31]

Since many of the most popular songs of the musical had already become hits in East Germany as well, especially songs such as "Maria," "Tonight," and "America," GDR reviewers regularly noted the lateness of the release of this historical musical. Nevertheless, they overwhelmingly agreed that it was a great choice, since it combined popular musical hits with trenchant social criticism and reflected the hopelessness facing many American youth, which had only become more pronounced and pressing since the musical's original release. None of the East German film reviews, however, made reference to the musical series scheduled to start in the fall on West German television, with *West Side Story* as the premiered feature.[32]

Because of the sheer popularity of American films and for variety's sake, GDR film selectors bent their ideological rules and assured at least a steady trickle of musicals and comedies onto East German cinema screens during the course of the 1970s. Traditional American westerns and especially their standout star John Wayne, by contrast, were despised by GDR film officials because of the rewriting of America's ruthless colonial history they entailed. Less common than the lighthearted genres, American westerns were nevertheless included in most of the yearly cinema programs during the 1970s.[33]

In this latter case as well, New Hollywood movies made the choice for the East German film selectors a great deal easier because they included revisionist westerns. Unlike the traditional films, the revisionist western reversed the role of hero and outlaw. Now it was the US military who savagely slaughtered innocent Native American women and children, plundering their villages and ruthlessly exploiting their vulnerability. Cowboys, too, were no longer men of steel with laser-sharp aim, but more often dark and brooding, capricious and self-serving. In these films, which David Cooke labeled "Vietnam Westerns," the genocidal war against Native Americans stood front and center.[34]

A film like *Little Big Man*, then, was indeed seen as a welcome addition to the GDR cinema program and was rushed to the East German movie screens with relative speed: it premiered in November 1972, three years after its release in the United States. Predictably, it was celebrated for the novel approach of the film and Dustin Hoffman's convincing performance. Through Hoffman's character the viewer is led to take side with Native Americans, thereby reversing stereotypical white-Native relationships. These combined themes, Dustin Hoffman's star performance, and the critical revisionist history of the American West, dominated the published film reviews in the GDR. And with the Vietnam War still raging at the time, several GDR reviewers made sure to link it to the US brutality and barbarism in Vietnam, including regular references to the My Lai massacre.[35] In general, the westerns that appealed most to East German cultural officials were those that either reversed or parodied familiar archetypes of the traditional American western. This probably also explained the very late release of *Destry Rides Again* (*Der grosse Bluff*) in March 1971 in the GDR (originally premiered in 1939 in the United States). As GDR selectors saw it, the film's appeal lay in the fact that it parodied many of the familiar western clichés—almost anticipating some of the late 1960s revisionist films. In addition, it featured James Stewart and especially Marlene Dietrich, which, the officials hoped, would draw a crossover audience of both old and young moviegoers.³⁶

It is also interesting how closely these revisionist westerns mirrored the overall plotlines of the GDR's own Indian films (Indianerfilme), which were produced by DEFA between the mid-1960s and early 1980s and which often ranked among the more popular films produced in the GDR. The hallmark of DEFA *Indianerfilme* was the noble savage, inevitably portrayed by the Yugoslav actor Goyko Mitic. As Gerd Gemünden emphasizes, these films originated as a dual response to the Karl May films, which emerged in the early 1960s in West Germany, and in order to "articulate an outspoken critique of the colonialism and racism" of traditional American westerns. While they were often more concerned with relaying a hidden socialist message rather than portraying a historically realistic image of Native Americans, they nevertheless predated the American rewriting of this film genre that started in the late 1960s.³⁷

When one approaches the selection of US movie imports from the opposite end of the spectrum—films that were rejected—the contours of the GDR import policy become even more apparent. It also becomes clear that in the early 1970s at least, ideological and political criteria were still applied fairly rigorously. In terms of genres, for example, hair-raising horror movies like *The Exorcist* or pure action spectacles (what GDR selectors called *Katastrophenfilme*) were simply deemed unsuitable for East German audiences. Likewise, any film that featured John Wayne was rejected or, in the case of one film (*Zirkuswelt* or *Circus World*, 1970), banned after initial approval, because the first rounds of approval had overlooked Wayne's bellicose support for the Vietnam War.³⁸

Another movie rejected by GDR censors was *Viva Zapata* by Elia Kazan in 1971. The film seemed like it was made for GDR screens: it celebrated a popular Mexican revolutionary, it had been made by one of the most radical and blacklisted directors of 1950s Hollywood (the film had officially premiered in the United States in 1952), and it contained a thorough condemnation of the Mexican authoritarian regime. However, in a later round of reviews, DEFA Export officials realized that the script had been written by John Steinbeck, who also had come out in support of the war in Vietnam, and therefore retroactively banned the film. Another classic Kazan film, *On the Waterfront* (premiered in the United States in 1954), seemed like it, too, was tailor-made for GDR ideological purposes, since it showed the crooked and corrupt side of American business and society—with an appealing Marlon Brando in the lead role no less. The selectors saw the film as a powerful vehicle to portray "a disillusioning image of America" but ultimately rejected it because of its critical view of labor unions, which in the film were a central aspect of the corrupt practices on the waterfront.[39]

DEFA Export officials were also rather selective when it came to choosing from among the wide variety of socially critical films of the New Hollywood. Cultural portrayals without overt political messages, like *Alice's Restaurant*, did not make the cut in 1975. In a similar vein, they passed on many classic features of the New Hollywood. *Bonnie and Clyde*, *Who's Afraid of Virginia Wolff?*, and *Midnight Cowboy* were never exhibited on East German screens, nor were other popular late 1960s movies like *The Graduate* or *Easy Rider*. Films like these were considered either too violent or simply too inaccessible for East German audiences or were rejected because they dealt with potentially explosive taboo topics (drug use, homosexuality, and the hippie culture, for example). Finally, there was the danger, as one report warned, "that these films could be superficially attractive to GDR audiences."[40]

When the discussions of these selection reports are surveyed closely, it is apparent that a significant shift took place right around the mid-1970s: compared to the early part of the decade, selection criteria were becoming noticeably more lax in the late 1970s and especially the early 1980s. When in doubt in terms of politics and ideology, GDR selectors generally rejected even crowd-pleasing films in the first half of the decade. In the latter half of the 1970s and early 1980s, selectors emphasized the role of mass appeal more and more—even to a degree where ideology was forced to take a back seat. One of the clear indications of this changing trend is apparent in the acceptance of *Jaws* in 1976. Earlier this film would most likely have been rejected as another apolitical *Katastrophenfilm* (catastrophe movie), yet the leading officials of the Central Film Administration proved themselves more generous in their discussion in 1976. In their summary approving the film, they wrote, "In judging this movie, it is important to view the film by itself and not by its assumed categorization with the so-called catastrophe films." The film was appealing and ultimately deserved to be shown because of "its suspenseful entertainment [. . . and] man's fight against natural forces and his ultimate success."[41]

Another indication of these accommodations was that GDR cultural officials were rolling back most outright bans against specific genres by the early 1980s. American science fiction films, once a genre not welcome on East German movie screens, made an entry into the official film program. Even in films that were rejected, a different tone prevailed in the deliberations. When DEFA Export officials discussed the potential adoption of *Blade Runner* in 1982, for example, they definitely saw the appeal of the film: "This movie combines reactionary ideas of bourgeois futurology with a perfectly implemented action story." And although the GDR officials ultimately rejected the film, they conceded that "in terms of the future-oriented vision of the movie an adoption would be interesting, especially also concerning its technological appeal and its special effects."[42]

Political reasons for the rejection of certain Western imports were markedly decreasing at the same time in the late 1970s and early 1980s. To be sure, certain films were still taboo, like the rabidly pro-American series of *Rocky* and *Rambo* films, which began to debut in the late 1970s in the United States, or historically dubious adventure spectacles like the *Indiana Jones* series of the early 1980s. Yet increasingly, political rejections seemed to be reserved for proposed import films that either directly denigrated a communist country and for those movies that featured actors who had fled an Eastern Bloc country. The film *The Turning Point* (premiered in 1977), for example, was rejected because Mikhail Baryshnikov, a former dancer at the Kirow Theater in Leningrad, played a central role in the movie. Likewise, the acclaimed and appealing film *Witness* (with Harrison Ford; premiered in the United States in 1984) was banned from purchase in the GDR in 1985 because of the participation of Alexander Godunov, who had danced for the Bolshoi Theater in Moscow until the early 1970s.[43]

It is also apparent that a political concern of a different kind was creeping more frequently into the considerations and deliberations: GDR officials were becoming ever more concerned that Western—and especially American—film imports might actually stir up and magnify political trouble or cultural opposition to their regime. This concern was very clearly the main reason why an otherwise appealing film on Woody Guthrie, *Bound for Glory*, was not imported in the late 1970s. Coming on the heels of the tumultuous protests against the expatriation of the controversial East German folk singer Wolf Biermann, the East German officials were in no mood to stir up further trouble despite their positive appraisal of the film: "All in all, this is a well-made film on a topic that has barely been represented on American screens. Guthrie's critical and uncompromising attitude [... however,] would provide unnecessary discussion material in light of the current events (the so-called dissident problem)."[44] Unlike the rejection of this film, however, GDR film selectors generally opened the gates further simply because they needed even ideologically troublesome Western imports in order to subsidize East German cinema as well as to placate the growing popular demand.

The concern about potentially misfiring or backfiring film imports increasingly made its way into the official assessments of the GDR film selection process by the late 1970s. Officials were still set on introducing more American films, especially socially critical movies of the New Hollywood. But they were also worrying that these films might get re- or misinterpreted by GDR viewers. There was an ever-present danger that these films could be "wrongly judged or received by our viewers," as one report put it, "especially since, aside from the political criticism, they are very appealing in terms of their artistically attractive milieus and detailed . . . scenes."[45] It is hard to know which films exactly the GDR officials had in mind when they voiced these concerns. Yet the potential troubles can be re-created in rough outlines at least when one looks at three of the most celebrated films of the late 1970s: *Chinatown*, *All the President's Men*, and *One Flew Over the Cuckoo's Nest*. All three of these films were devastating in their criticism of US politics and society, and all three of them were rushed to East German screens as quickly as possible, which was two years after their original release in the United States.

Roman Polanski's *Chinatown* (United States, 1974; GDR, 1976) and Alan Pakula's *All the President's Men* (United States, 1976; GDR, 1978) most clearly share a thematic focus. Although Polanski's neo-noir film is set in 1930s Los Angeles and chronicles the corrupt politics surrounding water rights at that time, its real focus is not far removed from Pakula's Watergate film. Both movies dealt with the corruption at the heart of much of American politics and the greedy and manipulative culture this bred. In many ways, *Chinatown* cut even deeper because it highlighted the incestuous relationship of Los Angeles' most powerful man, Noah Cross, with his daughter and ended with him remaining at the top of his politically corrupt and morally bankrupt empire. In *All the President's Men*, audiences at least had the satisfaction to see democracy in action, which ultimately removed Nixon from office. Not surprisingly, GDR officials were effusive in their praise of both movies and recommended that both films be shown in the biggest theaters to reach the widest possible audiences.[46]

It is very likely that East German movie audiences were riveted by these films, and these movies might well have chipped away at the ever-enduring appeal of the American way of life. However, it is just as likely to imagine that the same GDR audiences might have admired and even envied the openness with which American film directors could portray the flaws of the United States and its capitalist, politically corrupt system without being prosecuted, imprisoned, or expatriated for their actions. In addition, similar to earlier films like the popular *Strawberry*

Statement, they conveyed an aesthetically pleasing milieu and landscape: the appeal of the hippie culture, the allure of big American cities like Los Angeles and New York, or, as in *All the President's Men*, the advantages of a free press and free speech, which, in this case at least, could bring even the most powerful men to their knees. They highlighted that capitalist countries periodically seemed capable of purging themselves of their evil demons, while few in East Germany in the late 1970s saw this potential for political regeneration in the GDR, since only the wrong people seemed to get purged.

This open, and potentially troublesome, room for interpretation and reinterpretation was probably no more evident than in the film *One Flew Over the Cuckoo's Nest* by Miloš Forman, which premiered in East Germany in April 1978. The film classic starred Jack Nicholson in the role R. P. McMurphy as a dishonorably discharged Korean War veteran and troublemaker. When McMurphy finds himself confronted with a prison sentence, he instead feigns mental illness and is transferred to a mental institution, which is run with an iron fist by the omnipotent and feared Nurse Ratched. McMurphy, recognizing that most patients in the mental institution are actually quite sane, is able to alleviate the monotony of the patients and wakes them from their collective slumber. He even manages to take them for an unauthorized joyride outside the walls of the institution, temporarily eluding the iron grip of the authorities. Yet upon his return, McMurphy is punished for his transgressions and subjected to electroshocks and ultimately brain surgery in order to heal his insanity. The authorities win, although McMurphy's social rebellion has at least revived his Indian friend "Chief" Bromden, who in an act of kindness kills the comatose McMurphy and escapes the walls of the mental institution.

Figure 2.3. East German film poster for *One Flew Over the Cuckoo's Nest*, which premiered in the GDR in 1978. (Courtesy of DEFA-Stiftung.)

GDR selectors insisted that this film represented a perfect metaphor for the repressive capitalist system ("bürgerlicher Unterdrückungsapparat"), but East German viewers could probably have been forgiven if their thoughts strayed a little farther than that. After all, Miloš Forman had left Czechoslovakia after the brutal suppression of the Prague Spring uprising in 1968 and was intimately familiar with the oppressive nature of the communist system. None of the GDR reviews referenced Forman's émigré status. In articles titled "Taming a Rebel the American Way" or "Dead Souls," they viewed McMurphy's rebellion as well as the film one-dimensionally through a narrow ideological lens as a critique of the capitalist system. To be sure, this was one possible way to read this film. But there certainly were others.[47]

It is clear that GDR cultural officials feared that this film contained the potential for multiple readings. The final report to the head of the Progress film distribution stressed that "while propagating this film we need to make sure that we enable viewers to judge the content and the critical potential of this film properly [as criticism confined only to the capitalist system]." In an interview, Miloš Forman, however, argued that the character McMurphy stood for rebellious heroes everywhere: "Well, individuals fighting or rebelling against the status quo, the establishment, is good for drama. And also I feel admiration for rebels, because I lived twice in my life in totalitarian society [sic], where most of the people feel like rebelling but don't dare to. And I am a coward, because I didn't dare to rebel there and go to prison for that. That's, I guess, why I admire the rebels and make films about them." And while clear documentary evidence about the precise impact of the film is lacking, what is clear is that Jack Nicholson's rebellious character McMurphy was celebrated as one of the most sympathetic and admired film heroes by East German youth in the late 1970s and that they embraced him as one of their own.[48]

Economic Crisis, Political Fear, and the Surrender of GDR Film Control in the Late 1970s and 1980s

By the late 1970s, a perfect storm was brewing over the East German film industry, which would unload its destructive energies on the East German cinema throughout the 1980s. First and foremost, the financial bottlenecks were becoming ever more restrictive in the late 1970s, and the film sector was being squeezed as well. In 1981, for example, GDR film selectors had to pass on importing Francis Ford Coppola's antiwar opus *Apocalypse Now* because they simply could not afford it. "Based on the current economic situation, an adoption of the film is not possible," the DEFA Export summary conceded. In the more detailed notes, it was apparent that the film would have cost almost twice as much as most other imports, something that was still done in exceptional cases in the mid- to late 1970s, but which was increasingly out of the question by the early 1980s.[49]

Economic concerns were certainly nothing new when it came to the purchase of Western import films, but financial considerations became ever more pressing and decisive by the turn of the decade. The 1970 film *Aristocats*, for example, had finally been imported to West Germany in 1980 and ran in FRG movie theaters, to the delight of family audiences. Hoping to utilize this already dubbed film version, GDR selectors admitted that it would also have been an appealing addition to the family program in East German theaters but concluded that "considering the well-known price demands of the Walt Disney Company an adoption cannot be recommended." Likewise, other appealing films like *Barry Lyndon*, which was available in a dubbed West German version, and *F.I.S.T.*, which was considered by GDR cultural officials "an important contribution concerning the problems of the union movement in the United States," were rejected based on an increasingly more common refrain: "rejected because of the current economic situation."[50]

In order to deal with this restrictive financial situation, officials in the Central Film Administration were developing two coping mechanisms. One was to give previously rejected, and slightly older, films a second look, and a number of them were now finding their way into the yearly cinema programs in the early 1980s. The second strategy was to delay the purchase of US films until they had aged enough to become economically feasible. Following the first path, the western *A Man Called Horse* (*Der Mann, den man Pferd nannte*; premiered in the United States in 1970) finally was scheduled for viewing in GDR movie theaters in 1983 because selectors expected a strong appeal among youth audiences and because "the reasons that led to its rejection years before [competition with East German *Indianerfilme*]" were no longer valid. Likewise the children's film *Black Stallion* (*Der schwarze Hengst*; United States, 1979) was postponed even though a dubbed West German version was available. As the report highlighted, "An adoption should take place only under improved economic conditions, even if the purchase is delayed as a consequence."[51]

There is no doubt that these bottlenecks in the area of film imports were directly related to the larger economic woes that were sending shock waves through the state budgets in the GDR. By the late 1970s, as Andreas Malycha highlights, the indebtedness of the GDR to Western lenders had increased tenfold when compared to the early years of the decade—from 2 billion Valutamarks (VM) in 1972 to 22 billion VM in 1979.[52] Much of this was due to the fact that Honecker ran many of his social and consumer policies on a credit card and ignored the advice of his economic experts who told him that this course of action was unsustainable. Yet money was running out by the late 1970s, and the Ministry of Culture, and with it the film industry, was not spared. Every stone was turned and all avenues were explored to generate more Western currency during those years, including the sale of famous artworks as well as rare books. For the film sector, this meant that vital technical upgrades were delayed or cut, materials for color films were unavailable, and long-overdue renovations of movie theaters never took place.[53]

The second major complication for East German cinema in the late 1970s was the increased political insecurity and fear in the wake of the drawn-out fight after the Biermann Affair. Concerned about its domestic stability, GDR politicians clamped down on East German filmmakers starting in the late 1970s. This renewed curtailment largely suffocated domestic filmmaking under a blanket of restrictive policies. Simultaneously, the SED leadership was watching with consternation as other Eastern European countries—even before Mikhail Gorbachev's perestroika initiatives of the mid-1980s—allowed greater freedom to their respective filmmakers in terms of exploring previously taboo social and political topics.[54]

All of this caused increasing tensions between Warsaw Pact countries in terms of their cultural cooperation in the late 1970s, when all of them seemed to be experiencing similar economic troubles and oppositional pressures. In 1978, for example, DEFA Export officials were complaining bitterly that they could not sell the required number of DEFA films to other socialist countries in order to fulfill revenue expectations. Even more frustrating was the fact that more and more socialist countries were offering their films to Western, and especially West German, television stations first before they were even offered to their East German counterparts, which they attributed "to the national interest and economic profitability" of their socialist neighbors.[55]

These problems deteriorated to a point well beyond repair by the mid-1980s. DEFA films were hardly finding any takers even among socialist countries, and GDR films were harshly criticized for being one-dimensionally focused on the private sphere with (often single) women in leading roles. In 1986, even the Soviet Union cut back to purchasing just two East German films, and countries like Czechoslovakia, Bulgaria, and Hungary each bought only one DEFA production. The GDR reports emphasized other increasingly powerful trends among socialist partner states, especially the desire of Eastern Bloc countries to sell their movies to Western European markets in order to gain access to hard currencies: "Film as a product is gaining priority over political, ideological considerations," and films from socialist countries were overall seen as less appealing by their domestic audiences, which led to "a higher import of Western films" in all countries of the Warsaw Pact.[56]

By the early 1980s, GDR cultural officials basically gave up on enforcing any consistent, politically driven policy when it came to the importation of Western and American films. Their only insistence was that the movie drew crowds and made money. In a 1983 report, SED officials conceded that GDR cinema was dependent on Western entertainment films, "because their high viewership and high economic profitability contribute to the fulfillment of the target goals of GDR cinema." Western imports that guaranteed at least one million viewers (Millionenfilme) were becoming absolutely vital in order to sustain the East German film industry. In the process, East German officials were willing to throw overboard most political reservations. In the most sobering part of the report from an official East German perspective, the film selectors admitted that "the majority of films from capitalist countries interpret their heroes, their history, and their worldview not in line with our ideological perspective," but the GDR cultural censors had run out of viable alternatives.[57]

Aside from the cultural repercussions of these trends and accommodations, there were political consequences as well. One of the most significant ones was the further deterioration of Honecker's policy of demarcation (Abgrenzung), which he had announced in the early 1970s as a corollary to increased cultural tolerance and openness. This policy was intended to keep the cultural influences of the West at bay while East Germany was developing more fully into its uniquely socialist identity. Yet similar to the Faustian bargain that the GDR had made by signing the Basic Treaty (Grundlagenvertrag) of 1972, which normalized relations with its West German enemy, the increased importation of Western and American films backfired for East Germany and ultimately undermined its independence and autonomy.[58]

The third major challenge to East German cinema in the late 1970s and the early 1980s was the overpowering nature of television competition, especially since the East German film industry had to contend not only with East German television but with West German TV as well. The dynamic unleashed by the 1973 decision to allow free access to West German television in the GDR was felt ever more powerfully in the film sector by the end of the 1970s and into the 1980s. In order to compete with the rapidly escalating film offerings on West German television in the 1970s, East German television was left with no option but to follow suit, as the next chapter will highlight. What this meant for the East German film industry was that it encountered ever-greater pressure to satisfy heightened audience expectations and demands.[59]

One of the most important findings of the youth survey of 1980 was that East German youth watched six times as many films on West and East German television by the end of the 1970s compared to films they watched in movie theaters, and the vast majority of these TV films were Western movies. As in the theaters, they preferred adventure, comedies, and entertainment movies of all kinds as well as films that dealt with both contemporary and utopian themes. West German television was only too eager to satisfy this demand. For example, the two main FRG TV channels (ARD and ZDF) broadcast a combined 332 films in 1977. Only 5 percent of these movies were from socialist countries, yet nearly 50 percent originated from the United States. At the turn of the decade, these numbers had further increased, and not to be completely

Figure 2.4. Movie theater in Wurzen, East Germany, 1990. Smaller GDR cities like Wurzen had a hard time maintaining their movie theaters and keeping them open in the 1980s as cinema budgets tightened even further. (Courtesy of ullstein bild / Granger, NYC—All Rights Reserved, New York; Image ID 0642795.)

outdone, East German television had joined in the fray. By 1980, East German viewers could watch 644 films per year on GDR TV, 31 percent of which were Western movies. By 1988, East German television was showing 983 films per year, and by then 56 percent of these were Western imports.[60]

What is sure is that this escalating entertainment war between East and West German television put enormous pressure on the GDR film policy. As mentioned above, one consequence of this was that films in movie theaters had to be unique, which often led to an emphasis on American blockbuster films, especially by the 1980s. Just as important was that combined with the financial restrictions, the television competition made the selection of films more difficult, since US films appeared on West German television with shorter delay times. By the late 1970s and the early 1980s, DEFA Export officials could no longer wait three to four years to import an American film unless they wanted to risk the chance that GDR viewers would see it on a West German TV channel first. The film *Cabaret* (United States, 1972), for example, was released on GDR movie screens in 1975, and was available one year later on West German TV. A few years later, *Missing* (United States, 1982) was first seen in East German movie theaters in 1984, followed by its West German TV debut in 1985.[61]

The fourth and final development responsible for the gradual capitulation of the cinema control on the part of East German officials was the fact that East Germany was being sucked into an international film culture heavily dominated by US imports, especially Hollywood blockbuster movies. And this gravitational pull of American films extended far beyond the East German borders into the rest of the Eastern Bloc countries. While cinema in the Soviet Union was more broad-based and generally drew from a wider variety of countries, largely because of its sheer size and differing regional cultural affinities, many Eastern European countries especially by the 1980s were most influenced by American films, similar to the GDR. One country that stands out in this respect is Poland, where moviegoers demanded US movies and became intimately familiar with the cinematic tradition and genres of Hollywood. Because of the generally vast influence of Hollywood culture in Poland, Andrzej Antoszek and Kate Delaney go so far as call the country "a translator and transmitter of American culture, making American works accessible to others in the Eastern Bloc," a position similar to that of East Germany. By the late 1980s, Hungarian cinema was likewise heavily dominated by Hollywood blockbusters: in 1989, no Hungarian-made film ranked in the list of top-ten movies in the country, while the US-produced *Rain Man* emerged as the top-grossing film. Also that same year, as the number of Hungarian-produced films declined, a total of eighty-five US movies were screened in Hungarian cinemas, compared to only ten from the Soviet Union.[62]

Because of the GDR's close proximity and continuous cultural interaction with its West German neighbor, the development of East German cinema in the 1970s and 1980s even more closely mirrored what was happening in other Western European countries during the same decades. As Joseph Garncarz highlighted, this was an overwhelming trend that had played out in West Germany since the 1960s in a pronounced manner. During the watershed decade of the 1970s, Hollywood films were beginning to dominate West German movie theaters—and by extension FRG television. Beginning in 1973, for example, the United States and West Germany already shared two to three films in their respective list of top-ten movies; after 1983, that overlap of top-ten movies further increased to three to five films per year. Likewise, after 1973 and through the late 1980s, US films consistently comprised the majority of movies shown on West German television, with roughly 40 to 50 percent of all FRG TV film offerings.[63]

And this trend was not limited to West Germany alone, although it happened earlier there and more pronounced than in other Western European countries. Even in countries with more robust film industries, like France and Italy, a very similar development occurred in the 1970s, although delayed by about five to eight years. By the late 1970s, French films had decreased to 55 percent of films shown in France; by the 1980s, their share further shrank to 35 percent. American films, by contrast, surged to 45 percent of market share in France by the late 1970s and captured a dominant position with 55 percent of featured films by the 1980s. By the 1980s, the top-ten film lists of the United States, West Germany, France, and Italy showed a 30 to 40 percent overlap.[64]

Conclusion

By the mid-1980s, the GDR film policy was a bundle of contradictions. Western, and in the 1980s especially American, film imports had become the lifeblood of the GDR film sector. In addition, still vainly chasing the mirage of the socialist cinema that was the ideal of GDR policy makers and deadly afraid of further political turmoil, SED cultural officials ultimately suffocated their own filmmakers with this failed and unpopular vision. Because of an equally restrictive import policy against progressive socialist films in the 1980s, it cut off the last avenue that might have ensured the continued relevance of socialist films. All in all, then, GDR officials inadvertently paid for their domestic political stability with the de facto surrender of their cultural, ideological film vision.

Looking back from the vantage point of the mid-1980s, the potential opportunities of the first GDR Film Week in New York in November of 1975 must have seemed very far removed indeed. At that time, GDR officials had still hoped to crack open the Western market for DEFA films, which in their rosiest view must have appeared like a feasible way forward. Yet in the ten years since those heady days, very few DEFA films had made their way across the Berlin Wall in the other direction. In the United States, only four GDR films had been distributed in that ten-year period since 1975, and Great Britain, France, and West Germany likewise had only purchased eight films each.[65]

Instead, the cultural reach of an international and heavily Hollywood-dominated film culture had been extended to East Germany by the 1980s. Similar to Western European countries, a few—often American—blockbuster films brought in the vast amount of film revenue. In the GDR in the late 1980s, 7 percent of new films drew about half of all film viewers into the movie theaters. And although the number of American films did not increase significantly in the years during the 1980s, their respective audience share became decidedly larger. Finally, the top-rated films in the GDR in the 1980s significantly overlapped with the top-rated films in West Germany, although often with a few years delay. This trend became especially pronounced in the last years of East Germany's existence: in 1987, *Beverly Hills Cop* was the top-rated film in the GDR (it took second place in the FRG in 1985); one year later, *E.T.* took top billing in East Germany (top-rated film in FRG in 1982); and in 1989 *Dirty Dancing* was seen by over five million viewers in East German theaters, to take first place (in West Germany, it had dominated the top-ten film list one year earlier).[66]

This increasing cultural convergence between the two German film markets—as well as those in Western and Eastern Europe—in the 1980s was highlighted by very similar trend lines, which was also one of the key developments in the television industry, discussed in the next chapter. The commercial European film culture of the 1980s was an entertainment-driven and youth-dominated industry, which feasted largely on blockbuster movies. Because West Germany was in the lead of this internationalizing, US-dominated film culture in Western Europe, it swept across the Berlin Wall and reached into every corner of the GDR. As a consequence, East Germany was pulled into the cinematic cultural vortex of its political archenemy and cultural nemesis. Combined with the internal crises and popular demand in the GDR in the late 1970s and early 1980s, these dynamics led to the surrender of cultural film control on the part of the GDR leadership and the cultural capitulation of their film vision in the face of inexorable and overpowering economic, political, and cultural trends.

Notes

1. Bericht über die Teilnahme an dem Programm "Filme aus der Deutschen Demokratischen Republik" in den USA, eingegangen 15 January 1976, SAPMO-BArch, DR1 18857, pp. 3 and 5. The films covered the whole thirty-year period, from early films like *Die Mörder sind unter uns* and *Wozzek* to films from the early 1970s such as *Legende von Paul und Paula* and *Jakob der Lügner*.
2. Ibid., pp. 6–9; seventeen DEFA films were ultimately sold, but only to a non-commercial film distributing company.
3. For an outstanding and broader discussion of these financial difficulties of the GDR in the late 1970s, see Andreas Malycha, "Ungeschminkte Wahrheiten: Honeckers Wirtschafts- und Sozialpolitik—ein zentrales Konfliktfeld im SED-Politbüro. Ein vertrauliches Gespräch von Gerhard Schürer, Chefplaner der DDR, mit der Stasi über die Wirtschaftslage der SED im April 1978," *Vierteljahrshefte für Zeitgeschichte* 59, no. 2 (2011): 283–305. The worsening financial situation of GDR cinema will be discussed later in this chapter.
4. See Elizabeth Prommer, *Kinobesuch im Lebenslauf: Eine historische und medien-biographische Studie* (Konstanz: UVK Medien, 1999), 352.
5. For an outstanding introduction and general overview of this topic, see Rosemary Stott's book *Crossing the Wall: The Western Feature Film Import in East Germany* (Oxford and Bern: Peter Lang, 2012).
6. "Analyse der Lage im Lichtspielwesen der DDR und Einschätzung dieses Bereiches bis 1975" (1971; no specific date provided), SAPMO-BArch, DR1 13273. In terms of the changing movie audiences, see Prommer, *Kinobesuch im Lebenslauf*.
7. "Analyse des Planablaufs 1970," eingegangen 3 March 1971, SAPMO-BArch, DR1 4918; the quote is from p. 56 of the report.
8. For a good overview of the institutional GDR film sector, see Daniela Berghahn, *Hollywood behind the Wall: The Cinema of East Germany* (Manchester and New York: Manchester University Press, 2005), 23–35.
9. On Honecker's overall policy reversal, see Mary Fulbrook, *The People's State: East German Society from Hitler to Honecker* (New Haven and London: Yale University Press, 2008), 41–42. On the liberalization on the film industry, see Dagmar Schittly, *Zwischen Regie und Regime: Die Filmpolitik der SED im Spiegel der DEFA-Produktionen* (Berlin: Ch. Links, 2002), chapter 5. On the

impact of the 1965 policy, see ibid., chapter 4; and Berghahn, *Hollywood behind the Wall*, chapter 4.

10. Joshua Feinstein, *The Triumph of the Ordinary: Depictions of Daily Life in the East German Cinema, 1949–1989* (Chapel Hill and London: University of North Carolina Press, 2002), chapter 7; and Berghahn, *Hollywood behind the Wall*, chapter 5.
11. Seán Allan and John Sandford, eds., *DEFA: East German Cinema, 1946–1992* (New York and Oxford: Berghahn Books, 1999), chapter 1.
12. "Konzeption zur Erhaltung und Entwicklung der materiell-technischen Basis des Kulturbereiches für 1976–1985," April 1973, SAPMO-BArch, DR1 14462a; the quote is on p. 1 of the report.
13. "Dokumentation des Haushaltsplanes 1975," 26 March 1973, SAPMO-BArch, DR1 14434; and report of the Staatliche Zentralverwaltung für Statistik, 10 January 1973, SAPMO-BArch, DR1 14503a.
14. "Auswertung der Ergebnisse des Filmeinsatzes nach Produktionsländern bzw. Gruppen von Produktionsländern per 27.11.75," 29 December 1975, SAPMO-BArch, DR1 14920. On the variety of ticket prices in the GDR, see Jens Michalski, *…und nächstes Jahr—wie jedes Jahr: Kinogeschichte Kreis Döbeln, 1945–1990. Das Beispiel für das Lichtspielwesen der SBZ und der DDR* (Berlin: topfilm, 2003), 59–60. As Michalski highlights, the most common pricing was a 50 percent increase for recent films from the West. As he also points out, attendance at screenings of socialist films were artificially inflated, so that the actual revenue advantage of Western films might well have been higher.
15. "Jahreseinschätzung der Zulassung ausländischer Spielfilme im Jahre 1978," no date given, SAPMO-BArch, DR1 12852; the quotes are on pp. 10 and 15, respectively.
16. Kristin Roth-Ey, *Moscow Prime Time: How the Soviet Union Built the Media Empire That Lost the Cultural Cold War* (Ithaca and London: Cornell University Press, 2011). The quote is from p. 53, and her discussion of the development of the Soviet film is covered in chapters 1 and 2. As in East Germany, the discussed trends started well before the 1970s, but accelerated especially in the last two decades. A significant increase in capitalist film imports in other Eastern Bloc countries in the 1980s especially is also highlighted by Richard Oehmig, *"Besorgt mal Filme!" Der internationale Programmhandel des DDR-Fernsehens* (Göttingen: Wallstein Verlag, 2017), 157–59.
17. For a more in-depth discussion of this oppositional dynamic of DEFA films, see Berghahn, *Hollywood behind the Wall*, chapter 1; Dieter Wiedemann, "Der DEFA-Jugendfilm und seine empirische Erforschung," in *Zwischen Bluejeans und Blauhemden: Jugendfilm in Ost und West*, ed. Ingelore König, Dieter Wiedemann, and Lothar Wolf (Berlin: Henschel Verlag, 1995), 121–27; and Schittly, *Zwischen Regie und Regime*, chapter 5.
18. For the 1971 report, see "Grundsätze für die Zulassung ausländischer Filme im Zeitraum 1971–1975," 8 July 1971, p. 14; the 1975 quote is from the report

"Grundsätze für die Zulassung ausländischer Filme im Zeitraum 1976–1980," no date provided, p. 2; both are in SAPMO-BArch, DR1 14971.
19. "Zu einigen aktuellen Fragen der Filmrezeption bei Jugendlichen: Problemmaterial aus neueren Untersuchungen des ZIJ," no specific date provided (1977), SAPMO-BArch, DR 1 4828, pp. 3–13; the quote is from p. 3.
20. "Spielfilm-Einsatz in der DDR nach Ländern, 1970–1982," no date provided, pp. 1–2, SAPMO-BArch, DR1 14971a. By 1989, however, American film imports outweighed all others from the West, constituting about 40 percent of all Western import films; see "Analyse über die Zulassung ausländischer Spielfilme 1989," 2 June 1990; SAPMO-BArch, DR1 4717. On GDR television, as Richard Oehmig highlights, British imported series were most prominent in the 1970s because US programs were usually too expensive; see *"Besorgt mal Filme!,"* chapter 5.
21. See Stott, *Crossing the Wall*, chapter 1; and Hans Joachim Meurer, *Cinema and National Identity in a Divided Germany, 1979–1989: The Split Screen* (Lewiston, NY: Edwin Mellon Press, 2000), 123–29.
22. Stott, *Crossing the Wall*, 44–47.
23. See Irmela Schneider, "Ein Weg zur Alltäglichkeit: Spielfilme im Fernsehprogramm," in *Das Fernsehen und die Künste*, ed. Helmut Schanze und Bernhard Zimmermann, Geschichte des Fernsehens in der Bundesrepublik Deutschland 2 (Munich: Fink Verlag, 1994), 227–301; and Eberhard Fensch, *So und nur noch besser: Wie Honecker das Fernsehen wollte* (Berlin: edition ost, 2003), 195–96.
24. Stott, *Crossing the Wall*, 99–100, 153–55.
25. For an overview of the New Hollywood films, see David A. Cook, *Lost Illusions: American Cinema in the Shadow of Watergate and Vietnam, 1970–1979* (Berkeley and Los Angeles: University of California Press, 2000); and Jonathan Kirshner, *Hollywood's Last Golden Age: Politics, Society, and the Seventies Film in America* (Ithaca and London: Cornell University Press, 2012).
26. "In der Hitze der Nacht," Einsatzhinweise; Hochschule für Film und Fernsehen "Konrad Wolf" [hereafter HFF "Konrad Wolf"], Pressedokumentation, Schlüssel-Nummer 45003035. For the GDR reviews, see *Freie Presse* (Karl-Marx Stadt), 17 November 1970; and *Der Neue Weg* (Halle), 1 October 1970; for a more critical East German review, see *Eulenspiegel*, December 1970 (no. 49). The collection of reviews in the HFF "Konrad Wolf" does not provide page numbers for these or any of the following reviews cited.
27. "Nur Pferden gibt man den Gnadenschuss," HFF "Konrad Wolf," Pressedokumentation, Schlüssel-Nummer 45004735. For the reviews, see "Keine Welt der schönen Bilder," *Ostsee-Zeitung* (Rostock), 26 January 1973; and "Sie tanzen für eine Handvoll Hoffnung," *Sächsische Zeitung* (Dresden), 23 January 1973.
28. "Blutige Erdbeeren," HFF "Konrad Wolf," Pressedokumentation, Schlüssel-Nummer 45005135; "Blutige Erdbeeren" nicht mehr aktuell?," *Sächsisches*

Tageblatt, 26 July 1973; and "Nachdenken über einen Film," *Junge Welt* (Berlin), 5 April 1973.
29. For the 1970s, this list included the following films: 1970—*Funny Girl*, 1971—*Cat Ballou*; 1972—*Hello Dolly* and *The Fortune Cookie*; 1973—*West Side Story*; 1975—*Cabaret* and *Some Like It Hot*; 1976—*For Pete's Sake*; 1977—*What's Up, Doc?*; 1978—*Lucky Lady*; see Stott, *Crossing the Walling*, appendix 1, pp. 251–54.
30. "Funny Girl," HFF "Konrad Wolf," Pressedokumentation, Schlüssel-Nummer 45002750. For a representative and fairly detailed review, see "70-mm-Märchen vom Broadway," *Thüringische Landzeitung* (Weimar), 6 June 1970.
31. For the political assessment of the musical, see "West Side Story," HFF "Konrad Wolf," Pressedokumentation; Schlüssel-Nummer 45005340. For a West German review, which discusses the new musical series on ZDF in the fall 1973, see "Millionen für Musicals," *Frankfurter Rundschau*, 2 May 1973, section "Fernsehen und Funk."
32. See, for example, "Im Armenviertel New Yorks," *Junge Welt* (Berlin), 5 June 1973; and "Um den Platz in der Sonne," *Der Neue Weg* (Halle), 11 June 1973.
33. Stott, *Crossing the Wall*, appendix 1, pp. 251–54.
34. Cook, *Lost Illusions*, 173–82.
35. "Little Big Man," HFF "Konrad Wolf," Pressedokumentation, Schlüssel-Nummer 45004640. See "Ein Krieg nach dem anderen," *Sonntag* (Berlin), 7 January 1973; or "Little Big Man," *Der Morgen* (Berlin), no date provided.
36. "Der Grosse Bluff," DFF "Konrad Wolf," Pressedokumentation, Schlüssel-Nummer 45003440. For a fairly representational GDR review, see "Klischees werden parodiert," *Thüringische Landeszeitung* (Weimar), 31 March 1971.
37. Gerd Gemünden, "Between Karl May and Karl Marx: The DEFA Indianerfilme (1965–1983)," *New German Critique* 82, no. 4 (2001): 25–38; the quote is from p. 26. As Gemünden highlights in connection with the implied socialist vision, one of the films actually ended with the motto "Indians of all lands, unite!" (p. 27).
38. "Der Exorcist," September 8 1975, 6847C; "Airport 77," 27 October 1977, 6614C; and "Zirkuswelt," 12 December 1969, 7772C; Filmarchiv Berlin [hereafter Filmarchiv].
39. "Viva Zapata," 1 March 1971, 7768C, and "Die Faust im Nacken" (*On the Waterfront*), 23 February 1970, 7727C, Filmarchiv. For the quote, see p. 3 of the report from 19 January 1970. In the late 1960s, even a seemingly innocuous musical like *Mary Poppins* could fall victim to the political sensibilities of the GDR censors. It was accused of being too conciliatory—advocating the slogan "Seid nett zueinander"—and showed a clear trend toward the reconciliation between social classes in the minds of GDR officials; see "Mary Poppins," 25 March 1968, 7748C, Filmarchiv.
40. "Alices Restaurant ist keine Kirche," 18 November 1975, 6622C, Filmarchiv. Other American film classics like *Casablanca* and *American Graffiti* were also rejected in the mid-1970s as too apolitical or inaccessible: "Ameri-

can Graffiti," 18 November 1975, 6605C, and "Casablanca," 14 August 1974, 6753C, Filmarchiv. For the potential danger implied in these films, see "Grundsätze für die Zulassung ausländischer Filme im Zeitraum 1971–1975," 8 July 1971, SAPMO-BArch, DR1 14971, p. 12.
41. Discussion of movie *Jaws* (*Der weisse Hai*), 8 November 1976, SAPMO-BArch, DR1 4741.
42. Stott, *Crossing the Wall*, 168–83. For the discussion of *Blade Runner*, see "Blade Runner," 22 December 1982, 6669C, Filmarchiv.
43. "Rocky," 20 May 1977, 7377C, and "Raiders of the Lost Ark," 4 January 1982, 7374C, Filmarchiv; "Am Wendepunkt," 1 December 1980, 7877C, and "Witness," 31 July 1985, 6817C, Filmarchiv. When the GDR selectors imported *Beverly Hills Cop II* for their program in 1987, they were careful to point out that it first had to be edited in order to remove the reference that referred to the leader of one gang as the former cultural attaché of a Central American GDR embassy; see "Beverly Hills Cop II," 15 October 1987, 6642C, Filmarchiv.
44. "Dies Land ist mein Land," 7 February 1978, 6788C, Filmarchiv. By comparison, an earlier film on folk music, *Festival*, was not shown only because of irresolvable technical issues. The film premiered in the United States in 1967 and was requested for import into the GDR in 1971; see "Festival," 18 June 1971, 7728C, Filmarchiv.
45. "Jahreseinschätzung der Zulassung ausländischer Spielfilme im Jahre 1978," no specific date provided, SAPMO-BArch, DR1 12852.
46. "Chinatown," HFF "Konrad Wolf," Pressedokumentation, Schlüssel-Nummer 21507. For *All the President's Men*, see memo from Harkenthal to Kranz, 10 March 1977; SAPMO-BArch, DR1 13236, pp. 2–3.
47. "Einer flog über das Kuckucksnest," HFF "Konrad Wolf," Schlüssel-Nummer 24696; film summary. For such narrowly focused East German reviews, see, for example, "Taming of a Rebel the American Way," *Neues Deutschland* (Berliner Ausgabe), November 1978; "Tote Seelen," *Das Volk* (Erfurt), 20 December 1978; or "Einer flog über das Kuckucksnest," 16 January 1979, *Volkswacht* (Gera).
48. Memo to Harkenthal, 21 June 1977, SAPMO-BArch, DR1 13236. McMurphy's particularly strong appeal to East German youth is mentioned in Lothar Bisky's and Dieter Wiedemann's study *Der Spielfilm—Rezeption und Wirkung. Kultursoziologische Analysen* (Berlin: Henschelverlag, 1985), 85–86. For the 2002 interview with Miloš Forman by Tasha Robinson, see AV Club, 24 April 2002, accessed 2 July 2013, http://www.avclub.com/articles/milos-forman,13764/.
49. "Apocalypse Now," 28 October 1981, 7881C, Filmarchiv.
50. "Aristocats," 4 February 1981, 6600C; "Barry Lyndon," 23 January 1980, 7886C; and "F.I.S.T.," 23 January 1980, 7909C; Filmarchiv. The average price for a Western import film in the late 1970s was around 40,000 Valutamarks (VM), but top-rated films went for as much as 60,000 VM, plus fees for the renting of film negatives; see "Bericht des Hauptbuchhalters zur Rechen-

schaftslegung über das Planjahr 1978," no specific date provided, SAPMO-BArch, DR1 15199a.

51. "Der Mann, den sie Pferd nannten," 9 January 1984, 7946C (the quote is from the memo from 10 October 1983), and "The Black Stallion," 30 July 1981, 7979C, Filmarchiv.
52. Valuta or Valutamarks was a currency designation for internal use in the GDR. One Valutamark was roughly equivalent to the value of one Deutschmark; Valutamarks were used to purchase imports from Western countries. Ostmarks were generally not accepted outside of the Eastern Bloc.
53. See Malycha, "Ungeschminkte Wahrheiten," 286–87. On the proposed sale of valuable artistic items, see "Erhöhung des Exports und der Exportrentabilität kultureller Erzeugnisse in das nichtsozialistische Wirtschaftsgebiet," 24 January 1977; the technical and material shortages for the film industry are discussed in a memo to Gerhard Schürer, 27 November 1978; both in SAPMO-BArch, DY 30 IV B2/2.024/76 (Büro Hager).
54. Schittly, *Zwischen Regie und Regime*, chapter 6; Meurer, *Cinema and National Identity in a Divided Germany*, 97–108; and Feinstein, *The Triumph of the Ordinary*, epilogue.
55. On the reduced sale of DEFA films, see "Einschätzung der Planerfüllung I. Quartal 1978," 3 May 1978, p. 5, SAPMO-BArch, DR1 12855, and "Rechenschaftsbericht 1977," p. 14, SAPMO-BArch, DR1 15199b.
56. "Einschätzung der Verkaufsvorführung für die sozialistischen Länder vom 22-25. 9. 1986 in Neubrandenburg," pp. 9–10, SAPMO-BArch, DR1 13239.
57. "Zu Problemen der Zulassung und des Ankaufs ausländischer Spielfilme für den Einsatz in den Filmtheatern der DDR (Positionen und Aufgaben)," no specific date provided, SAPMO-BArch, DR1 14971a; the quotes are on pp. 1–11.
58. For a comparative view, see M. E. Sarotte's *Dealing with the Devil: East Germany, Détente, & Ostpolitik, 1969–1973* (Chapel Hill and London: University of North Carolina Press, 2001), especially the conclusion "The Costs of Dealing with the Devil."
59. For very helpful overviews on this topic, see Peter Hoff, "Wettbewerbspartner oder Konkurrent? Zum Verhältnis von Film, Kino und Fernsehen in der DDR," *Rundfunk und Fernsehen* 33, no. 3/4 (1985): 437–55; and Claudia Dittmar, "GDR Television in Competition with West German Programming," *Historical Journal for Film, Radio and Television* 24, no. 3 (2004): 327–43.
60. For the 1980 youth survey, see section "Kino," SAPMO-BArch, DR1 4826. For the 1977 statistics, see Bisky and Wiedemann, *Der Spielfilm—Rezeption und Wirkung*, 40; and for the 1980s statistics, Dieter Wiedemann, "Wo Bleiben die Kinobesucher? Daten und Hypothesen zum Kinobesuch in der neuen deutschen Republik," in *Medien der Ex-DDR in der Wende*, ed. Peter Hoff and Dieter Wiedemann (Berlin: VISTAS, 1991), 89. Peter Hoff argues that the high percentage of Western import films on GDR TV was a particularly

powerful trend from the mid-1980s through the latter part of the decade: "Wettbewerbspartner oder Konkurrent?," 454.

61. On the increased reliance on US blockbuster films in the 1980s, see Stott, *Crossing the Wall,* 240–41. For the viewing dates of films of West German television, see Irmela Schneider and Christian W. Thomsen, eds., *Lexikon der britischen und amerikanischen Spielfilme in den Fernsehprogrammen der Bundesrepublik Deutschland, 1954–1985* (Berlin: Wissenschaftsverlag Volker Spiess GmbH, 1989: *Cabaret* (p. 546) and *Missing* (p. 318).

62. For an analysis of Poland's cultural development, see Andrzej Antoszek and Kate Delaney, "Poland: Transmissions and Translations," in *The Americanization of Europe: Culture, Diplomacy, and Anti-Americanism after 1945*, ed. Alexander Stephan (New York and Oxford: Berghahn Books, 2006), 218–50; the quote is on p. 224. The development of Hungarian cinema is analyzed by John Cunningham, *Hungarian Cinema: From Coffee House to Multiplex* (London and New York: Wallflower Press, 2004), chapters 8–9; see pp. 118–20 and 143–44 in particular. For a broader discussion of the varied influences of Hollywood and US cinematic culture in different European countries, see Thomas Elsaesser, *European Cinema: Face to Face with Hollywood* (Amsterdam: Amsterdam University Press, 2005); and Ewa Mazierska and Zsolt Győri, eds., *Popular Music and the Moving Image in Eastern Europe* (New York: Bloomsbury Academic, 2019).

63. Joseph Garncarz, "Populäres Kino in Deutschland: Internationalisierung einer Film Kultur, 1925–1990" (Habilitationsschrift, 1996), 133, 152.

64. Ibid., 138–151.

65. Meurer, *Cinema and National Identity*, 128–29.

66. On the increasing reliance of the blockbuster hits, see Wiedemann, "Wo Bleiben die Kinobesucher?," 86. The comparison of top-ten films in East and West Germany is based on the tables provided by Meurer, *Cinema and National Identity*, 293–94. See also Sabine Hake, *German National Cinema* (London and New York: Routledge, 2002), chapters 5–6.

CHAPTER 3

The Westernization of East German Television in the 1970s and 1980s

> The competition that takes place in millions of TV households every night is part of the class conflict through which the two systems and their irreconcilable ideologies face off against each other: [it is] a non-military but nevertheless an existential class struggle—and certainly not an electronic social game.
> —SED Ministry of Culture report, 1988

In the socialist shorthand, "class struggle" referred to the international Cold War and the irreconcilable antagonism between peaceful communist countries representing the power of workers and farmers and the imperialist West, which was ruled by capitalist oligarchies intent on political dominance and military expansion. As the previous chapters have highlighted, this conflict was fought through numerous venues: through the proxy war and propaganda exploits in Vietnam, through international athletic competitions—particularly the Olympic Games—as well as through the fight over movie audiences and cinematic influence. While many of these areas were not directly political in nature, all of them mattered greatly and took on deeply political overtones when placed in the context of the powerful and inescapable Cold War conflict.

Because of the unique division of Germany and Berlin, the Cold War was waged more strenuously and felt more intensely in East and West Germany than in most other parts of the world. And while the partial reconciliation and normalization of the early 1970s had eased the likelihood of military conflict, it only further heightened the social and cultural competition between the two countries and their respective ideologies. Especially after Erich Honecker's announcement in 1973 that effectively condoned the viewing of West German TV programs in East Germany, television became the daily battle zone where the two sides fought over audience and ratings and read the results as symbolic indicators of the appeal and acceptance of their respective social and political systems. As the quote above indicates, this cultural competition was not takien lightly in East Germany and was viewed as an important measuring stick of the success and failure of its own political ideology.[1]

After its rise to media dominance in the 1960s, television was seen as the primary and most vital of all media by the East German political and cultural officials. Because of its stature and significance, GDR television received more support by the SED and its cultural officials in the 1970s and 1980s than did cinema. They also fought much harder to keep East German viewers loyal to their television channels. In the 1970s especially, East German cultural planners and TV producers premiered several new family series, for example, which proved to be popular with their general TV audiences.[2] Yet despite these efforts, the eventual outcome would be similar to the movie sector: ultimately, East Germany's television planners would lose control over the industry due to popular demand, increasingly tight economic budgets, and international developments well beyond their control.

The increasing degree of synchronicity between media cultures in Western and Eastern Europe already discussed in connection with cinema in the previous chapter also applied to socialist television. In all European countries, for example, television officials initially tried to use this medium primarily for education and cultural uplift, yet these initiatives frequently failed because of popular disinterest and an increasing necessity to respond to the overwhelming demand for entertainment through TV programs. Socialist television officials generally resisted this widespread call for relaxation and entertainment by audiences slightly longer than TV officials in the West. Because of this continued insistence on education and cultural uplift in television programming, media compromises that combined the ideological priorities of the socialist government with the popular demand for light entertainment frequently prevailed in the 1960s and early 1970s on Eastern Bloc TV channels. However, the overwhelming popular demand for entertainment ultimately forced communist regimes to prioritize consumer satisfaction over political messaging in their television programming in the late socialist era, which included a heavy dose of Western imports or adoption of Western models as a significant portion of this entertainment mix.[3]

Hand in hand with this dynamic, it is also important to correct one popular misconception about GDR TV and the impact of Western and primarily FRG television. Nightly emigration to Western TV did occur regularly, and on some nights it included the majority of the East German viewing public. However, on many weekdays and especially weekend evenings in the 1970s and 1980s, half or more than half of the East German population actually tuned in to their own TV channels during the prime-time hours. The average yearly ratings for the primary GDR TV station during these two decades fluctuated between the low thirties and low forties for the all-important prime-time shows starting at 8:00 p.m. If one considers that no more than 70 percent of East German households tuned in on any given night, GDR programming held its own against the West German competition in the two decades prior to the fall of the Berlin Wall and, in fact, throughout most of its existence.[4]

Yet this general statistic tells only half the story, because it does not say anything about what GDR viewers were actually watching and what kept them loyal to their own TV stations in these years. A closer look reveals that while the overall ratings remained relatively steady for prime-time GDR TV, the content did not. In fact, what happened in the late 1970s and accelerated far more rapidly in the 1980s was that GDR cultural officials accommodated viewer demands with an ever-increasing importation of Western films as well as TV series modeled after US and FRG shows. This ensured that East German TV viewers at least kept tuning in to their own stations, but the nightly television competition and rating successes based on importing Western influences into socialist TV channels created clearly pyrrhic victories. By the 1980s at the latest, the strategy of importing Western films and copying capitalist genre formats amounted to abandoning the socialist cultural vision of GDR TV planners and officials in the face of overwhelming challenges.

Stemming the Tide in the 1970s: The Embrace of Entertainment Television in East Germany

Unlike some of the political and athletic victories of the early 1970s, East German television was in a slump during these same years. Increasing numbers of viewers tuned out GDR channels in favor of West German television programming, a tendency that was even further encouraged by Honecker's decision to condone the viewing of FRG television in 1973. Ratings reports confirmed decreasing yearly ratings from the late 1960s through the mid-1970s. In 1968 and 1969, for example, the average yearly ratings for GDR television had hovered right around 40 percent. It started to decline in the early 1970s and reached rock bottom in 1975 with an average yearly rating of about 33 percent for the prime-time hours of both East German TV channels. By 1976, after some of the political television shows were abandoned or shortened and substituted with entertainment programming, the trend started to reverse itself.[5] Not surprisingly, GDR TV planners decided to respond with more frequent and more varied entertainment programs in order to placate public discontent and to arrest the desertion to Western TV in more parts of its programming schedule. During the decade from 1967 to 1977 in particular, political TV programs decreased significantly. In the same time period, entertainment and music programming increased by nearly 200 percent, and television programming time for feature films skyrocketed by over 400 percent by 1977 compared to the latter part of the 1960s.[6]

Surveys from the mid-1970s provide more illuminating and detailed insights into the position of GDR TV and the emerging strategy developed by its planners. Looking back to 1971, when the first major reform of GDR television was undertaken after Erich Honecker's rise to power, a 1975 report referred to Honecker's own demand to overcome "a certain boredom" prevalent on East German TV and echoed his call for more appealing and entertainment-oriented television shows. Even though the ratings for GDR channels still remained relatively low in 1975, the attempted reforms produced some positive changes. Especially in the all-important weekend prime-time slots, GDR television actually increased its viewership. On Sunday nights at 8:00 p.m., for example, an average 36 percent of viewers were now tuning in to East German TV channels by 1975 (compared to 32.8 percent in 1972). On Saturday evenings, the percentage had likewise increased from roughly 38 percent (1972) to over 41 percent (1975). Not coincidentally, these were two of the evenings for which GDR TV reserved its most successful music, variety, and crime shows produced by East German writers, producers, and artists. But there was also still plenty of room for improvement. On Tuesday and Thursday evenings, which were mostly reserved for political shows and programs, ratings had gone into a nosedive. Compared to 1971, when the ratings had stood at a yearly average of 34 percent on Tuesday evenings, the audience had shrunk to only 19 percent by 1974. On Thursday evenings, the development was just as bad—with a decline from roughly 35 percent for GDR political shows in 1971 to less than 20 percent three years later. As an explanation for these dramatic decreases, the authors pointed out that the two main West German television stations featured popular entertainment programs in their lineup on those two evenings, which received the lion's share of East German television audiences. Not surprisingly, then, the report called for more entertainment programming starting early in the evening to compete with the FRG TV channels.[7]

The overwhelmingly critical assessment of GDR television in the early 1970s was also echoed by audiences. In 1973, an SED party member and work supervisor complained about shows like "72 Hours at the Furnace," which in his opinion did not reflect what viewers wanted to see after a full day of work. As he put it, "I'm already preparing myself for the heated criticisms and debates when I return to the construction site tomorrow. Even as a party member, I'm not sure what to say anymore." Another viewer was less discriminating in his response when he complained that there had been nothing worthwhile to see on GDR TV for the past six to eight weeks and added pointedly, "Moreover, you provide the viewers who live within the range of West German television ever more reasons to switch to their programming." One final viewer scolded especially the frequent repeat programming and took aim at the second East German TV channel, referring to its reputation as the "repeat TV station": "To be honest, all [GDR] TV broadcasting is developing into repeat TV programming. There's hardly a show that doesn't run two or three times, initially on the first TV channel, then on the second, and a year later it's warmed up again for another viewing."[8]

Reports and audience responses like these point to several larger trends of GDR television planning and programming in the early 1970s. First of all, East German television was generally speaking a reactive medium in its competition with Western TV, largely playing defense in its attempts to parry new initiatives and programming changes undertaken by its West German rival especially. Very closely related to this, GDR TV was engaged in asymmetrical cultural warfare because it was not in a competitive position. A GDR assessment from 1971 acknowledged, for example, that FRG television had the advantage in every important category: financially, it had three times the resources available to East German TV, and in terms of technical equipment the advantage was even higher. In addition, the number of programs broadcast by East German television was more limited. In the early 1970s, the GDR budget and production capacity really only secured enough resources and programs for one robust channel. The second GDR TV channel, which started in 1969, was limping along with frequent repeat shows as well as a heavy dose of Russian-language programming. West German television in the meantime was broadcasting over three fully resourced and distinctive channels, and most of these channels were able to penetrate far more deeply into East German territory than GDR TV was able to do on the other side of the border. In short, the competition was already lopsided in the early 1970s, and it would only get more so as the decade progressed.[9]

Added to these troubles were the difficulties that the East German television industry encountered in trying to create color television programs as well as in featuring a truly competitive second TV channel. Only 25 percent of all GDR programming was broadcast in color in 1975; SED officials hoped that this might increase to 50 percent by 1980. In contrast, all TV shows in West Germany were broadcast in color by the mid-1970s. At the same time, the second GDR TV channel was severely under-resourced and hampered by exceedingly low ratings. Between 1972 and 1974, the average yearly ratings for this station fluctuated between 2 and 3 percent. Even those in charge of programming conceded that nearly 20 percent of all TV shows broadcast on the second East German station in the early 1970s had no measurable audience whatsoever.[10]

To be sure, some television trends converged in the FRG and GDR in the 1970s. For example, East Germans closed the gap of TV ownership by the late 1970s. Roughly 90 percent of households in both German states owned a television set by the early 1980s. In 1970, the rate had been 69 percent ownership in the GDR versus 77 percent in West Germany; by 1982, it stood at 90 percent for East German and 92 percent for West German households. In both countries, TV was the primary and most popular leisure pursuit in the 1970s, with two-thirds listing it as their favorite activity. And not surprisingly, both audiences favored entertainment and music programming by wide margins. But there were also significant differences. Since the East German population had about ten hours less leisure time per week compared to West Germans and less money and opportunity to go out, the importance of TV viewing was further elevated in the GDR. In addition, East Germans paid far more for their TV sets than on the other side of the Berlin Wall: in the early 1980s, a black-and-white television set cost about five times as much in the GDR, while average incomes were half those of their counterparts in West Germany. There is also little doubt that the opportunity to watch West German television stations, which were available in close to 90 percent of GDR territory by late 1970s, added significantly to this higher status of television viewing in East Germany.[11]

Faced with these challenges, GDR officials responded in a number of ways. One of the more attractive as well as popular strategies was to produce more of their own TV series, especially entertainment shows. While there were certainly precedents for this kind of programming in East Germany prior to 1970, it was the 1970s that saw both the expansion of family series on East German television as well as significant revisions of this genre.[12]

The first GDR TV family series of the Honecker era, which premiered on East German television in November 1972, was titled *Our Dear Fellow Men (Die lieben Mitmenschen)*.[13] It was a seven-part series broadcast on Friday evenings at 8:00 p.m. over the first GDR television channel. In the announcement to the East German press, the production officials referred to the series as "an interesting experiment." This series provided a relative innovation for GDR television, since it was neither focused on crime nor adventure stories. Instead, it "told 'everyday stories' and treated 'everyday problems' that were familiar and interesting to large segments of the audience." The two main characters of the series crossed the generational divide: Carola Bärenburg, played by the well-liked actress Friedel Nowack, was described as a "likable, but also rather stubborn old lady." Her great-nephew and physics student Hans Hochheim (actor Frank-Otto Schenk) portrayed an attractive young man, who also happened to be a member of the SED Party. The purpose of the humorous stories was to "support the viewers' perspective that understanding and compassion ease our lives and will create more harmonious and stronger communities."[14]

From the opening scene of the first episode, it was apparent that *Our Dear Fellow Men* also had clear political messages; one of them was that East Germany had moved up in the world and that it could hold its own when compared with its West German neighbor. The opening of each episode was accompanied by upbeat music with rapid cuts of attractive scenes of everyday life in East Germany. In the first episodes, Carola Bärenburg was not the most effusive salesperson for the socialist GDR system. In fact, there were several aspects that she disliked about the government and its policies, but Carola eventually came around to a deeper appreciation for the socialist way of life as the series continued. A particularly good example of this trend was highlighted in an episode that aired in mid-December 1972, in which Carola was visited by her childhood friend and her friend's son from West Germany. Reflecting the nagging sense of inferiority that many East Germans felt when they came in contact with their FRG counterparts, Carola was concerned about a number of things: she fretted about her renter who was a captain in the GDR army, the (inferior) quality of life in East Germany, and the impression that her friend might have of her house and community.

As it turned out, she and her great-nephew were easily able to match the cosmopolitan flare and classiness of her West German visitors. In fact, her friend's son especially was deeply impressed by the advantages of GDR socialism, especially its university system, and her renter captain turned out to be a charming and polite host. In fact, it was her West German friend who finally brought out the socialist in Carola because of her relentlessly critical attitude. By the end of the episode, Carola had become a staunch advocate of her country and the socialist way of life, and she politely but firmly rebuked the pettiness of her friend's criticisms.[15]

Audience responses to the new family series were overwhelmingly positive and congratulatory. "The film [sic] *Die lieben Mitmenschen* was

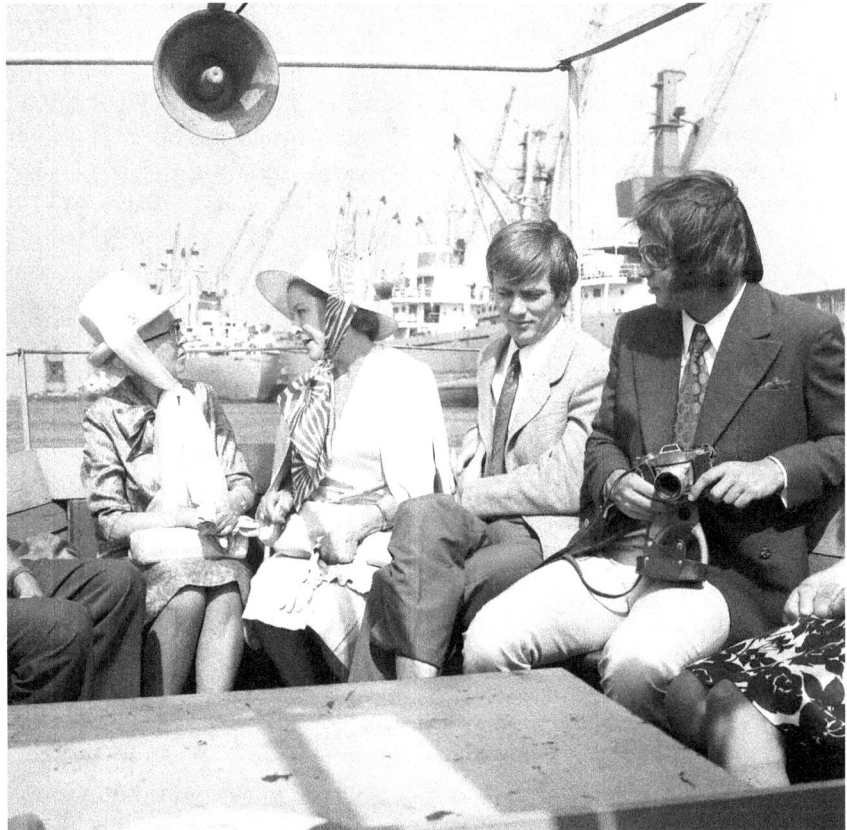

Figure 3.1. Scene from *Our Dear Fellow Men*. The East German pair is hardly distinguishable in terms of fashion from its West German counterpart. Friedel Nowack (playing Carola Bärenburg) is on the left, and Frank-Otto Schenk (her great grandnephew in the series) is second from the right. (Courtesy of Deutsches Radio Archiv; rbb media GmbH, Berlin; ID 1561509.)

very good. It would be great to see something like this more often," wrote one enthusiastic female viewer. A couple from Dresden agreed and added that they really enjoyed watching the series "because the show dealt humorously with everyday problems and searched for ways to solve them through smart and commonsense solutions." When the last episode of the series had aired, one viewer appealed to the TV producers not to let the show die and highlighted what he saw as its invaluable political contribution: "I cannot imagine a better civic education than this TV series. Thanks a million to the author, the producers, and all those who contributed to it."[16]

Carola Bärenburg was a savvy choice as the main character of this series. Because of her age and past, she had retained many bourgeois traits, and her skepticism toward the SED and official policies was quite likely shared by many viewers. However, she slowly came around to understand the advantages of the East German life and even defended the policies of the SED government. As Sebastian Pfau put it succinctly, "At the end of each episode Carola Bärenburg has shed one prejudice and has moved one step closer to the ideal of the socialist person." The formation of her socialist personality, aided by her great-nephew's steady support for the government and SED party, was reflected in her everyday deeds, especially her caring and community-oriented interaction with her fellow citizens.[17] It is also important to emphasize the willingness of the GDR television officials to engage in this kind of cultural bargaining with their audiences. Inspired by calls for more creative and entertaining television programs as well as buffeted by the political and international rise of East Germany in the early 1970s, this kind of openness and willingness to take risks was relatively rare and ultimately short-lived in GDR television as well East German media culture as a whole.

The popularity of the TV series *Our Dear Fellow Men* ensured that the producers were allowed to air three more well-received episodes of the series in 1974, after which the series disappeared from GDR TV screens. East German producers' tendency to limit all of their family series to between seven and, at the very most, twenty episodes in the 1970s and 1980s begs the question why they did not extend such popular series for years or even decades—similar to television programming in the West. After all, they did just that for popular music and variety shows as well as crime series that received high ratings, but never in the case of family series. The best answer to this puzzle is provided by Ursula Damm-Wendler and Horst Ulrich Wendler, two former East German TV writers who worked on family series during these two decades. They argued that long-term family series were unthinkable on GDR television because of the financial and logistical limitations. As they highlighted, the financial budgets and talent ceiling in East German television was far too limited to reserve actors and actresses for a long time. Just as important, GDR TV lacked the technological production equipment to keep multiple series going for several years.[18] Another factor contributing to short-run family series was that television was looked down upon by East German artistic professionals in the 1970s. Actors, writers, and producers often considered television entertainment less serious and less important in its artistic value and rather worked on theater productions or serious drama instead.[19]

Nevertheless, the success of *Our Dear Fellow Men* jump-started a trend of popular GDR TV family series, which continued into the late 1970s and throughout the 1980s. Another particularly successful show aired in the late 1970s and was titled *Retired People Are Always Busy* (*Rentner haben niemals Zeit*). It featured a likable retired couple, Paul and Anna Schmidt (Herbert Köfer and Helga Göring), who were even more folksy and relatable than Carola. Despite the focus on retirees, the appeal of the series was not limited to older viewers. Paul and Anna had married children as well as grandchildren, whom they frequently babysat, which provided a ready-made setup for a TV show with an appeal for all viewers. Moreover, they were very active in their neighborhood and inclined to help out wherever they could, which included going back to their old workplaces when things got tight. Encouraged by the success of earlier TV family series, GDR producers saw the potential of the show and scheduled twenty episodes, which was the longest run for any GDR family series in the 1970s.[20]

The writers and producers directly connected *Retired People Are Always Busy* to the format established by *Our Dear Fellow Men* and referred to it as an "entertaining family series." The shows consisted of unpretentious and friendly everyday stories that were meant to reflect "the strong ties of citizens to their communities and country [Heimatgefühl] as well as the kindness of everyday life under socialism." The goal of the episodes was to make "viewers smile rather than have them break out in laughter." The two main characters were sympathetic and full of life as well as eager to help family, friends, and neighbors, but they also displayed some of their own humorous and quirky foibles. Paul in particular was not yet ready to settle into retirement and frequently overdid his community involvement, but always with a humorous and generous spirit. His wife, Anna, was at times a bit stern, but she always meant well and was often the more reasonable of the two. The time she spent supporting her household and her family as well as with her neighbors was usually more than enough to fill her days.[21]

When the series finally aired on Saturday evenings at 7:00 p.m. on the first GDR television channel between December 1978 and April 1979, it proved to be a veritable television hit in East Germany. The lowest rating for any of the episodes was around 40 percent, and the highest-rated episodes attracted close to 60 percent of all GDR TV households. One typical episode focused on Paul's leather jacket, which was a special present from his family. For weeks he was afraid to wear it and just kept it locked up at home, but he finally decided to sport his new coat and wear it outside the house while he ran some errands. Of course, his coat did not survive the outing and was ruined not just once, but twice because of Paul's exuberant friendliness and readiness to help anyone in need. Although Anna scolded him for his careless attitude, they both agreed that helping others was ultimately more important than wearing fine clothes and were able to laugh off the loss of the jacket at the end of the episode.[22]

As in the case of *Our Dear Fellow Men*, audiences responded very favorably to *Retired People Are Always Busy*. They lauded stories that were relatable and believable, "taken directly from everyday life," as one viewer put it. Others wrote that their family was "looking forward all week to the next episode of their favorite show." To be sure, some of the responses were critical, pointing out that Paul and Anna seemed to have a better living standard than most retired people in East Germany and hinting at the lack of GDR-specific settings or topics. Both criticisms were well justified, because while the main characters lived modest lives, they never lacked for anything. However, the few critical responses were drowned out by the overwhelming chorus of positive responses. Yet despite the popularity of the show, there was no extension or second life for the series.[23]

The other feature of the series that deserves special emphasis was its rather nonpolitical nature. This sentiment was highlighted by the writers of the show and clearly speaks to larger cultural trends in East German television in the late 1970s. As one of the writers, Horst Ulrich Wendler, stated in an interview after the fall of the Berlin Wall, he and his wife purposefully avoided political references or discussions of the SED policies in the TV series. In addition, neither one of them was a party member. When asked about the lack of politics in their TV entertainment, Wendler commented flatly, "The older ones of us were more or less done with [politics] by the late 1970s and 1980s."[24] This comment correlates closely with the fact that GDR television in general became

Figure 3.2. This scene from *Retired People Are Always Busy* captures the simple but comfortable apartment of its lead characters, Paul and Anna Schmidt (Herbert Köfer and Helga Göring), as well as the three generations of their family. (Courtesy of Deutsches Radio Archiv; rbb media GmbH, Berlin; ID 1561507.)

less politically focused as the 1970s progressed—very similar to cinema, where ideology increasing took a back seat by the end of that decade. Family series on East German television in the late 1970s and early 1980s were a clear reflection of the increased focus on family, the private sphere, and everyday problems. Just as importantly, these shows exhibited growing similarities and convergence with family series on West German and US television, which were increasing in number and becoming more popular with GDR audiences as well. As Sebastian Pfau emphasized, "This convergence of GDR television with FRG TV was seen as a legitimate means by those in leading positions to keep their audiences loyal to East German programming." The two GDR family series discussed were indeed important markers along this trajectory and reflected this accelerating trend.[25]

The relative popularity and successes of GDR TV family series also caught the attention of neighboring Eastern European countries. One country in particular was Czechoslovakia, where the political leadership desperately sought to renew audience enthusiasm for its own television programming in the early 1970s after the crushing of the Prague Spring reform efforts several years earlier. In fact, according to Paulina Bren, it was television officials in the Soviet Union who encouraged their counterparts in the CSSR to take a page from GDR television and introduce more lighthearted entertainment serials. Part of the Czech government's challenge was similar to East Germany: especially German-language speakers of its population could receive and preferred West German or Austrian television channels. With the anticipated arrival of satellite TV, this problem was only going to increase. In addition, the political leadership had cleansed Czech TV production studios of much of its personnel due to the fact that many members had actively participated in the Prague Spring activities in 1968. The ensuing loss of professional and creative talent and fear of subversive broadcasting had left television in the CSSR paralyzed. Looking across the border to East Germany, Czech officials began to utilize family series as a way to rekindle the audiences' love affair with CSSR television. They often succeeded in remarkable fashion, especially with the TV series written and produced by Jaroslav Dietl, as Bren highlights. And since there was relatively less Western competition in the CSSR compared to the GDR, Dietl's television series achieved far higher ratings among its domestic audiences than the East German TV series he emulated. In addition, he managed to insert more subtle and regime-friendly political messages at the same time. Finally, in a relatively rare reversal of the highly asymmetrical cultural exchange between East and West, Dietl and Czech television were even able to sell one of his less political family series to West German television, which broadcast the dubbed version in its evening programming in the second half of the 1970s.[26]

To be sure, even in 1980s' East Germany television there were still series and episodes of domestically produced entertainment programming that reflected political priorities directly or indirectly. One of the most popular series in the mid-1980s, *Meeting Place Airport* (*Treffpunkt Flughafen*), for example, frequently involved flights to other socialist countries and at times connected the crew's adventures directly to current international events or crises, which sought to emphasize the solidarity with socialist countries. In this vein, one episode focused on a flight of the GDR crew to Nicaragua and their adventures in assisting the Sandinista government in its fight against US-supported rebels. Yet, similar to another series from the later 1970s, *At Sea* (*Zur See*), its audience appeal also significantly depended on the beautiful sceneries and the travel to foreign countries. Political themes might play their part, then, but even more important was the human and emotional drama involved in these series, as well as the virtual travel adventures to locations that remained out of reach for the vast majority of East German viewers.[27]

In line with the increasingly nonpolitical nature of GDR series, East German television planners scheduled more family series in the 1980s. While only nine short-lived TV series were produced in the 1970s, twice as many went into production and were ultimately aired in the 1980s. But despite this increase, GDR television still could not keep up with the growing audience demand for entertainment programming as well as the expanding schedules of the two East German television channels.[28] That gap had to be filled with imported programming, which was ultimately cheaper, ready-made, and usually popular with GDR audiences, especially when it consisted of appealing Western films, as the last section of this chapter will highlight.

Insurmountable Financial and Technological Challenges

What complicated and hampered the production of additional GDR TV series more than anything else by the late 1970s was the lack of technological equipment as well as a meager infrastructure and aging production facilities, all of which pointed to the same key problem: lack of financial resources. As indicated in the previous chapter, Honecker's financial gamble of increasing average living standards and consumption began to implode by the late 1970s. As Hans Hermann Hertle so aptly put it, East Germany was caught in "a debt trap" starting in 1978: "Loans and interest that were due had to be covered by new loans. The solvency of East Germany depended on the willingness of Western banks to authorize new credits for the SED government." And because the GDR government was deathly afraid of public protests if it were to increase prices or reduce subsidies, it further weakened its economic foundation by pulling desperately needed money from capital investments and from funds for research and development.[29] The combination of these ill-fated decisions made the economic decline of

East German television, as well as its increasing reliance on Western TV imports, all but irreversible.

The financial troubles were building gradually and steadily during the 1970s. Between 1972 and 1981, there was not a single year when East Germany produced a surplus or even close to a balanced budget. The worsening debt burden grew slowly, starting with an extra 1 billion Valutamarks (VM) in 1972. An additional 2 billion VM was added in 1973 and another 2.5 billion in 1974. By the end of the decade, the indebtedness of the GDR had grown tenfold: while East Germany owed 2.7 billion VM to Western banks and lenders in 1970, the debt stood at close to 28 billion VM by 1980.[30]

In the East German television industry, as in the movie sector discussed previously, the fallout of the economic mismanagement was felt more harshly by the late 1970s when significant cuts were depleting TV budgets. Starting in 1978, the director of the GDR TV division, Heinz Adameck, wrote increasingly urgent letters to his superior, Joachim Herrmann in the Central Committee of the SED, asking him to reverse some of the cuts or provide emergency funding in order to keep television productions afloat through the year. In early April 1978, for example, Adameck sent two urgent letters within one week, pointing to the dire situation in many areas of the television sector. At this time, the second GDR TV channel still could only be received by two-thirds of all East German households, and in order to raise this to the targeted 90 percent by 1980, an additional 300 million Ostmarks would be needed. Even based on this trajectory, it would take until 1990 to service all areas of East Germany with full access to both GDR TV stations. In addition, the construction costs for a newly planned studio in East Berlin were higher than initially anticipated, and the technological equipment in all sectors of East German broadcasting, both television and radio, was stretched to the breaking point. When he received notification of further cuts planned for 1979, Adameck warned in no uncertain terms that they would seriously impact television as a whole and jeopardize the planned production schedule for that year.[31]

Even though Herrmann passed these concerns on to the man ultimately in charge of economic planning for the GDR, Günter Mittag, there was little the latter could do, because all sectors of the East German economy were equally affected. In addition to the items mentioned by Adameck, East German television struggled due to shrinking and insufficient film stock available for GDR movie productions as well as a basic lack of equipment to produce competitive color films and TV series. The announced 20 percent cut for the overall budget of the Ministry of Culture in 1979 seriously jeopardized the badly needed expansion of production facilities as well as the replacement of aging and dilapidated equipment. And since the GDR had stopped investing in many of these technological areas, the demand could only be met by increased purchases of high-tech equipment from the West with hard currencies.[32]

The impending debt trap and the accelerating budget crisis in the GDR did not bode well for East Germany's political and economic well-being as a whole nor for GDR broadcasting or the television sector in particular. When the new five-year plan for television was unveiled in 1980, for example, GDR television officials again warned that the allotted funds would at best cover the replacement of already existing technological equipment, but it would not allow for purchases of desperately needed newer and up-to-date technology nor be enough to fund any significant expansion of GDR programming. As they emphasized, the requested "*accelerated development* [emphasis in original] of the self-produced programming could not be achieved based on the allocated funds." Moreover, much of the equipment had to be purchased with Valutamark funds in the West, which amounted to almost 40 percent of the GDR television budget in 1980.[33]

All of this severely impaired the cultural battle with West German television. The reports and letters by GDR television officials from the early 1980s reflect the sinking feeling on their part that the odds were getting longer. Surveying the developments of West German television in the early 1980s, for example, they enviously commented that their FRG counterparts were in the process of creating more programming of their own in order to reduce West German television's dependence on imported US series. In addition, they noted the expanding collaboration between different national television stations, which West German officials were eagerly pursuing even with other Eastern European television partners. This also meant that these collaborative series could not be aired on GDR TV, because West Germany retained the exclusive right to broadcast them in all German-language regions of Central Europe.[34] Finally, West Germany was able to expand its investments in technological TV infrastructure, which increased both the production of competitive television series and the reach of its respective TV channels. By 1981, this meant that the first West German TV station could be received in 84 percent of GDR territory, while the second FRG station reached 77 percent; several of the third regional West German channels were accessible in over 40 percent of the East German territory. By contrast, even the strongest first GDR television channel could be received in less than half of FRG territory by the early 1980s.[35]

In general, East German cultural officials were well aware of the development of private cable and satellite TV, which was well underway in West Germany and scheduled to go into effect by the mid-1980s. With this development, West German television would be able to reach into every corner of the GDR, and numerous additional new program options would open up to East German audiences. A study undertaken on behalf of the East German television sector in the late 1970s conceded that there was no conceivable way for the GDR to tackle this looming technological leap or even contemplate embarking on a similar expansion into cable or satellite TV.[36]

Amid the escalating budget crisis and fear of financial insolvency, which hung over the GDR in the mid- to late 1980s, the increasing depoliticization of GDR programming became more widespread as well. And despite its privileged status as the primary GDR media, television was not spared from further financial budget cuts. After years of decreasing budgets, television planners sent an urgent message to Joachim Herrmann in 1986, warning him that more than 80 percent of allocated funds for salaries, travel, and technology had already been

Figure 3.3. Store for radios and televisions in Bad Salzungen, March 1974. The purchase of electronic devices was a major investment for families in the GDR and usually far more expensive than in the West. (Courtesy of Bundesarchiv Koblenz; Bild 183-N0311-026.)

spent halfway through the year. By 1988, things had gotten even tighter: East German television was running huge deficits, and a report from late 1987 pointed out that the allocated budgets lacked funds for the coverage of the Olympic Games and the European Soccer Cup in 1988 as well as the anticipated TV costs for the 1990 World Cup.[37]

One of the last initiatives undertaken to breathe new life into East German television programming was to seek out collaborative projects with West German public television. As Woo-Seung Lee has pointed out, this cooperation between the television officials of the two Germanys—though relatively limited—was mutually beneficial in the 1980s. East Germany received much sought-after Western currency, and West German TV stations were able to purchase programs of famous plays or important historical dramas shot on location on the other side of the Berlin Wall. This collaboration intensified even more with the onset of the competition of private TV stations in the FRG in the mid-1980s, when West German public television officials looked for any help they could get to save costs and expand their programs and schedules. The final outcome of this tentative rapprochement was a general Cultural Agreement as well as a Television Agreement between East and West Germany in 1987, which solidified the ongoing collaboration. Yet it was too little and too late to significantly re-energize the East German television industry.[38]

It was in connection with this agreement that Adameck and several of his East German TV colleagues traveled to West Germany in May 1987 and successfully negotiated several projects, especially for dramatic productions of major literary works. What impressed Adameck far more than the new collaboration was the high-tech television studio into which the second West German public TV channel had moved in 1984. It was built with a total budget of 600 million Deutschmarks, almost half of which had been dedicated to the most up-to-date technology. This studio was part of an effort by FRG public broadcasting stations to compete with the expected onslaught by private commercial channels after the mid-1980s. Adameck's West German counterparts told him that they expected at least a dozen more (private) TV channels in West Germany by 1990. They highlighted as well that they assumed satellite television to be the norm by the early 1990s, which would allow for a much-improved television image with a far higher resolution. Even his FRG counterparts expressed concern over technological investments needed to survive "the merciless competition" from private TV channels coming their way. Adameck merely reported these conversations in his letter to Honecker, but he surely must have contemplated how hopeless the situation was for his own GDR TV division if his far better-equipped West German colleagues had trouble keeping up with the coming challenges.[39]

All of these developments came to a head in the late 1980s. At this point, even high-ranking SED cultural officials were beginning to voice far more honest, and at times harsh, assessments of the failings of East German TV, especially since yearly ratings were decreasing once again toward the end of the decade. A 1988 report stated matter-of-factly that GDR television was falling short: "For the first time since the VIII. Party Congress [1976], we will not be able to fulfill our yearly programming in terms of quantitative and qualitative programming or in terms of variety." At a gathering of TV professionals a year later, the concluding protocol likewise acknowledged a clear decrease in appeal of East German TV programming, especially during the vital prime-time hours, and ended on both a combative and somewhat desperate note: "The GDR is not located on an island. Rather it is situated at the focal point of the confrontation between capitalism and socialism. What are our offensive responses? We have to confront the competition more directly—and with an offensive strategy!"[40]

The Expansion of GDR TV and Wholesale Embrace of Western Films and Genres in the 1980s

Despite these dire circumstances, East German officials embarked on one last initiative in the early 1980s, which had been discussed and promised for almost a decade. Since West German television offered three all-day public channels, their East German counterparts committed themselves to offering at least two fully developed and competitive GDR TV channels with complementary programming in 1982. GDR television officials called it "the alternative program structure," and it amounted to the second and last major television reform undertaken during the Honecker years. The fact that this expensive expansion was bankrolled as the financial noose was tightening around the GDR's neck highlights the important role of television and, closely tied to it, the political significance that the cultural competition with FRG television held in the minds of leading SED officials.[41]

Yet as the officials in the East German television began to discuss this second major TV reform, it quickly became apparent that they did not have a well-developed strategy to move forward. They bemoaned the fact that GDR television "lacked outstanding programming quality and highlights" and agreed that they were not delivering East German audiences the attractive broadcasting that they had been promised. Moreover, they were financially squeezed. By late 1981, East German officials had secured programming for only the first four months of the 1982 television schedule. With their backs against the wall, they eventually settled on the one strategy they knew would work—increasing the usage of import films from the West. As the internal discussion emphasized, "We have secured too few top film hits with which we can defeat West German television.... The situation is critical, and our competitive disadvantage is dire."[42]

In connection with the television reform of 1982–83, then, GDR TV programming officials made a decision that exemplifies both East Germany's cultural dilemma as well as the future direction of GDR television, which eventually also had a very negative impact on GDR cinema. In May 1982, they decided to show an increasing number of Western import films on GDR TV before first releasing them in East German movie theaters. Naturally, this further drained GDR cinema of attractive first-run films, making its task of drawing in movie audiences even more difficult. Yet by the early 1980s, the key question was no longer how to revitalize the flailing movie sector; in many ways, its decline was well beyond repair already. Instead, their main concern shifted to the more vital aspect of East Germany's media landscape—television—and the key challenge of how to keep as many GDR viewers dialed in to East German TV channels as possible. The most significant goal was to compete with, and possibly beat, West German television on as many nights as possible in terms of ratings, especially in the all-important prime-time slots. As far as the movie selection for GDR TV was concerned, by the early 1980s the most important selection criterion became whether a film had already been shown on FRG TV. If that was not the case, GDR cultural officials were intent on beating their West German counterparts to the punch and score a victory for their television channels in the perpetual ratings war.[43]

When Adameck and his colleagues in the East German television division assessed the impact of the alternative programming reform in mid-1983, they saw cause for optimism: "In comparison to the first quarter of 1982 we have gained on average one million viewers per day during the same period in 1983," they confidently claimed and pointed to the entertainment-driven approach as the secret to this success. Indeed, for the next years until the late 1980s, the average yearly ratings for GDR prime-time television remained strong. After having declined to below 34 percent in 1982, the ratings returned to a solid 40 percent by 1983 and remained close to this yearly average through the mid- to late 1980s.[44]

At the same time, the introduction of the television reform and the goal to offer two fully competitive TV channels came at a high price—mainly because it necessitated a vast increase of imported Western or Western-style programming for East German television. In light of the budgetary crisis and the limited production capacity, a mid-1983 study noted that the number of self-produced programs had declined dramatically. For the prime-time evening hours, the percentage of GDR-produced programming declined to 40 percent in the first three months of 1983, while it still had represented over 60 percent for the first three months a year earlier. In a paradoxical manner, the report called for the significant increase of GDR-produced series but also signaled that the all-decisive means for future programming selection was "the central and all-important criterion of popular appeal." International films mainly from the West, as everyone knew, had clearly proved themselves as ratings successes. In the new prime-time schedule for early 1983, imported, and primarily Western, films made up half of all the programming on GDR television.[45]

When one surveys the prime-time schedule of East German television a few years after the 1982–83 TV reform, it becomes very apparent that GDR cultural officials put their emphasis squarely on airing international and primarily Western films in their TV programming. Planning their TV schedule for 1985, for example, East German officials inserted a Western film series into every evening during the TV prime-time hours in the GDR. The planned weekly schedule for the 1985 East German television season highlights this very clearly.

On the generally successful Monday evenings, East Germans were offered international films on the first GDR TV channel through a program titled *For the Movie and TV Friend*, which also included more movies in color than in previous years. On Tuesday nights, the first GDR TV channel extended its popular series entitled *Films of Your Choice* for the summer months in addition to the usual program, which featured films by famous international actors and actresses (Schauspielreihen). These new offerings on Tuesdays were supposed to revitalize the ratings of one of the weakest nights on GDR TV. Wednesday evenings showcased a series of films by famous actors and actresses on the second channel. On Thursday evenings, which had been reserved for political shows in the past, GDR planners added more self-produced quiz and entertainment shows on the first channel as well as attractive international films on the second GDR station. Friday prime-time television was reserved for popular GDR TV series, but in 1984 only one such series, *Tooth for Tooth* (*Zahn um Zahn*), was ready to be aired, which meant that more international films had to anchor the all-important opening of the TV weekend in 1985. On Saturday nights, East German television showcased its own popular music programs for family audiences and variety series, especially for older viewers. Yet planners also scheduled what they promised would be attractive international films for the same evening on the second channel. For Sunday evenings, finally, which traditionally highlighted popular GDR shows on the first channel, planners added ten Western movie hits. Overall, while GDR TV still had a small reservoir of popular TV series that it produced domestically by the mid-1980s, the reliance on Western import films and shows had grown exponentially.[46]

This shift in programming strategy had a number of significant implications. First of all, it highlights the fact that under the financial constraints and budget cuts of the early 1980s, television was given clear priority over film production and cinema. Those who argue that TV and film were collaborators and not competitors in East Germany might have been right as far as the 1970s are concerned.[47] But when things got tight and crucial decisions had to be made, as was the case in the 1980s, TV was the golden child, and cinema got the cold shoulder. The accelerating demise of GDR cinema was reflected in crumbling movie theaters and woefully underfunded production equipment and facilities. By the late 1980s, even a new housing development near Potsdam, which was advertised as a "film city" (Filmstädtchen), had to be content with having its streets named after famous film actors and actresses, yet it did not feature even a single movie theater. Overall, the resulting dynamic gradually turned GDR television into a home movie theater for primarily Western films, which ensured much of its continued popularity with East German audiences through the end of the decade.[48]

Second, the race to show international film hits on GDR television only intensified in the coming years. When the East German television officials planned their lineup for 1986, international films were essential in order to support the alternative programming strategy. As an internal report acknowledged, "The purchase of popular international films for the TV prime-time (8:00 p.m.) has absolute priority." Equally important, this increasingly meant that these films should not have previously aired on West German television or been featured in East German movie theaters: "We need to significantly increase the number of top movie hits, which means films that have neither been shown in our theaters nor on FRG TV."[49]

Despite these accommodations, East German television audiences were nevertheless getting impatient with the offerings by GDR TV by the mid-1980s. In 1984, for example, close to ninety films broadcast on East German television scored less than a 10 percent rating, and over thirty films had ratings of less than 5 percent. In addition, the number of repeat screenings was clearly on the rise as film offerings accelerated. By 1986, more than half of films shown during the prime-time hours on East German television were repeats, and only 25 percent of films broadcast at 8:00 p.m. on both GDR TV channels were films released in the 1980s. By comparison, 20 percent of movies aired had been released in the 1970s, and another 25 percent originated from the 1960s, with the rest being even older.[50]

Hand in hand with the increased emphasis on Western imports, a parallel redefinition of the ideological battle between East German television and its capitalist opponent took place by the mid-1980s. In the 1960s and 1970s, this competition was framed in terms of challenging the appeal of Western culture with equally attractive socialist film releases and television productions. By 1986, the ideological battle had completely shifted onto the terrain of the capitalist opponent. From an East German perspective, the question was no longer whether socialist TV series or DEFA films would be able to compete with their Western rivals; by the mid-1980s it was clear that the vast majority could not. The battle now often became which television system—GDR or FRG— would first air popular Western films in order to win favors with its audiences. As a report from the GDR media import agency put it in 1986, "As we know, the purchase of top international films occurs through an intense battle with our opponents and is the crowning achievement in the constant wrestling over the core of our quality programming [Qualitätskern]."[51]

It does not take much to recognize the ultimately short-sighted nature of this East German television strategy. Beating West German television stations by being the first to televise a Western film is indeed a telling measuring stick. However, it encapsulates the increasingly desperate situation in which GDR planners found themselves and how truly limited their choices had become. Ultimately then, GDR TV followed the path of GDR cinema rather closely. It ended with the cultural capitulation by SED and GDR media officials by the mid-1980s when they wholeheartedly embraced the import of Western films as the most significant and most reliable strategy to keep East German viewers tuned to their own television stations.

With every passing year, the calls for acquiring top movie hits became louder and the cultural accommodations more urgent. As they planned for 1987, GDR television officials called for the purchase of ten to twelve "international film hits" as well as an additional twenty-five to thirty "international films of outstanding quality and appeal." In fact, the report pointed out that the "quality core" of GDR TV broadcasting consisted of these very movies and again referred to the tough battle that GDR selectors had to fight in order to secure them. In another sign of the significance of this competition, the Ministry of Culture was willing to add four more selectors to the film acquisition teams despite the increasingly tight budget restrictions.[52]

In the process, the number of films shown on East German television mushroomed from over six hundred in 1980 to close to one thousand by 1989; by the end of the decade, 40 percent of all GDR TV programming consisted of movie programming. More importantly, the percentage of Western film imports increased even more over these years because Russian and other East Europeans films became too threatening to East German television officials. As mentioned in the last chapter, Mikhail Gorbachev's policy of glasnost and perestroika in the Soviet Union and the liberalization of the media in other Eastern Bloc countries created movies and TV series that were unacceptable to SED officials. From this vantage point, Western imports were actually the lesser of two evils by the late 1980s.[53]

To put it into a larger context, television in other communist countries was heavily saturated with Western and especially American imports by the 1980s as well. The visionary plans to use the Soviet Union's vast satellite network for the distribution of socialist television programs had already fizzled out in the 1970s. Instead, all Eastern Bloc countries had gained access to Western television programming, either by importing series directly or by accessing broadcasts through cross-border viewing. When Romanian TV officials decided to turn their national channels primarily into vehicles for the development of Nicolae Ceaușescu's personality cult in the 1980s, for example, Romanians learned foreign languages and fled to other countries' channels in even greater numbers, especially Hungarian and Yugoslav television, frequently focusing on imported US or Western series in particular.[54]

The other ironic development in the GDR was that from the mid-1980s onward, East German television actually broadcast more imported Western films and series, especially from the United States, than the public television stations in West Germany. The high point of the reliance on imported and especially US-based programming in West Germany lasted from the early 1970s through the early 1980s. British and American imports, predominantly feature films, took up nearly 50 percent of FRG television programming in the late 1970s, which was no doubt driving the East German trends as well. Starting in the mid-1980s, however, the imported TV programming decreased slightly on FRG public broadcasting stations. Part of this reversal was a whole new dynamic that was added to the mix: 1984 was the year when private television programming was introduced in West Germany. Unlike the public channels, these private, commercial newcomers relied almost completely on imported entertainment series and films, primarily from the United States. By 1988, the US-program share on the two dominant private TV channels in West Germany was 68 percent (SAT 1) and 54 percent (RTL plus), respectively. Like their West German public broadcasting competitors, these private channels too were now broadcasting across the Berlin Wall and could be received in many parts of East Germany. For GDR television, therefore, the media landscape and the cultural battle became vastly more complicated and competitive from the mid-1980s onward.[55]

All of these developments led to a further devaluation of political and news programming on East German TV channels from the mid- to late 1980s. Unlike the earlier decades in the GDR, when its own programming and political broadcasts had reigned supreme and when political news programs at least held their own against entertainment series, political broadcasts and magazines clearly took a back seat by the 1980s, with the hope that they would not alienate or drive away too many viewers. When they planned the TV schedule for Tuesday evenings in 1984, for example, GDR cultural officials emphasized that political shows should be used on only fifteen evenings of the year on one of the prime-time evenings reserved for political programming. Even then, as they pointed out, "they should be scheduled in three- to five-week intervals only." By 1987, when quality prime-time programming was regularly equated with entertaining film imports or entertainment shows, GDR TV planners emphasized that "necessary broadcasts focused on the politics of the GDR should be utilized *to the least extent possible* [my emphasis]."[56] This depoliticization of GDR TV programming was a reflection of the main trends in the 1980s: East German television had become primarily focused on meeting popular demand for entertainment and Western cultural imports in order to maintain viewer numbers and ratings.

This trend clearly expressed itself in the GDR-produced TV series of the 1980s as well. Similar to those in West Germany, more series focused on hospital settings or physicians' clinics, often providing lighthearted glimpses into the professional lives of medical staff. In 1985, East

German television premiered the previously mentioned series *Tooth for Tooth* (*Zahn um Zahn*), which centered on the likable professional pair of Dr. Wittkugel and his charming and witty office assistant Häppchen. In one of the earlier episodes, audiences learned that the dentist himself was afraid of the dentist. Dr. Wittkugel tried to avoid ending up in the dentist's chair despite excruciating toothache. Even more threatening to this middle-aged and rather chauvinist professional was the thought of landing in the chair of a female fellow practitioner. Of course, Häppchen came up with a clever ruse that accomplished both. By the end of the episode, Dr. Wittkugel was cured of his toothache as well as some of his misogynistic prejudice. The series was popular among GDR viewers, receiving an average 30 percent rating for the first seven episodes. Eventually, its popularity led to two short-lived extensions in the 1986 and 1988, with seven episodes each.[57]

Equally popular was another series that aired later on in 1985, which reflected the emerging soap-opera quality of many GDR shows more explicitly. *New Stories over the Garden Fence* (*Neues übern Gartenzaun*) was the continuation of a 1982 TV series *Stories over the Garden Fence* (*Geschichten über den Gartenzaun*). The original as well as the sequel were reflections of the quintessential retreat into the private sphere in East Germany: it was set in a garden community where many East Germans spent their weekends and summer evenings. Like *Retired People Are Always Busy*, the series focused on a three-generation family. Life in this stereotypical garden community focused on leisure-time activities, interactions with family and friends, and a host of everyday and interpersonal challenges. In a typical episode, one of the main characters, Mr. Timm, confronted and advised his son-in-law about an extramarital affair, which he uncovered by coincidence; ensuing episodes focused on its eventual resolution. Like the earlier seven-episode series, the second run in late 1985 proved equally popular and attracted an average 40 percent of GDR viewers.[58]

What is noticeable about these GDR series of the 1980s is how much they mirrored the themes and genre formats of their Western counterparts. Just as significantly, GDR family series also increasingly employed similar narrative strategies and dramatic devices that were directly influenced by Western TV. Most notable among these was the all-important cliff-hanger, which had become the prime signifier of US-produced TV series by this time.[59] Likewise, GDR TV began to make plans for the previously unthinkable: they began to lay the foundation for long-running TV series that would air not just for months but years. Two such shows were in the early planning stages in 1986. The first, tentatively entitled

The Sanatorium (*Das Kurheim*) was to focus on an East German rehabilitation clinic. It would have provided ample opportunities for human-interest stories as well as chances to highlight one of the great benefits of life under socialism: the fact that most GDR citizens could expect one or two all-expenses-paid, multi-week spa visits in the course of their lives. The other long-term series was to center around the busiest train station in East Germany, Leipzig (tentative titled *Train Station Leipzig* [*Hier Leipzig Bahnhof*]). As the concept paper pointed out, a quarter million people made their way through the station every day. In addition, there were one hundred emergencies daily, some of them life-and-death situations, as well as over a thousand people who worked there—including eighteen families who actually lived in the train station. Yet none of these long-term series ever made it beyond the planning stage, because of dwindling budgets and the lack of sufficient technological and production infrastructure.[60]

In preparation for its 1990 Party Congress, SED officials in 1989 asked academics at the Karl Marx University in Leipzig to provide them with an overview of the media development in the GDR. The final report was unusually blunt and insightful. Overall, as the academics concluded, GDR television as a whole and the media reforms in particular had failed their audiences in East Germany. First of all, the lack of political freedom led citizens to a retreat into the private sphere by the late 1970s and what the authors called a "privatization of social communication": "People constructed arcs and searched for niches in order to discuss those topics that everyone believed could not be discussed publicly or that were simply eliminated from public discourse." In terms of media technology and the entertainment industry, the report bluntly stated that East Germany was not competitive in either area: "The biggest competitive disadvantage exists in terms of the development of a coherent strategy for mass entertainment that can meet the demands of the new international and global challenges of the 1990s." The GDR had no comprehensive and appealing "theory for a socialist mass culture," the report's authors stated flatly. In addition, there was too little actual competition between East German artists, and the technological backwardness of GDR visual culture was becoming ever more noticeable. The resulting provincialism of East German popular culture, as the media experts concluded, was rather evident by the late 1980s: "The audiences, which are well informed about the international standards through Western TV or the import of popular music, are becoming more critical than ever before in light of the East German provincial constraints and amateurism."[61]

One group had reached these conclusions even sooner than the general public: the youth of East Germany. GDR television had precious little to offer to them, and they turned their backs on most of East German television programming, especially youth-oriented shows, starting in the late 1970s. As studies from the late 1970s and early 1980s confirmed, young people in the East watched Western TV more frequently than did their fellow citizens and found West German television more entertaining by a two-to-one ratio. While many still watched individual youth music shows specifically produced for their age group in the late 1970s such as *Round* (*Rund*), much of the other youth programming fell flat. The most appealing East German TV shows, aside from an occasionally popular youth program, were GDR-produced crime series like *Police Call 110* (*Polizieruf 110*) as well as attractive international films. In fact, by 1982 young people were watching on average 120 to 150 mostly imported films on East German television. The one recommendation that the reports agreed on was to air more international, primarily Western, films and series to lure more young people back to East Germany's own TV channels.[62]

When GDR researchers conducted another study by early 1987, the preference for Western television and media had accelerated even further among young people in East Germany: "There has been an increasing trend to listening to Western radio stations and watching West [German] TV programming between 1982 and 1985. Correspondingly, the attraction of our programming has decreased, including our TV youth programming." East German television was rated far lower by East German youth than by the general GDR public. As a clear indicator of this accelerating dynamic, they pointed to the fact that Western TV had provided the topics for discussion for 82 percent of young people in the week of the survey. GDR TV, by comparison, had sparked conversations among 59 percent of young people in East Germany during that same time period. Simultaneously, the number of young people who regularly watched GDR TV youth programming had slipped below 10 percent by the mid-1980s.[63]

Conclusion

In her analysis of the psychological mind-set of the leaders of the GDR TV industry in the last two decades prior to the fall of the Berlin Wall, Claudia Dittmar argues that they, together with the SED leadership as a whole, suffered from collective delusion and had become "victims of their own propaganda." There is certainly much to support such a view. In his retrospective, Eberhard Fensch, who supervised television for the Central Committee of the SED, repeatedly stated that Erich Honecker stopped reading public opinion surveys by the late 1970s and ignored evidence or comments that contradicted the official party line. Others highlighted that Honecker ran the Politburo meetings in the 1980s like a stern schoolmaster, allowing no room for either dissenting or critical voices. The continued rhetorical insistence on a uniquely socialist TV culture and the call for socialist fictional heroes, which persisted all through the 1980s in the face of overwhelming evidence to the contrary, certainly corroborates this willed ignorance and isolation on the part of those in charge of East German politics and culture.[64]

Yet by the mid- to late 1980s, at the latest, officials increasingly came face-to-face with the inescapable reality of GDR TV's gradual demise. The most damaging and ultimately debilitating factor was the worsening financial crisis and the crippling technological and infrastructure shortfalls. When Adameck was standing in the brand-new West German television studio in 1987 and came face-to-face with the future of television broadcasting, the contrast could not have been any starker: while West German TV was gearing up for the future competition against private commercial providers and the looming switch to cable and satellite TV, Adameck's colleagues in East Germany were still struggling with basic problems such as extending the range of TV reception throughout all of the GDR or increasing the use of color television—problems that were long in the rearview mirror in the West.

While the slow economic strangulation was one of the root causes of the dilemmas facing the GDR cultural leadership, the increasing political crises and gradual opening in other parts of the Eastern Bloc further weakened East German television's viability, very similar to the GDR cinema sector. The fact that more and more television series and films from communist allies dealt with taboo social topics as well as frank political criticisms was unacceptable to the GDR leadership and was viewed as a dangerous political experiment. By censoring all of this new programming, East Germany further isolated itself and became even more dependent on Western cultural imports than before. By the second half of the 1980s, East German television officials had exhausted all possible avenues, and they played the one trump card still left to them: they ultimately relied on popular imports, especially Western international movie hits, in order to hold on to as many TV viewers as possible. But the cultural battle for viewers was now fought almost exclusively on the terms and with the weapons of the capitalist class enemy.

Notes

1. The single best book on this topic is Claudia Dittmar's study, *Feindliches Fernsehen: Das DDR-Fernsehen und seine Strategien im Umgang mit dem Westdeutschen Fernsehen* (Bielefeld: Transcript Verlag, 2010). For another outstanding overview, see Rüdiger Steinmetz and Reinhold Viehoff, eds., *Deutsches Fernsehen Ost: Eine Programmgeschichte des DDR-Fernsehens* (Berlin: Verlag für Berlin-Brandenburg, 2008).
2. For additional studies on GDR television, see Knut Hickethier, *Geschichte des deutschen Fernsehens* (Stuttgart and Weimar: Verlag J. B. Metzler, 1998); the special issue "East German Television History," ed. Rüdiger Steinmetz, *Historical Journal of Film, Radio and Television* 24, no. 3 (2004); and Peter Goddard, ed., *Popular Television in Authoritarian Europe* (Manchester and New York: Manchester University Press, 2013), part 3.
3. For a discussion of the TV compromise reached in the 1950s and 1960s in East Germany, see especially Heather L. Gumbert, *Envisioning Socialism: Television and the Cold War in the German Democratic Republic* (Ann Arbor: University of Michigan Press, 2014). The gradual convergence of Eastern and Western European television programming is most comprehensively analyzed in Anikó Imre's excellent book *TV Socialism* (Durham and London: Duke University Press, 2016). For more focused studies, see among others Paulina Bren, *The Greengrocer and His TV: The Culture of Communism after the 1968 Prague Spring* (Ithaca and London: Cornell University Press, 2010); Martin Štoll, *Television and Totalitarianism in Czechoslovakia* (New York: Bloomsbury Academic, 2019); Kristin Roth-Ey, *Moscow Prime Time*, especially chapters 4 and 5; and several essays in the anthology edited by Goddard titled *Popular Television in Authoritarian Europe*.
4. The average yearly ratings for prime-time East German television fluctuated between 40 percent in 1969 to a low of about 33 percent in 1975 and returned to roughly 40 percent or the high 30s by the early to mid-1980s; see "Massnahmen zur besseren Profilierung und Abstimmung des I. und II. Programms," 1 February 1977 (p. 2), SAPMO-BArch, DR8 160; and "Ergebnisse der Programmarbeit im Zeitraum 06.01.-30.06.1986," 30 July 1986, SAPMO-BArch, DR8 189. See also Michael Meyen's study, which most forcefully argued the case for parity or even the preference of GDR TV among East German viewers: *Einschalten, Umschalten, Ausschalten? Das Fernsehen im DDR-Alltag* (Leipzig: Leipziger Universitätsverlag, 2003).
5. "Massnahmen zur Profilierung und Abstimmung des I. und II. Programms," 1 February 1977, SAPMO-BArch, DR8 170.
6. "Zur Entwicklung des Arbeitsvermögens im DDR-Fernsehen," 30 June 1977, SAPMO-BArch, DR8 161. A number of popular GDR TV shows such as *Ein Kessel Buntes* and *Polizeiruf 110* had their origin in this early 1970s television reform as well; see Hickethier, *Geschichte des deutschen Fernsehens*, chapter 11.

7. "Zu programmstrategischen Überlegungen über die weitere Profilierung des I. und II. Programms des DDR-Fernsehens," 27 June 1975, SAPMO-BArch, DR8 151. The ratings are listed on pp. 3–4, and the quote is from p. 2; for the recommendation, see p. 43.
8. "Auszüge aus Zuschauerbriefen, Juni-November 1973," SAPMO-BArch, DR8 378.
9. Dittmar, *Feindliches Fernsehen*, chapters 4–5; the report of the comparison of FRG and GDR TV from 1971 is quoted on p. 315. In terms of the defensive and adaptive mode of East German television, see also Knut Hickethier, "Das Fernsehen der DDR," in *Wie im Westen, nur anders: Medien in der DDR*, ed. Stefan Zahlmann (Berlin: Panama Verlag, 2010), 119–30.
10. "Zu programmstrategischen Überlegungen über die weitere Profilierung des I. und II. Programms des DDR-Fernsehen," 27 June 1975, SAPMO-BArch, DR 8 151. The ratings for the second channel are cited on p. 9.
11. Meyen, *Einschalten, Umschalten, Ausschalten?*, pp. 38–72. The table with the ownership comparison is on p. 38. For his comments about leisure time and the cost of TVs in the GDR, see pp. 63–65 and pp. 38–40, respectively.
12. For an excellent overview of this TV genre and its development in East Germany, see Sebastian Pfau, *Vom Seriellen zur Serie—Wandlungen im DDR-Fernsehen: Die Entwicklung der fiktionalen Serie im DDR-Fernsehen mit dem Schwerpunkt auf Familienserien* (Leipzig: Leipziger Universitätsverlag, 2009).
13. For an intriguing discussion of this show, see also Sascha Trültzsch and Reinhold Viehoff, "Undercover: How the East German Political System Presented Itself in Television Series," in *Popular Television in Authoritarian Europe*, ed. Goddard, 141–58.
14. "Die lieben Mitmenschen," Unterhaltung/Dramatik, HA-Serienproduktion, Presseabteilung; 23 October 1972, Deutsches Rundfunkarchiv Babelsberg [hereafter DRA Babelsberg]; "Die lieben Mitmenschen," Sendeunterlagen und Einzelfolgen.
15. Episode 5: "Um des lieben Friedens Willen," *Die lieben Mitmenschen*, 15 December 1972, DRA Babelsberg AD 5740/1.
16. "Auszüge aus der Zuschauerpost zu Die lieben Mitmenschen," DRA Babelsberg, *Die lieben Mitmenschen*, Sendeunterlagen und Einzelfolgen.
17. Pfau, *Vom Seriellen zur Serie*, 118; for the broader discussion, see pp. 110–25.
18. "Gespräch mit Ursula Damm-Wendler und Horst Ulrich Wendler am 8. Juli, 2002," in *"Die Liebenswürdigkeit des Alltags": Die Familienserie "Rentner haben niemals Zeit,"* ed. Reinhold Viehoff (Leipzig: Universitätsverlag Leipzig, 2004), 119–20.
19. Discussion between Heide Hess and Martin Heinzel, "Serien im DDR-Fernsehen in den 70er und 80er Jahren," in *Zum Fernsehspiel und zur Fernsehserie in der DDR*, ed. Helmut Heinze and Doris Rosenstein (Siegen: Bildschirmhefte 71, 1997), 92, 109.

20. For an informative overview of the episodes of the series, see Sebastian Pfau and Sascha Trültzsch, "Stabangaben der Einzelfolgen mit Inhaltsangaben zur Serie *Rentner haben niemals Zeit*," in *"Die Liebenswürdigkeit des Alltags,"* ed. Viehoff, 129–52.
21. "Inszenierungskonzeption zur Serie 'Rentner haben niemals Zeit'," 25 April 1977, DRA Babelsberg, "Rentner haben niemals Zeit," Sendeunterlagen, 1–5.
22. Episode 17, *Rentner haben niemals Zeit*, 24 March 1979, DRA Babelsberg, AC 6633. For the ratings of the series, see Sebastian Pfau and Burkhard Raue, "Kostproben aus dem Deutschen Rundfunkarchiv: Eine Auswahl von Leserzuschriften und Pressestimmen," in *"Die Liebenswürdigkeit des Alltags,"* ed. Viehoff, 109.
23. "Auszüge aus der Zuschauerpost für 'Rentner haben niemals Zeit'," DRA-Babelsberg, *Rentner haben niemals Zeit*, Sendeunterlagen. See viewer responses from 17 March 1979, 13 February 1979, and 23 April 1979.
24. "Gespräch mit Ursula Damm-Wendler und Horst Ulrich Wendler am 8. Juli 2002," in *"Die Liebenswürdigkeit des Alltags,"* ed. Viehoff, 121.
25. See Pfau, *Vom Seriellen zur Serie*, 110–57; the quote is on p. 151.
26. Bren, *The Greengrocer and His TV*, see especially chapters 5–6. The inspiration that GDR television provided for this new approach in Czech TV is discussed on pp. 121–23.
27. For *Treffpunkt Flughafen*, see for example Episode 7, 6 April 1986, DRA-Babelsberg, AD 7658/1.
28. See Pfau, *Vom Seriellen zur Serie*, 184–89.
29. Hans Hermann Hertle, "Die DDR an die Sowjetunion verkaufen? Stasi-Analysen zum ökonomischen Niedergang der DDR," *Deutschland Archiv* 42, no. 3 (2009): 476.
30. "Zur Zahlunsbilanz NSW 1975," Report from Günter Mittag to Erich Honecker, 30 October 1974, SAPMO-BArch, DY 3023/964. For the broader discussion, see Falk Küchler, *Die Wirtschaft der DDR: Wirtschaftspolitik und die industrielle Rahmenbedingungen 1949 bis 1989* (Berlin: FIDES Verlag, 1997), 51–55; and Matthias Judt, "Periodisierung der Wirtschaft der DDR," in *Die Wirtschaft im geteilten und vereinten Deutschland*, ed. Karl Eckart and Jörg Roesler (Berlin: Duncker und Humblot, 1999), 180.
31. Letters by Heinz Adameck to Joachim Herrmann, 4 April and 11 April 1978, SAPMO-BArch DY30 IV2/2.037 40; for the 1979 letter, see SAPMO-BArch, DY30/2.2037 41.
32. Letters by Joachim Herrmann to Kurt Hager, 12 April 1978 and 19 October 1978, SAPMO-BArch, DY30 IV B2/2.024 76.
33. "Planprojekt zur Entwicklung des Fernsehens der DDR im Fünfjahresplan 1981–1985," Staatliches Komitee für Fernsehen, 1980 (no specific date), SAPMO-BArch, DR8 169; the quote is on p. 8.
34. "Serien im Fernsehen der BRD," 14 January 1981, SAPMO-BArch, DR8 178.
35. The reception rates of West German TV are discussed in a letter to Joachim Herrmann, 1 July 1981, SAPMO-BArch, DY30 IV2/2.037 42.

36. The late 1970s reference to cable television is discussed in a letter to Herrmann from 3 April 1978, SAPMO-BArch, DY30 IV2/2.037 40.
37. "Analyse Ergebnisse der Programmarbeit im Zeitraum 06.01.-30.06.1986," SAPMO-BArch, DR8 189, pp. 1–3; and "Planentwurf 1988: Ökonomie und Bilanzierung, Künstlerische Gestaltung, Fernsehbetrieb," 29 October 1987, SAPMO-BArch, DR8 193. For the overall escalating budget crisis in the late 1980s, see Hertle, "Die DDR an die Sowjetunion verkaufen?" 484–487.
38. Woo-Seung Lee, *Das Fernsehen im geteilten Deutschland (1952–1989): Ideologische Konkurrenz und programmliche Kooperation* (Potsdam: Verlag für Berlin-Brandenburg, 2003), chapters 6–7.
39. Schreiben by Adameck to Honecker, 12 May 1987, SAPMO-BArch, DY30 IV 2/2.037 42.
40. For the 1988 report, see "Rechenschaftsbericht auf der GO-Wahlversammlung am 24. Oktober 1988 (Unterhaltung und Musik)," p. 7, SAPMO-BArch, DY30 518. For the later report, see "Protokoll über die Beratung des Sekretariats der Kreisleitung am 16. Juni 1989," 16 June 1989, SAPMO-BArch, DY30 520, p. 6. The quote is on p. 11.
41. See Dittmar, *Feindliches Fernsehen*, chapter 6; and Steinmetz and Viehoff, *Deutsches Fernsehen Ost*, chapter "1980–1989." Richard Oehmig also highlights both the necessity for the *"Massenwirksamkeit"* of GDR programming and the ever-tightening budgets in his analysis of the 1980s East German television in his study *"Besorgt mal Filme!" Der internationale Programmhandel des DDR Fernsehens* (Göttingen: Wallstein Verlag, 2017), chapter 6.
42. For the first quote, see "Zur Arbeit des Fernsehens der DDR," Abteilung Agitation, letter and report to Erich Honecker, 6 September 1982, SAPMO-BArch, DY30 IV 2/2.037; for the second quote, see "Referat der zentralen Parteileitung," 7 September 1981, SAPMO-BArch, DY30 479, p. 7.
43. "Konzeption 'Abrechenbare Schritte für einen raschen Leistungszuwachs des DDR-Fernsehens in den 80er Jahren'," 28 May 1982, p. 100, SAPMO-BArch, DR8 181; see also "Vorlage für den Plan 1986," p. 4, SAPMO-BArch, DR8 186.
44. "Erfahrungen und Schlussfolgerungen aus der Arbeit des Fernsehens der DDR seit dem 13.12. 1982," p. 1, 31 May 1983, SAPMO-BArch, DR8 184. For the 1980s yearly ratings, see "Ergebnisse der Programmarbeit im Zeitraum 06.01-30.06.1986," 30 July 1986, SAPMO-BArch, DR8 189, p. 7.
45. "Erfahrungen und Schlussfolgerungen aus der Arbeit des Fernsehens der DDR seit dem 13.12.1982," 5 May 1983, SAPMO-BArch, DR8 184, 4-10; the quote is on p. 8.
46. For the day-by-day planning for 1985, see "Konzeption zur Erschliessung von Effektivitätsreserven in grösseren Dimensionen," 27 January 1984, SAPMO-BArch, DR8 185. For a detailed discussion and comparison of the GDR television schedules in the mid-1970s and the mid-1980s, see Dittmar, *Feindliches Fernsehen*, 333–41, 395–401.
47. Peter Hoff, "Wettbewerbspartner oder Konkurrent? Zum Verhältnis von Kino, Film und Fernsehen in der DDR," *Rundfunk und Fernsehen* 33, no. 3/4

(1985): 437–55. Hoff argued that "cinema and television cannot face off as competitors in a socialist state" (p. 437), but his statement does not accurately describe the developments of the 1980s.

48. For the reference about the GDR (film city) housing development, see letter by Karl Gass to Erich Honecker, 4 January 1989, SAPMO-BArch, DY30 27357.
49. "Vorgabe für den Plan 1986 mit den herausragenden Vorhaben bis zum 40. Jahrestag der DDR," p. 4, 26 April 1985, SAPMO-BArch, DR8 186.
50. For the 1984 ratings, see ibid., 67. The information for 1986 comes from the report "Ergebnisse der Programmarbeit im Zeitraum 06.01-30.06.1986," 30 July 1986, SAPMO-BArch, DR8 189.
51. "Bericht Internationaler Programmaustausch," p. 3, 15 May 1986, SAPMO-BArch, DR8 188.
52. "Entwurf der Vorgabe für den Plan des Fernsehens der DDR 1987," 16 May 1986, SAPMO-BArch, DR8 188, pp. 3–6.
53. For the increase in films on GDR TV, see Hans-Jörg Stiehler, "Disappearing Reality: The End of East German Television," *Historical Journal of Film, Radio and Television* 24, no. 3 (2004): 486. The fear of SU films is discussed by Franca Wolff in the study *Glasnost erst kurz vor Sendeschluss: Die letzten Jahre des DDR-Fernsehens (1985–1989/90)* (Cologne: Böhlau Verlag, 2002), 201–9. As Wolff points out, since several of these Soviet films were shown on West German television, the East German censorship of them actually had little real impact.
54. Dana Mustata, "Re-Staging the Popular: Televising Nicolae Ceaușescu," in *Popular Television in Authoritarian Europe*, ed. Goddard, 107–23. For a discussion of the expansive television vision of the Soviet Union, see Roth-Ey, *Moscow Prime Time*, chapter 5.
55. Gerd Hallenberg et al., "Programmstrukturen in BRD und DDR," in *Zwei Mal zur Wende: Fernsehunterhaltung in Deutschland*, ed. Wolfgang Mühl-Benninghaus (Berlin: Avinus Verlag, 2008), 60. For overviews on the West German TV development, see Irmela Schneider, "American and British Feature Films Broadcast by the ARD between 1954 and 1985: An Outline of Their Development," and Udo Michael Krüg, "U.S. Productions on West German Commercial Television," both in *Cultural Transfer or Electronic Imperialism? The Impact of American Television Programs on European Television*, ed. Christian W. Thomsen (Heidelberg: Carl Winter Universitätsverlag, 1989), 71–76 and 77–87, respectively; the quoted ratings are on p. 78. On the reduction of imported programs on the second FRG TV channel (ZDF), see Hans-Günther Brüske, "Europe to the Europeans? Or: An Objection to the Distorted Reality," in ibid., 161–69.
56. For the 1985 planning, see "Konzeption zur Erschliessung von Effektivreserven in grossen Dimensionen," 27 January 1984, SAPMO-BArch, DR8 185, p. 119. Concerning the 1987 planning, see "Entwurf der Vorgabe für den Internationalen Programmaustausch," 23 April 1987, SAPMO-BArch, DR8 191.

57. For episode 4 of *Zahn um Zahn*, 7 June 1985, see DRA-Babelsberg, AC 5881/1. For the ratings, see "Dramatische Kunst—Eigenserien," Sehbeteiligungskartei, DRA-Babelsberg.
58. For the episode of *Neues übern Gartenzaun*, see episode 4 from 30 October 1985, DRA-Babelsberg, AD 5949/1. The ratings are listed in "Dramatische Kunst—Eigenserien," Sehbeteiligungskartei, DRA-Babelsberg.
59. Pfau, *Vom Seriellen zur Serie*; for the discussion of the cliff-hanger, see p. 150. He discusses the increased adjustments in later parts of his book as well (pp. 184–85, 193).
60. For the discussion of the two long-term series, see "Recherchebericht für eine Langserie unter dem Arbeitstitel 'Das Kurheim'," 5 April 1986, SAPMO-BArch, DR8 189. For the lacking funds, see Pfau, *Vom Seriellen zur Serie*, 189–94; and Dittmar, *Feindliches Fernsehen*, 343–79.
61. "Tendenzen und Widersprüche der Massenkultur und Medienentwicklung in der DDR" (Analysematerial zur Vorbereitung des XII. Parteitages der SED; Karl-Marx-Universität, Sektion Kultur- und Kunstwissenschaft, Leitung Prof. Günter Lehmann), 1989, SAPMO-BArch, DY30 26287; the quotes are on pp. 5, 10, and 12.
62. "Zum Verhälnis Jugendlicher zu den Sendungen des DDR-Fernsehens," ZIJ Studie von August 1979, SAPMO-BArch, DC4 624; and "Fernsehrezeption Jugendlicher," ZIJ Studie von Juli 1982, SAPMO-BArch, DC4 676. The show *Rund* is discussed in the 1979 study, p. 8; for the appeal of specific TV genres and the overall preference for FRG TV, see pp. 16–21.
63. "Probleme der ideologischen Klassenauseinandersetzung auf dem Gebiet der elektronischen Massenmedien," ZIJ Studie vom Januar 1987, SAPMO-BArch, DC4 637; the quote and reference are on pp. 7 and 14, respectively. For the final statistic, see Stefan Krüger and Wolfgang Mühl-Benninghaus, "'Fragments of Freedom': Fernsehunterhaltung und das Unterhaltungsverständnis für Jugendliche in Ost und West (1965–1990)," in *Zwei Mal zur Wende*, ed. Mühl-Benninghaus, 217.
64. Claudia Dittmar, "Opfer ihrer eigenen Propaganda: Die Eliten des DDR-Fernsehens und ihre Auseinandersetzung mit dem 'Westfernsehen,'" in *Rhetorik der Selbsttäuschung*, ed. Bettina Radelski and Gerd Antos (Berlin: Frank und Timme, 2014), 223–44; and Eberhard Fensch, *So und nur noch besser: Wie Honecker das Fernsehen wollte* (Berlin: Neue Berlin Verlags GmbH, 2003), 119–20, 200–202. For other insightful analyses of this phenomenon, see Stefan Wolle, *Die heile Welt der Diktatur: Alltag und Herrschaft in der DDR, 1971–1989*, 3rd ed. (Berlin: Ch. Links Verlag, 2009), part 4; and Michael Schmidt, "Fernsehen—aus der Nähe betrachtet," *UTOPIE kreativ*, Sonderheft 2000, pp. 32–41.

CHAPTER 4

Fighting against All Odds
GDR Popular Music and Youth Radio in an International Context

Since they were integral parts of East Germany's media and culture, it is not surprising that popular music and radio broadcasting developed along similar lines as GDR cinema and television in the 1970s and 1980s. There are indeed numerous parallels between all of these media in the last two decades before the fall of the Berlin Wall. All of them struggled mightily with the continuous tension—and ultimately irreconcilable conflict—between their political mandate to educate a new socialist personality and the entertainment demands of the vast majority of the East German audiences. Likewise, the GDR media generally fought reactive battles against more fully resourced and rapidly multiplying channels and stations crossing the border, especially from West Germany, which kept up a relentless pace of cultural competition and technological innovation. Finally, cultural officials in East Germany were confronted with a population for whom cultural border crossings became ever more routine in the 1970s and 1980s—in a hybrid media milieu where Western capitalist culture and East German socialist expressions coexisted, competed, and clashed on a daily basis in an uneasy and unresolved tension. And it was a conflict in which the scale was tipping ever more decisively in favor of the Western opponents by the 1980s: it was indeed a fight against all odds.[1]

East German radio, along with its accompanying popular music, was particularly exposed to this continuous confrontation because of its technological effervescence and the quickly multiplying options that East Germans had at their fingertips. With a turn of the dial, they could tune in to Cold War broadcasting stations like Voice of America, Radio Free Europe, or the popular Berlin-based Radio in the American Sector (RIAS). More options were made available by proliferating West German radio stations that were in close proximity to the border and that were a ubiquitous part of the daily East German media diet. By the late 1970s and especially by the mid-1980s, private, commercial Western radio stations added their channels to the already plentiful mix that penetrated deep into the GDR, making the task of East German radio officials trying to hold onto their audiences increasingly difficult.[2]

GDR youth radio, in particular, was integrally linked to international popular music and the related lifestyles of various subcultures that flourished in East Germany in the 1970s and 1980s as well. Rock and pop music, hippies, long hair, and provocative fashions as well as the succeeding waves of punk, new wave, and hip-hop left deep imprints on the GDR youth and transformed their cultural sensibilities and identity. GDR youth radio was the nexus to the officially approved culture, which ensured near-continuous conflicts between the SED policy makers, the professionals in charge of programming, and their audiences who demanded change at a faster pace. All of this ensured that youth radio broadcasting represented a particularly rife site for never-ending friction and cultural contests as well as an intriguing reflection of the changing nature of East German cultural transformations in the last two decades of its existence. And it is no coincidence that the headwinds for GDR cultural and media policies became especially strong in the 1980s, because this decade saw the rapid acceleration of technological changes in the international media landscape. As Stig Hjarvard has pointed out, the 1980s "witnessed the start of a series of structural changes in both the media sector and society in general" in large parts of Europe and the United States. Prominent among these were the end of the monopoly of "public service radio and television [in Europe] and the expansion of broadcasting services via satellite and cable, [which] created a more commercial and competitive climate in radio and television."[3] For East Germany, these challenges proved especially vexing—and ultimately insurmountable.

In fact, the influence of Western popular music and the deep penetration of Western radio stations posed the most significant and difficult challenges to all Eastern Bloc countries as far as the dissemination of Western media and culture were concerned. Starting in the immediate postwar period, but especially accelerating in the late socialist phase of the late 1960s to the 1980s, Western rock, pop, and ultimately punk, hip-hop, and new wave became integral parts of the mainstream culture of every socialist country. It seeped in over international broadcasting channels like Radio Free Europe or Radio Luxembourg, was increasingly sanctioned and included in official youth programming by communist governments, condoned through concert performances by Western bands in socialist countries, accessed in cross-border cultural transfers between socialist countries, or smuggled in, duplicated, and disseminated through underground exchanges. In addition, there was no uniform or coordinated Soviet or Eastern Bloc approach toward the ubiquitous influences of Western popular music. Individual communist governments in Eastern Europe pursued an inconsistent set of policies depending on the political crises and cultural mood they faced in their countries at different times. These approaches vacillated between periods of greater liberalization and tolerance followed by years of restrictive pushback, jamming, and increased censorship. And since none of these policy shifts were coordinated across the Eastern Bloc as a whole, young audiences always knew where to find the most promising access to their cherished bands and music, even if this meant cross-border poaching or traveling to more open socialist societies such as Hungary. This also highlights that youth cultures in each Eastern Bloc country developed differently and uniquely, just as was the case in other cultural arenas, weaving together homegrown bands and milieus with international influences into creative and nationally specific hybrid cultures.[4]

This chapter addresses the two most prominent strands of these rapidly unfolding transformations as they affected East Germany's radio broadcasting industry and popular music scene. The first focuses on the diverse impact of popular music and its related subcultures as well as lifestyle choices in the GDR. Rock, pop, and punk music forever altered the cultural life in the GDR and the identity formations of a large number of East German youth. It also created, for a short time at least, an authentic and robust GDR rock music scene with international reach and ambitions. Second, this analysis investigates the role and status of youth radio broadcasting within the GDR media environment. As the development of East German youth programming emphasizes, SED policy makers and radio officials made significant accommodations in order to stay at least somewhat relevant and competitive in light of the appeal of Western competition. But East German officials were facing a myriad of obstacles that went well beyond the challenges of Western radio broadcasting: GDR political and cultural leaders were battling relentless popular demand for more liberal cultural expressions, rapidly changing musical and broadcasting standards, as well as multiplying technological transformations in an international media environment, against which their initiatives and responses proved ineffective in the end.

International Popular Music and East Germany's Alienated Youth

The overt political and ideological fight for the hearts and minds of the East German population, and particularly its youth, was a continuous feature of the cultural East-West confrontation and a central component of the larger Cold War. As insightful analysts at the Central Institute for Youth Research in Leipzig (Zentralinstitut für Jugendforschung Leipzig) as well as researchers within the Ministry of Culture argued by the mid-1980s, East German officials had to properly understand the challenges that the GDR faced if they wanted to have even a fighting chance of implementing part of their cultural socialist vision for radio broadcasting. As their 1984 report confirmed, radio remained the favored medium for young people in particular, even though it was often used as an accompanying medium rather than the sole focus of attention. When it came to relaxation, East German youth preferred radio over television by a wide margin, and almost all young people listened to the radio longer on a daily basis than they watched TV.[5]

The report also clearly diagnosed the multiplying obstacles for East German media in connection with the "internationalizing trends" of the media in general. It pointed out that the GDR was irrevocably and deeply enmeshed in an international exchange and that it had become "an import-dependent country" in this transnational cultural process. Several factors highlighted this trend particularly clearly. One was the ease and normality with which the East German population daily and even hourly chose from a broad range of international media selections by the 1980s and the high degree of competitive pressure that this put on East German cultural institutions. The other aspect that the researchers emphasized was less visible but equally powerful. As the authors pointed out, this international culture imposed certain styles and modes of expression on East German media because "the modification of standards, expectations, and experiences [of] international offerings" were hard to circumvent or escape.[6]

In a similarly revealing 1985 analysis, Peter Wicke, one of the foremost youth and popular music experts in the GDR, insightfully analyzed the growing deficits in terms of cultural infrastructure and creative energy in East Germany. He convincingly tied these to both subtle and overt cultural transformations of lifestyles, especially among young people. As Wicke argued, the new media environment of the 1980s was swiftly being transformed, which directly affected the sensibilities, lifestyle, and identity of East German youth. What all the novel popular music expressions had in common was that they were attractive, emotionally appealing, and honest, as well as defined by expert craftsmanship and artful composition. In terms of the prospects for GDR-produced popular music, Wicke's outlook was not encouraging: "It is hard to ignore that in an international comparison the rock and pop music of the GDR does not meet world standards both in terms of its technological level as well as the originality and authenticity of its music."[7]

The bleak assessments from the mid-1980s almost make one forget that East Germany had had a rather successful and thriving rock scene, especially in the mid- to late 1970s. In fact, in terms of German-language rock music, East German bands were among the most successful in Europe for a short decade in the 1970s, when they performed abroad and sold tens of thousands of albums in a number of Western European countries. Prime examples of such success stories were bands like City, Karat, and Puhdys, all of which were popular among East German youth as well as internationally. These groups were part of the GDR traveling bands (Reisekader), which was a select group of carefully chosen bands that represented the GDR abroad and were provided with exclusive privileges. A good example of this was the folk-rock band City, which developed its international appeal with the 1978 hit "At the Window" ("Am Fenster"). The song was a rock ballad, based on a poem by a well-known East German poet, and performed with the accompaniment of a violin. This creative mix became one of the trademarks of the band's folk-rock sound in the late 1970s and early 1980s—in a vein reminiscent of the British rock band Jethro Tull. The song and album were released in 1978 and became an immediate hit in East Germany and beyond. The releases in West Germany and parts of southern Europe put City on the map as an internationally recognized rock band. As its lead singer Toni Krahl argued, using German-language lyrics was initially imposed by the SED cultural officials, but ultimately embraced by East German bands because it lent their songs more authenticity and a close-to-home feeling for audiences.[8]

Even earlier than City, the Puhdys had made a name for themselves in the German as well as international rock scene of the early 1970s. Their 1973 rock anthem "When a Man Lives for a Long Time" ("Wenn ein Mensch lange Zeit lebt"), with its equivocating and existentialist lyrics and easy-to-hum melody, uniquely captured the countercultural moment in East Germany as well as broader Europe during this time. The fact that it emerged as part of the soundtrack for the GDR cult film *The Legend of Paul and Paula* (*Die Legende von Paul und Paula*) only added to its cultural appeal and longevity, similar to the 1969 American movie *The Graduate*, which was accompanied by Simon and Garfunkel songs.

Figure 4.1. The Pudhys performing on GDR television on New Year's Eve in 1984. By the time this image was taken, the Pudhys were well past the high point of their popularity in East Germany. (Courtesy of ullstein bild / Granger, NYC—All Rights Reserved, New York; Image ID 0642800.)

The Puhdys followed this up with multiple hit songs, most significantly "Old as a Tree" ("Alt wie ein Baum") in 1976, which climbed the charts in both East and West Germany as well as in several other European countries. This success also led to the first extended tour of the band, which took the Puhdys through many Western European countries and as far as Cuba in the late 1970s.[9]

A group of similar caliber and success was Karat, which emerged simultaneously with City on the German rock scene in the mid- to late 1970s. One of its most successful songs, "You Must Cross Seven Bridges" ("Über sieben Brücken must du gehen"), was a soft-rock hit, which was released as part of an album in 1979 that became the best-selling LP in both East and West Germany that year. Similar to City's hit "At the Window," this song by Karat was based on a literary work that had been adapted as a TV play in East Germany in the mid-1970s. The lyrics told about lost love and the heartbreak of separation, but it also spoke of hope and the confidence that the relationship might find a happy ending. Groups like City and Karat were representative of the high point of GDR rock music in the mid- to late 1970s and were given significant license and freedom within the popular music scene of East Germany.

Following its early successes, Karat was allowed to release the 1979 song "Albatross," which described a sailor's envy of the bird's unfettered flight and freedom—a thinly veiled allusion to the widespread East German longing to cross the Berlin Wall and travel freely. Likewise, in the late 1980s, City released such controversial songs as "Half and Half" ("Halb und Halb"), which bemoaned the state of a country and city (Berlin) in which one could only ever be half-free and half-satisfied and dealt with the central East German themes of isolation, limitations, and the gnawing sense of feeling left behind.[10]

What these brief examples demonstrate is that East German rock music bands were successful and genuinely celebrated by their young East German audiences. As in other areas of GDR popular culture, the peak of artistic vitality and popular approval stretched from the early to late 1970s. Estimates are that there were several hundred rock 'n' roll, folk, and blues bands in the GDR during this decade. Few were as successful as City or Karat, and most of them never traveled outside their own borders or had at best regional appeal, but all of them had a loyal group of followers who in many cases traveled all over the country to attend every single one of their concerts. As Michael Rauhut and Thomas Kochan have pointed out, "The jeans-and-parka movement [of the 1970s] was the longest-lasting and most energetic youth movement that existed in East Germany." And it created lifestyles and subcultures that deeply unnerved officials in the SED and the Stasi alike.[11]

The first aspect that greatly disturbed GDR officials was that these subcultures, like the music genres its followers admired, were largely inspired by Western and often American cultural models. As Christoph Dieckmann, who was both a participant in and later cultural historian of the GDR youth movements, attests, many of its impulses were inspired by the "other America"—the 1960s protest movements in the United States: films of the New Hollywood genre, groups like Crosby, Stills, Nash & Young, Woodstock and hippies, long hair and radical fashions. All of these were synonymous with freedom, rebellion, authenticity, and a "symbolic counter-reality," which could at least partly and temporarily remove one from the bleak and rather rigid East German society.[12]

Political battles, especially those between the political leadership and nonconformist youth, were often fought through symbols. Three of the most powerful rebellious symbols during the late 1960s and 1970s were long hair, jeans, and parkas, especially if the latter also included a US or Western emblem. The fights over their presence or absence from public life in East Germany created a relentless tug-of-war, one that the authorities usually lost. Jeans, for example, were officially prohibited in the GDR until the late 1960s and early 1970s. For its users, they reflected an appealing sense of personal liberation and nonconformity as well as an embrace of a youthful and adventurous international culture. By the latter half of the 1970s, the majority of East German youth possessed some form of jeans clothing, but as surveys showed, there was still a vast pent-up demand for more. Likewise, a majority of young people in East Germany did not object to wearing US emblems on clothing; only a third found it objectionable. The vast number of those who actually wore these symbols said that they did so because it was fashionable and not for political reasons.[13]

More powerful and conflict-laden than the choice of clothing, however, was the length of hair. Here, too, cultural officials ultimately had to relent, but the battle lines were drawn more deeply and the confrontation was fought more acrimoniously than over most other oppositional symbol. Similar to other parts of Europe, long hair was part and parcel of the rock and blues music scene that enveloped the GDR during the 1970s, and SED political and cultural authorities forcefully opposed it. If they wanted to appear on East German youth television programs, for example, GDR rock musicians had to tie up their hair in hair nets in order to set foot on the stage. Long-haired males were widely decried as tramps, asocial loafers, and political troublemakers. In the mid- to late 1960s, forced haircuts were not an uncommon penalty for those accused of disorderly conduct. The primary legal tool for this cultural enforcement was the infamous Paragraph 249 of the GDR penal code, which was labeled "Endangering the Public Order through Asocial Behavior." While forced haircuts slowly disappeared, enforcement of Paragraph 249 did not. Estimates are that as many as 25 percent of all East German prisoners were behind bars based on this statute by the mid-1970s. The key accusations were often very similar: decadence, asocial behavior, and a deformed personal identity.[14]

This intense state pressure and scrutiny created one of the decisive differences between the youthful subcultures in East Germany and those in the West: it was the degree to which young nonconformists were prosecuted and ultimately criminalized in the GDR. Youthful gatherings as well as concerts were continuous targets of Stasi surveillance and infiltration. Internal reports routinely commented on the dirty and unkempt appearance of the audiences, their loud and disorderly conduct, and their overt admiration for Western role models and promiscuous trends. Not surprisingly, such official reports always arrived at the same conclusion, which was that these "hippies and tramps" reflected an overall negative attitude toward the socialist state. As one author surmised rather broadly, "The 'commitment' to a specific beat-formation [rock music band] is an overt expression of a certain oppositional attitude as well as a symbol of a deformed relationship to the socialist society."[15]

As this Stasi report indicates, a nonconformist lifestyle and being identified as a member of a youth subculture had far more serious repercussions in East Germany than in the West. Being a rock musician or dedicated fan of the rock or punk bands marked someone not just as an outsider or marginal member of society. What was often and largely a commitment to cultural nonconformity and youthful rebellion in the West very quickly and routinely proved to be a decision with lifelong consequences in East Germany. Cultural nonconformity indeed was a life-altering commitment, which at a minimum cut one off from educational and professional opportunities. More consequently, it often entrapped members of these subcultures in the vicious cycle of a denigrating criminal justice system, which ironically increased the chances of turning cultural rebellion into political opposition. As one member of the GDR hippie movement recalled with the advantage of hindsight, "Hippies in the East dreamt of a Woodstock experience that would be as carefree and without personal consequences as the one on the fields of White Lake."[16]

In order to avoid the watchful eyes of zealous Stasi and district officials, popular music subcultures in East Germany were often driven deep into the countryside, where surveillance was less complete and where friendly pub owners or wide-open meadows provided more welcoming venues for concerts and open-air festivals. This phenomenon regularly set off waves of hitchhiking or free-riding youth on weekends all across the GDR when dedicated fans embarked on yet another adventurous journey, eager to follow their favorite band to the latest musical hot spot. It was a continuous cat-and-mouse game of canceled venues and spontaneous gatherings, which kept the rock bands nimble and flexible and its fans more committed to them than ever before.[17]

Based on this analysis, several important similarities to music cultures in other Eastern Bloc countries become apparent. What stands out is how much the later 1960s and 1970s represented a long decade when Eastern European rock bands emerged as part and parcel of mainstream youth cultures in all socialist countries. In the Soviet Union as well as in Hungary and Poland, for example, it was during this time period when native-grown rock bands hit their stride and established their inimical and vastly popular musical styles. Just as in East Germany, it reflected the birth of internationally successful socialist rock bands in these coun-

Figure 4.2. Roving groups of rock fans were visible signs of the increasing willingness of many young people in East Germany to more openly challenge the SED political control as well as its cultural vision in the 1970s and 1980s. (Courtesy of BStU Archiv; MfS-BV-Bln-AKG-1045-Seite-0005-Bild-0003.)

tries, although their reach was largely limited to mainland Europe. Yet a few of them, like the Hungarian band Omega, achieved greater success than its GDR counterparts and even toured the United Kingdom during its heyday in the 1970s, which was indeed a rarity for any socialist music band. In one significant respect, however, the East German rock culture differed from those of its socialist neighbors: while the GDR rock bands declined in their overall significance and popularity in the 1980s, elsewhere in the Eastern Bloc native rock bands and musicians increased their stature and influence in many countries, especially Poland and the Soviet Union. These dynamics were in no small part driven by political transformations such as the rise of the Solidarity movement in Poland in the early 1980s and the cultural opening of the Soviet Union under Gorbachev by the mid-1980s. These developments provided both the impetus and cultural space for energized and relevant rock scenes in these countries.[18]

And while successful socialist rock bands and musicians were able to leverage their popularity and status vis-à-vis government authorities all across the Eastern Bloc, they still had to put up with patronizing and meddling bureaucracies that could decisively impact their careers. Travel restrictions, prohibitions to perform, denial of opportunities to record songs, and tight control over public appearances were just some of the many limitations that bands had to navigate in order to pursue their musical careers. Most unsettling of all was that the restrictive censorship system was frequently unpredictable and operated according to rather arbitrary rules in the GDR and elsewhere. Of course, everyone knew that overtly oppositional lyrics could quickly end musical ambitions—let alone international success. Bands had to battle a thicket of bureaucratic layers, had to fight with incompetent administrators with little to no knowledge of the professional music scene, and often lived by the whims of small-minded local officials, who controlled which bands could legally perform within their jurisdictions. In East Germany, battles especially over lyrics were legion, and the use of the word "wall" could doom any otherwise acceptable song—or at least call for endless revisions. Moreover, most musicians depended on the studios of GDR radio, which were controlled by the only official GDR label, Amiga, and its production facilities. The central agency consisted of a group of music producers who listened to about two dozen songs every day and decided which ones deserved a release and which ones were to be revised or denied. Lyrics and talent, sound, fit for dancing, as well as political message and mass appeal all were key criteria in the decision-making process.[19]

Just as denigrating as the tiring battles over productions and lyrics was the clear realization that those in charge of musical production in the GDR prioritized classical orchestras and popular big bands over rock or blues. One important reason for this was that classical music made more money for the Ministry of Culture. Some of the renowned East German symphonic orchestras could compete with the best in the world and sold far more albums and recordings than did popular music, which brought in desperately needed and highly valued foreign currency. But this was also encouraged by a cultural bureaucracy dominated by older officials who maintained the traditional prioritization of what was referred to as serious music. This neglect and widespread ignorance about the popular music industry expressed itself in at times absurd proposals. When the popular GDR rock band Electra was preparing to tour West Germany in the late 1970s, for example, two of its members were banned from traveling by the local officials where they resided. In response, Ministry and Stasi officials advanced a plan that the group should just hire two other musicians who were cleared for travel in order to fill the open slots. In fact, officials in the Ministry of Culture seriously debated a proposal by which all travel-eligible rock musicians should be pooled and deployed as groups for concerts abroad when needed. As an opponent of the proposal sarcastically observed, unfortunately this attitude was not atypical for those in charge of many cultural agencies: "Clearly only someone with absolutely no knowledge of cultural and musical production could recommend this. Well, if work needs to get done and a plumber gets sick, we replace the plumber; why shouldn't the same apply to [rock] musicians?"[20]

Even under the best circumstances and at the height of their popularity, as in the early to late 1970s, GDR popular music hits were still overshadowed by songs of Western bands. In a survey conducted in 1978, for example, City's hit "At the Window" emerged as an audience favorite, but it still ranked behind a song by the Western band Smokie. The only other GDR band that was even in the top-ten ranking of East German youth that year was Puhdys. When researchers conducted another such study in the mid-1980s, they noticed a dramatic shift. While some GDR rock bands were still well-liked by young people in the GDR, overall East German rock had suffered a precipitous decline. One factor was that the fresh and hard-hitting lyrics of the West German musical movement "New German Wave" had captured the hearts of East German youth and upstaged some of the GDR bands. The general preference for Western and English-language rock also increased during the same years. In 1979, 40 percent of surveyed young people in East Germany had still mentioned a GDR hit among their favorite songs; by 1984 that number had shrunk to 25 percent. Likewise, the percentage of favorite hits from Western countries increased from just over half in 1979 to well over 70 percent by 1985.[21] And the demise of East German rock got even more pronounced in the second half of the 1980s. By 1988, only around 15 percent of East German youth liked specific GDR groups and their hits, and half stated categorically that they did not even listen to their own rock musicians anymore.[22]

A 1984 assessment within the East German Ministry of Culture corroborates this radical shift in the early 1980s. The report argued that GDR rock music underwent a rapid expansion in the mid-1970s and emerged as the most significant German-language rock music in Europe. Citing several prominent East German bands, the authors argued that "the high poetic level of many songs" particularly distinguished their rock music—with lyrics that were close to reality, connected to GDR society, as well as highly expressive. By 1983, however, the authors argued that the East German rock scene had gone into a precipitous nosedive, which had both external and internal reasons. One of the most important external ones was the rise of the "New German Wave" rock movement in West Germany, which represented the blossoming of German-language rock in the FRG in the latter years of the 1970s. Largely free from political restrictions and censorship, its music and lyrics expressed a critical edge and freedom that could not be matched by East German groups. Simultaneously, internally East Germany popular music suffered the long-term consequences of the patronizing and restrictive SED attitude toward its musicians and bands. In addition, several of the most popular bands had left the GDR in early 1980s, which signaled the beginning of a mass exodus of cultural talent during these years. Just as galling as the restrictions and censorship were the continuous and debilitating lack of adequate technical equipment and the increased courting of mediocre West German bands for GDR visits at the expense of showcasing established and homegrown talent.[23]

In fact, in a desperate attempt to appeal to its own youth, East German policy makers began staging large open-air rock concerts in the GDR by the mid-1980s that featured Western rock, pop, and blues bands. When West Berlin's authorities launched a mammoth rock concert in June 1987 to celebrate the 750-year anniversary of the city, for example, East German officials countered it with an equally large three-day open-air festival in July of the same year. Over 100,000 GDR fans came together to hear folk and rock idols like Bob Dylan and Tom Petty and the Heartbreakers. In the following year, these concert series continued with even larger events. In June 1988, East German officials booked international stars like Pink Floyd and Michael Jackson as well as political renegades such as Udo Lindenberg and Nina Hagen for a multiday concert extravaganza. In July of the same year, 160,000 East German fans gathered for a Bruce Springsteen concert, which broke all previous records.[24]

Adding Fuel to the Fire: East German Punk

As the East German rock and blues scenes declined during the 1980s, a new musical style and subculture emerged in this transition period in East Germany, just as it did in much of Western Europe: punk. Inspired by British youth who had created this new movement, it shared some characteristics with the still continuing rock and blues subcultures. But it simultaneously and quickly set itself apart from earlier popular music: it was edgier, more aggressive, and less willing to make compromises and concessions. Much of the music of the GDR punk scene spoke for itself, like the 1983 song "The Nazis Are back in East Berlin" ("Nazis wieder in Ostberlin") by the GDR group Namenlos (Without a Name). As the song made clear, for punks the East German regime had long lost its legitimacy, and they perceived few differences between the SED regime and the Nazis who ruled Berlin before them: "Nazis, Nazis, Nazis are back in Ostberlin / Nazi pigs, Nazi pigs, Nazi pigs in Ostberlin!"[25]

While the punk movement of the 1980s was smaller in size compared to the popular rock and blues subcultures, it accelerated and intensified many of the trends that had emerged in East Germany in the late 1970s. It purposefully embraced provocative and shocking fashion symbols such as studded leather jackets, piercings, and the iconic Mohawk hairstyles. Because punks were often attacked in public places and because many punks themselves embraced violent behavior, their appearance was perceived as even more threatening, disorderly, and disruptive than that of earlier subcultures. Most importantly, unlike their predecessors, punks were overtly hostile to the society and politics of the GDR and unwilling to make concessions. As the refrain of the 1987 song "Without Sense" ("Ohne Sinn") by the group L'attentat made clear, in their minds the SED had robbed the East German youth of their future and were espousing a political system in which the politicians themselves no longer believed.[26]

As several studies have pointed out, while the slogan of British punks was "no future," which criticized the lack of jobs and authentic choices in the Western capitalist system, East German punks railed against "too much future," which implied that their lives in the GDR were planned out and prescribed, with little to no chance to create one's own choices and lifestyles. Despite this difference, the two movements in East and West had more in common than divided them: "Rather dead than conformed"—another GDR punk slogan that captured a key sentiment of its members—emphasizes that the two movements drew from the same reservoir of nonconformism and radical call for alternative choices. To GDR punks, even rock 'n' roll and folk subcultures had been co-opted into the system. They likened successful bands like Puhdys and Karat to "state-rock" bands, whose vitality and authenticity had been sacrificed by their collaboration with and accommodation to government prerogatives and priorities. This is also the reason why many East German punk bands refused to cooperate with the SED government even when the latter finally condoned playing punk songs on national radio in the late 1980s.[27]

Historians of the punk movement in the GDR trace its slow rise to the late 1970s, but agree that it did not coalesce into a significant East

German subculture until the early 1980s. It was also rather short-lived, continuing in a more diffuse form into the late 1980s. Its edgier public face became especially visible around the early to mid-1980s when radical skinhead followers split from the punk movement, and when it competed with new forms of independent musical influences such as new wave and hip-hop. The punk movement was also targeted more swiftly and aggressively by the Stasi than previous youth subcultures. From its start in the early 1980s, the Stasi focused with laser-sharp precision on dismantling the punk scene, although its declaration of war did not come until 1983, when several prominent punk musicians were sent to jail. The systematic attack against the punk movement in fact intensified the criminalization of nonconformist youth culture in East Germany to levels not seen before. Even more than before, cultural and societal opposition by punks was swiftly turned into political opposition and commitment. As Katrin Wissentz states rather insightfully, many punks were politicized precisely because of the politicization forced on them by the Stasi and the SED policy makers: "It is fair to say that through the regime's actions it created its own political opponents."[28]

Figure 4.3. Graffiti on a GDR bus stop. The punk movement in East Germany mushroomed in the early 1980s and was far more antagonistic toward the SED government and its integrationist policies than earlier East German youth subcultures. (Courtesy of BStU Archiv; MfS-BV-Bln-XX-3022-Seite-0004-Bild-0007.)

This criminalization of the lifestyle and identity of punks and skinheads was indeed no isolated occurrence. While they found some limited protection in the popular "Blues Masses" organized by progressive Protestant churches in the first half of the 1980s, punks were for the most part shunned by the GDR mainstream. For their part, punks did not hide from the public spotlight and often reveled in their public rejection. Yet it took an early and heavy toll. By 1983, several of the leading bands had been dismantled by the Stasi, and members of the punk scene were even more completely cut off from future opportunities because of the severity with which these groups were infiltrated and prosecuted. As Klaus Michael put it, "Whether consciously or not, whoever committed themselves to the punk scene severed their ties with the GDR state. . . . What was largely ignored in other countries was reinterpreted as an attack on the very foundation of the country's ideology."[29]

As emphasized earlier, this repressive backlash against nonconformist cultures actually created one of the greatest differences between youth subcultures in East and West. Because of the often severe consequences, completely bucking social norms and especially dropping out of society occurred less frequently in Eastern Bloc countries, largely because the penalties and personal costs of belonging particularly to drop-out communities were so much higher than in the capitalist West. However, during the 1970s and 1980s greater segments of socialist youth cultures across Eastern Europe were evading or living outside the boundaries of the officially sanctioned norms, which created wider cultural free spaces. Because of their rarity and unique position in communist countries, then, socialist drop-out communities often had more impact. At the same time, their members also frequently faced threats of criminalization and repressive treatment, which in a number of instances turned even initially apolitical communes toward more political activism or even outright subversive activities.[30]

Like all outright oppositional movements, the punk scene in East Germany was thoroughly infiltrated by a network of Stasi observers and informants. Surprisingly, as the post-1989 revelations demonstrated, even hard-core members of the East German punk scene, including some of its well-known musicians, became entangled as Stasi informers. Enticed by promises of reduced sentences, access to musical equipment, or privileges, they served the powers they were decrying in their songs and lifestyles—a betrayal that cut even deeper in the punk scene than in any of the other GDR subcultures in the 1970s and 1980s.[31]

The only youth subculture that achieved even more notoriety and risked a more abrupt break with the East German state were skinheads, who emerged in the GDR by the mid-1980s both as a further provocation and partially as a response to the intensifying prosecution of the punk movement around 1983. Nothing could be more provocative in the GDR than to openly espouse neo-Nazi rhetoric and insignia, because the whole existence of East Germany had been built on the premise that it represented the "other Germany"—the one not guilty for the Holocaust and World War II. Far less connected to music than the other independent movements of the time, the rise of the skinhead movement nevertheless further splintered the youth culture in the GDR in the 1980s, as did new and rapidly rising music trends such as new wave and hip-hop.[32]

One important aspect that all of these cultural movements had in common by the 1980s was that they were able to record and circulate their music independent of the official recording studios and systems. The reason for this was the cassette recorder, which proliferated rapidly in East Germany. With little chance of official recognition or dissemination, punk and other independent music bands started to record their own music and copied it through cassette tapes. In fact, some of them became so prolific that they created their own labels, even though the individual productions generally consisted of no more than one hundred copies at the most. These tapes were easy to produce and replicate while still ensuring reasonably good quality. Most important, they completely circumvented the established and tedious music production process in East Germany. Eventually, some of these recordings were used for music shows on GDR radio, but not until the last few years of the 1980s.[33]

In general, the previous two sections highlight three closely related trends of the popular youth culture in the GDR. The first noticeable trend emphasizes just how deeply and thoroughly East German youth were de-territorialized by the various musical and cultural influences of the 1970s and 1980s. To be sure, complex and contradictory affinities and cultural belongings remained until the late 1980s, but the degree of cultural displacement can hardly be overstated. As even the agency overseeing rock music in the Ministry of Culture had to admit, in the 1980s this created a completely unprecedented historical development: "We have to acknowledge that a large portion of our domestic audiences reject GDR rock music because of a lacking political commitment and identification with their country. This is almost unheard of in world history."[34]

Second, and directly connected to this sense of a highly de-territorialized youth culture, was the degree to which cultural decisions and commitments became political choices with lifelong repercussions in East Germany. Far more than in Western countries, lifestyle choices were politicized through frequent criminalization. Even for nonconformists who were never prosecuted, their identity formation was deeply and irrevocably imprinted by decisions over lifestyle and cultural preferences. Because of these unique historical and political circumstances, the cultural choices of nonconforming young people carried deeper and far more permanent significance in East Germany than in the West. The alienating effects of this process could still be countered in the 1970s when East German rock music provided identification with hybrid GDR bands and musicians. Once the last strands of such loyalties and affinities frayed in the 1980s, the impact of an international culture would be far stronger and more palpable than in most other countries.

The final thread was that most East German rock and pop bands lacked the technological equipment and artistic know-how to achieve the aesthetic and sound standards that defined international popular music by the early 1980s. As a 1979 report highlighted, the production technology and necessary equipment for popular music in the GDR reflected "an unacceptably high degree of backwardness." Most of the equipment had been bought in the mid-1960s, a technology termed "second-generation music production equipment," while the rest of international popular music had advanced to third-generation technology. Equally important, the training of "music production artists" had not kept pace with international standards. And the only place to purchase the necessary equipment was in the capitalist West, since East Germany had discontinued this electronic research and development years ago.[35] While some of this deficit could still be mitigated through the use of private music production studios of well-established GDR rock bands in the late 1970s, these technological limitations were a decisive factor for the demise of East Germany's popular music scene in the 1980s.

The Last Stand: Preserving Youth Radio in East Germany

As mentioned in the introduction to this chapter, the challenge of how to respond to Western broadcasting and especially how to keep young listeners tuned in to socialist stations was a nagging challenge and uphill battle for all communist governments in Eastern Europe. Even in the Soviet Union, which was much further removed from Western European influences than the GDR, foreign radio stations as well as Western music and news were ever present, forcing the Soviet government into concessions that were anathema to its socialist vision. In the mid-1960s, as part of the post-Stalinist Thaw, the Khrushchev government decided to respond to popular Western music with its own all-Union station, Maiak. The new station's programs heavily focused specifically on popular music and were able to win some Soviet audience groups back to domestic broadcasting channels. But the dominance of foreign stations persisted here as well during the late socialist era, especially as far as young Soviet listeners were concerned.[36]

The history of radio youth programming in East Germany goes back to the mid-1960s as well. In connection with a youth gathering organized by the feeder organization of the SED—the Free German Youth (Freie Deutsche Jugend [FDJ])—in May 1964, radio functionaries decided to develop a special youth-oriented program to accompany the weekend activities. This program was called *DT 64* (Deutschland-Treffen 1964). The broadcasts were received so positively—and fortunately fell into a short window of liberalized cultural policy—that it became a standard feature of the main East Berlin radio station starting in June 1964. It originally broadcast a two-hour program from 4:00 to 6:00 p.m. five days a week (weekdays only). Officially, *DT 64* was tied to the same rules as other GDR programming; one of the most important and controversial early requirements was the 60:40 ratio of music on East German radio—60 percent GDR or socialist music and only 40 percent music from the capitalist West. But based on surveys from the 1960s, it seems clear that even in its early years, *DT 64* circumvented this rule whenever and wherever possible in order to satisfy young people's demand for popular Western hits. Its mere presence also sparked the greater need for East German popular music and thereby contributed to the increased recordings of homegrown popular musicians and the rise of East German rock bands in the late 1960s and the 1970s.[37]

By the 1970s, GDR radio added several other programs hoping to attract East German youth, which aired several times a week on Voice of the GDR (Stimme der DDR). In addition, specific programs focused on listener requests as well as broadcasts featuring international popular music hits and shows designed to showcase specific bands. The additions also highlighted that already in the 1970s East German radio broadcasters had significantly relented in their ideological opposition to Western popular music. As Edward Larkey has put it, this shift "guaranteed Western pop music unequivocally a solid and permanent place in GDR youth programs."[38] Despite this expansion and the ensuing accommodations, by the late 1970s cultural officials in charge of radio programming were painfully aware that still more needed to be done. Researchers were particularly aware that young people listened to Western radio stations in far greater numbers than other population groups in the GDR. The official estimates were that at least 35 to 40 percent of young people in East Germany regularly or frequently listened to Western radio stations in the second half of the 1970s. On weekday evenings or weekends, when GDR radio offered very little competitive youth programming, the percentages of those listening to Western broadcasts were significantly higher.[39]

The ability to hear the latest international hits and to record music on cassette tapes in high sound quality were indeed two of the key attractions of all youth radio stations. The broadcasting programs for young people in the GDR were no exception. A very good example of such a popular show on GDR radio was *Duet: Music for the Cassette Recorder* (*Duett: Musik für den Rekorder*). Programs like it were very popular with GDR youth both in the 1970s and 1980s because they allowed listeners to create recordings of international artists whose albums were impossible to purchase for the vast majority. Such recordings became prized possessions of most young people in East Germany. In addition, the taping often involved a combination of planning, luck, and the cooperation on the part of the DJ because the artists featured in each program were often poorly advertised. Likewise, DJs occasionally talked over the beginnings or endings of songs, which was a frequent cause for irate listener responses to GDR radio stations.[40]

Shows like *Duet* also had the advantage that they allowed GDR planners to shape the international popular music they deemed acceptable for East German culture, which showed an increasing tolerance of previously censored songs and albums from the capitalist West during the 1970s. By the late 1970s and early 1980s, the list of condoned Western artists included such British stars as Cat Stevens and Pink Floyd as well as American groups and singers like Chicago and Stevie Wonder. Guiding principles were popularity and lack of offensive lyrics or disorderly and rowdy image. Additional international performers welcomed on GDR radio by the late 1970s were bands and musicians like Aretha Franklin, Emmylou Harris, Neil Diamond, Queen, and Jethro Tull as well as other international groups, including some West German artists like Hannes Wader and Reinhard Mey. By contrast, musicians with explicitly critical lyrics like Udo Lindenberg or bands with a disreputable image like the Rolling Stones, punk groups like the Sex Pistols, or hard rock bands like Black Sabbath and AC/DC were frequently and for extended periods of time censored on GDR stations. But despite these exclusions, as the former music editor for *DT 64* Walter Bartel highlights, Anglo-American popular music was used as the main attraction for East German radio music programs—interspersed with some mixture of GDR and other international selections. The 60:40 rule was not a realistic target at any time during youth radio in the GDR, as he pointed out, especially not in the 1980s, when GDR rock and pop bands were in decline and international radio competition increased exponentially.[41]

The other endearing quality of these GDR youth radio programs was the ability of listeners to talk back to those responsible for the content of these broadcasts. Listener responses and some of the ensuing correspondence reflect a great degree of honesty and authenticity as well as at times sharp exchanges. This correspondence makes clear that program editors attempted to keep an open line of communication with East Germany's young people. The question of censored bands was a particularly frequent flash point in these exchanges. Why were GDR bands like the Klaus-Renft-Combo or Nina Hagen, who had either been expelled or left for West Germany, no longer played on East German radio? one young listener wanted to know. "Should one really pretend that they had never existed?" he added pointedly. Another noticed that around 1980 East German youth programs increasingly played songs by previously prohibited groups like the Rolling Stones and AC/DC. Was this because radio officials could "no longer resist them because they were faced with waves of requests?" the listener asked bitingly. In each case, one of the editors in charge of *DT 64* responded, generally in a conciliatory manner, often admitting the staff's mixed feelings on some of these matters. As an editor wrote in connection with ex-GDR bands, she too was a fan of some of these groups and still liked their lyrics. But she was simultaneously disappointed by what she deemed unacceptable and denigrating statements these artists had made about East Germany since their departure. Likewise, she defended her staff's decision to play previously censored Western music bands as a pragmatic and reasonable adjustment. As she put it, "I assume you would agree that we should not dogmatically insist on decisions from years past, but adjust according to changing times and circumstances." By contrast, when another letter writer complained about the censorship of songs by KISS a few years later, the response was far more clear-cut. The listener was informed that GDR broadcasting did not approve of a band that reveled in "horrifying symbolism" and in the eyes of the *DT 64* music editors flirted with "fascist tendencies."[42]

Questions about music genres and groups, which were temporarily or sporadically censored, occupied a significant bulk of the listener inquiries and responses. As in the case above, listeners were usually informed that there were reasons beyond the music itself that excluded some artists from East German youth radio shows. But the music editors of *DT 64* at times also surprised audiences with their responses, as in the case of one letter writer in 1982 who complained about too much openness on the part of music editors, especially that the youth station had played punk songs as part of one show. To the listener, this was yet another example of Western influences being imported without proper discernment or political rationale. One of the editors in turn suggested that the writer take a broader, more tolerant perspective and reminded him that not too long ago "long hair, jeans, and rock music as well were viewed with suspicion and accused of running contrary to socialism and respectable culture." She argued further that administrative restrictions were the least effective way to deal with such new musical genres and cultural influences.[43]

While there was often a search for reconciliation and common ground with listeners who questioned the music choices of program editors, the responses to criticisms of the political reporting on *DT 64* were frequently cause for harsher and less compromising editor responses. When a listener ridiculed what he perceived as a one-sided *DT 64* political report that painted the picture of a "happy and free GDR youth" in the face of travel restrictions and the absence of basic human rights, the editor did not mince words. The listener was encouraged to approach West German politics and lifestyle with the same critical attitude he applied to the GDR and was challenged to become active rather than to echo unfounded criticisms. The program editor closed on a rather exasperated note: "Thank you for your letter, but I have—quite frankly—heard enough from you."[44]

Based on the discussions in this chapter thus far, it is apparent that 1986 was not an auspicious year in East Germany's cultural history to launch a new youth radio station. The popularity of GDR rock and popular music was in decline, the technological broadcasting infrastructure was antiquated, and financial resources were dwindling. In light of these circumstances, it is probably not far-fetched to view the launch of a new youth radio station in 1986 as a last-ditch effort on the part of the political and cultural leadership to counter the increased competition from the West. It was an attempt to reconnect with its disenchanted youth and maybe even to gain back some lost ground over time. In this spirit, East Germany's radio officials mobilized their last reserves and resources to give this new station a fighting chance to compete. And in the final analysis, it proved to be more successful than seemed possible under the circumstances. Jugendradio DT 64, as it was called, actually regained some trust, respect, and even loyalty among a portion of East German youth in the late 1980s.[45]

By the mid-1980s, all of West Germany's regional broadcasting stations had established additional channels focused exclusively on young listeners. By 1984, an internal GDR assessment highlighted that there were about twenty Western radio stations that could be received in some or most parts of East Germany. East German radio officials realized that their one-size-fits-all approach was not making any listeners happy and further encouraged the increasing habit to tune in to more appealing Western options. Around 1980, one report estimated that only as few as 20–25 percent of the GDR population was listening to morning programs on East German radio on many days of the week, for example. As the author of the report pointedly and facetiously asked, "We should therefore be interested in the question: where is the remaining 75–80 percent of the potential listeners?"[46]

The last push that finally convinced SED policy makers to embark on the establishment of their own youth radio station by the mid-1980s was that two of its fiercest Western competitors, first RIAS and then Station Free Berlin (Sender Freies Berlin [SFB]), decided to establish new youth channels in the mid-1980s in order to compete with new private stations unleashed by the introduction of the dual broadcasting system in West German in 1984. East Germany's response, Jugendradio DT 64, finally started to broadcast a daily eleven-hour program from 1:00 p.m. to midnight in March 1986—officially to celebrate the forty-year anniversary of the FDJ. The positive responses convinced the Central Committee of the SED to expand the programming even further. Starting in December 1987, the radio station added youth-oriented morning shows to its offerings and broadcast twenty hours daily (4:00 a.m.–midnight).[47]

None of this was accomplished easily, however. GDR radio technicians had to mobilize all remaining reserves in order to launch this new FM radio station in East Germany, and it further tightened the budgets for all other programs and stations. This was especially taxing because the station was directly competing with new Western channels, all of which sent their programs in stereo and with a high sound quality. The importance of sound reception was one of the important criteria for the listening choices of East German youth, and GDR cultural officials were well aware of this added competitive pressure: "The establishment of FM stations and quality stereo reception play a vital role [in the competition with the West]—a very good program has to be received in very good quality. Especially the excellent stereo sound on Western radio stations is often mentioned as a reason why [East German] young people listen to them, especially when it comes to recording music on tapes."[48]

When broadcasting officials finally launched the independent Jugendradio DT 64, many young people in East Germany responded favorably. Popular programs like *Duet* were absorbed into the new schedule. Probably one of the most welcome changes was that young people finally had an acceptable option to listen to GDR radio in the morning with the introduction of *Morning Rock* (*Morgenrock*). Surveys conducted shortly after the introduction of this morning program confirmed that its addition was particularly welcome. According to the majority of surveyed listeners, *Morning Rock* finally offered a real alternative to Western radio stations. What young listeners particularly appreciated were the short discussions about issues relevant to their lives as well as brief sports updates and a "more honest reporting style." For GDR listeners, what they desired the most was popular international popular music and relevant, timely information, as a 1988 report emphasized: "Eighty percent of listener music requests indicate a close familiarity with international charts and music video productions. [Listeners] are searching for the newest and most up-to-date information. They want to be informed so they can participate in topical conversations, which explains why they listen both to GDR and West radio stations."[49]

Under pressure to appeal to more GDR youth and widen its appeal in East Germany, Jugendradio DT 64 was even given license to venture into completely novel territory by 1986, which included punk music and the independent scene. To be sure, there had been some very sporadic and isolated forays into these music genres in earlier years, but what was called "the other bands" in the GDR had overall been ignored and censored as far as official radio broadcasting was concerned. The program *Parocktikum*, moderated by Lutz Schramm, would change this. In March 1986, he was given permission to air a two-hour weekly program on late Saturday evenings specifically dedicated to these marginalized and elusive audiences. One of the biggest challenges of the initial programs was that there were no official recordings of GDR punk bands, and Schramm had to use some of his own taped recordings or unofficially circulating tapes to debut his program. In his own recollections, he likened his program and work to that of a minesweeper. He had to both feel his way through the thicket of censorship rules and likewise establish links to a subculture that was highly suspicious of official contacts and channels. While he was able to make some headway in both directions, he also quickly learned that there were at times insurmountable limits in both camps.[50]

Complications arose rather quickly because some of the bands that Schramm featured in his program had not been given permission to perform by their local authorities. This made for rather awkward bureaucratic turf wars, since local SED functionaries furiously inquired why the music of censored GDR groups was suddenly being played over an official East German radio station. Likewise, many punk and independent bands were often not interested in having their music played on state radio. One reason for this was that they feared it would ultimately carry with it concessions and limits on their artistic freedom. Second, they knew that their loyal fan base viewed anything with an official stamp of approval with deep suspicion and even derision. For these reasons, a number of bands declined Schramm's entreaties and offers. Under trying circumstances, Schramm did what he could and was eventually able to record an official album of GDR punk music by 1989. But the opening toward the independent scene always remained half-hearted on the part of the SED leadership. It was an accommodation driven by desperation and an attempt to hang on as best as possible. But like so many of these last-minute reforms and innovations, they came too late in order to have a lasting impact.[51]

Nevertheless, programs like *Parocktikum* as well as the more open exchanges discussed earlier highlight that Jugendradio DT 64 had a unique place in GDR radio history. It was in closer contact with its listeners and attempted to win their trust and respect, stubbornly exploring new avenues as well as risking occasional acts of nonconformity in its political reporting. To add to this, its staff was generally more committed to its work and was willing to work hard under difficult circumstances. They were giving greater license and took greater risks, reluctantly condoned by a cultural leadership that understood their special role and link to young audiences in the GDR. The ultimate testimony of this closer connection and loyalty between station and listeners became apparent in the transition period from 1989 to 1991, when thousands of young people of the former East Germany protested and demonstrated against the impending closure of the station, which was threatened by a takeover from its arch nemesis RIAS. At the same time, Jugendradio DT 64 should not be celebrated as a rebel broadcasting station, as several previous staff members have argued. Very few openly rebelled, and most displayed what one observer called "middling courage"—enough to demonstrate dissent but not enough to become a dissident. Or as Marion Brasch, one of the staff members of Jugendradio DT 64 put it, ultimately the limits of dissension were clearly apparent in the big picture: "Maybe like no other media in the GDR we were privileged and allowed a longer leash. But rarely did we overcome the trained self-censorship. And if we did so occasionally, it largely created no more than tempests in a teacup."[52]

It is also important to remember that despite all of the relative accomplishments and successes, the new youth radio station in East Germany never became the favorite broadcasting program of GDR youth even during the height of its popularity. Surveys of young people in East Germany in the late 1980s all point to a very similar trend: many of the programs on Jugendradio DT 64 were popular with their audiences, and overall the station slightly increased the percentage of young people listening to East German broadcasting. As one report bluntly put it, Jugendradio DT 64 was the only radio station most GDR youth would even tune into by the late 1980s. But this was still a long way from making it their favorite. In fact, the vast majority clearly indicated that they listened most frequently to Western radio stations, and the front-runners in the late 1980s were RIAS 2 and regionally available FRG channels. The overall ratio of listening ran 3:1 in favor of Western stations by this time. While Jugendradio DT 64 at least remained part of the listener mix, thus, it could not reverse what one report characterized as "the overall shift toward Western media and against use of our own stations in the 1980s."[53]

A closer investigation revealed that it was not only popular music that attracted young people to GDR youth radio. In addition, what many listeners often appreciated most about their own station were short reports as well as discussions of problems that young people encountered in their everyday lives in East Germany—followed by other brief, topical reporting about their own country. When it came to the choice of music, the reporting on the international popular music scene, or the reporting style of the respective DJs, Western radio channels were favored by two out of three young people in the GDR.[54]

Clearly, East Germany continued to lose ground in its cultural competition with Western radio stations in the late 1980s—and the gap was widening even further. Despite numerous accommodations, radio broadcasting agencies ultimately jettisoned their vision of a socialist cultural alternative or identity by the mid-1980s, just as cultural officials in the movie and television industries did. In a desperate attempt to stay relevant to parts of their population and retain as many listeners as possible, they wholeheartedly embraced Western popular music by the 1980s—even if this meant throwing overboard the ideological policies and guidelines of the past. Peter Wicke has described the deep irony of these cultural reversals with pinpoint accuracy when he stated that

Figure 4.4. Springsteen concert in East Berlin, July 1988. Springsteen was one of many major Western rock stars allowed to perform in East Germany in the late 1980s. (Courtesy of Bundesarchiv Koblenz; Bild 1988-0719-4ON.)

toward the end of the GDR's existence this situation had all the elements of a grotesque farce: "Under the supervision of the Department for Propaganda of the Central Committee of the SED, the same Western music that it had previously wanted to erase from the hearts and minds of young people now advanced to become the central element and strategy of its ideological campaigns."[55]

In general, however, no accommodation could vault East German Jugendradio DT 64 toward the top spot of listener preferences by the late 1980s. Clearly, Western popular music and radio formats were the gold standard, and nothing short of matching it could change this. This included the specific style of DJ announcing unique to Western broadcasts (Moderation), which became yet another international standard that proved increasingly mandatory for East German broadcasters. Listener criticism of boring or rigid announcing styles on the part of GDR DJs was among the most common negative responses to Jugendradio DT 64. Working under political censorship and devoid of high-tech equipment made it indeed impossible to attain the same level of "confidence, relaxed attitude, and wit in relationship to the listeners," which analysts highlighted as the defining quality of youth-oriented Western radio.[56]

As Edward Larkey compellingly highlighted in his study on East German youth radio, the commercialization trends and the capitalist practices that defined West European media additionally impacted and forever transformed East German radio broadcasting by the 1980s as well. The ensuing reversal to a more Western-oriented broadcasting style and programming in the GDR was driven by a whole host of developments, which included the need for closer attention to the wishes and desires of audiences. The outcome was that radio on both sides of the Berlin Wall increasingly looked and sounded the same. This development and the expansion of Jugendradio DT 64 was yet another prime example of the increasing cultural convergence between Western and socialist media by the end of the 1980s.[57]

There were other similarly important dynamics at play that directly influenced East German culture and broadcasting. In the 1970s and 1980s, the GDR's inability to compete was directly tied to its failure to fund necessary infrastructure projects or keep pace with the technological structural media innovations. The newly developed East German foreign broadcasting channel, Voice of the GDR (Stimme der DDR), is a good case in point. Created in 1972 to represent East German perspectives abroad, GDR officials undertook a test in 1978 to find out how well this channel was operating. The rather disappointing outcome was that much of the programming could not even be received in satisfactory quality in large parts of the GDR, let alone outside its borders. The reception was poor in Warsaw, Budapest, and Rome. Even more disappointingly, the report emphasized that Voice of the GDR was almost impossible to receive in large parts of West Germany, especially in cities such as Munich or western and central parts of the FRG.[58]

Reading the internal Ministry of Culture reports from the late 1970s into the 1980s, it is very apparent how much GDR radio's infrastructure had begun to atrophy during these critical years. One aspect very reminiscent of the previous chapters was the increasing budget shortfalls and cuts that had to be implemented by the late 1970s in an effort to rein in ballooning deficits. In a report from 1977, for example, radio officials were informed that they would have to cut their budgets between 5 and 15 percent depending on the individual departments and that they should not expect additional personnel for the next few years. This situation deteriorated so dramatically over the next decade that by the late 1980s East German radio broadcasting had difficulty keeping their vans and trucks running in order to cover relevant news stories. As the head of GDR radio wrote in a pleading letter for more funds in 1987, the vehicle fleet was depleted, with more than 50 percent over the age limit and barely functioning. As he pointed out, radio had only received 20 percent of the necessary replacement funds over the past several years, and he could no longer vouch for the mobility and adequate news coverage by his reporters.[59]

And while the resulting delay in technological development was nothing new by the 1970s, it became particularly pressing in the 1980s. By the late 1970s, the technology gap was widening at a rapid pace. Just as challenging and fundamental was the fact that East Germany radio still kept wrestling with producing shows in stereo sound. By the mid-1980s, only about two-thirds of GDR radio programming was available in stereo, while quality stereo sound and reception had long become common features for all Western radio stations.[60] As one GDR radio engineer reflected in disgust, "[We] often had to produce or back-engineer the necessary equipment, units, or electronic parts from scratch or with very inadequate tools."[61] The other reason the technological delay became so apparent and paralyzing for the GDR was that the 1980s was a decade of major technological innovations. Music recording equipment and radio infrastructure was slowly digitized, and novel technologies, such as cable and satellite broadcasting, were implemented. In West Germany, the dual media system, which allowed private TV and radio stations to compete with public broadcasting channels, got underway in 1984. In turn, this greatly increased the pressure on public FRG broadcasters to increase their offerings and accommodate listener demands and choices. East German officials discussed these media revolutions, but any practical counter-steps remained in the planning stages.[62]

The reason for this was quite simple: the GDR lacked both the technological infrastructure and financial resources to match this accelerating technological revolution. As in other media sectors, it actually increased the vicious cycle that only further added to East Germany's cultural atrophy. East German media officials desperately needed to modernize their infrastructure and equipment, yet they lacked the technology and know-how to do so. And the only place where they could purchase the needed high-tech equipment was from the capitalist West, which meant that cultural agencies would have to spend increasingly unavailable Western currencies. As reports from the early 1980s highlighted, the political and cultural leadership realized this deficit and increasingly desperate situation, but they could not overcome their continued dependence on Western equipment and advanced technology.[63]

As a consequence, East German radio broadcasting stagnated in the early 1980s, paralyzed by overpowering domestic deficits and by the inescapable effects of the newly emerging international innovations based on revolutionary media technologies. For example, the introduction of the synthesizer and new electronic recording equipment established a base for international popular music by the 1980s; none of them were available in the GDR. While styles might differ, certain sound qualities and the ability to create specific sound effects were taken for granted and had become part of broadly shared musical standards by this time. By the end of the 1980s, East Germany did not have the talent, the technological infrastructure, or requisite spaces of political freedom and artistic autonomy to creatively respond to the manifold changes with which it was confronted.

Conclusion

Cinema and television as well as popular music and radio broadcasting developed along a similar trajectory in East Germany in the 1970s and 1980s. All of them began in the early 1970s, still hopeful to establish an independent and culturally vibrant socialist alternative that would compare favorably with that projected by the capitalist West. Buoyed by the political tailwinds of the early to mid-1970s, which included America's loss in Vietnam as well as political and economic crises in both the United States and West Germany, SED officials envisioned a robust GDR society and culture that could hold its own in the ideological and cultural competition with the West. By the late 1980s, this vision was lying in shambles. Plagued by an aging and increasingly inefficient economic and technological infrastructure as well as popular opposition and youth subcultures, the East German policy makers had to make one painful accommodation after another. Each step of the way, they had to concede a bit more of their cultural home turf to the relentless drive of Western media and the reach of ever more powerful international influences. At the same time, its population—and especially its youth—severed its cultural and ideological ties with its home country. By 1989, fewer than 20 percent of the GDR youth believed that the basic tenets of a Marxist-Leninist societal system provided effective social or individual guidelines. By the same overwhelming numbers, young people had lost any confidence in the SED and lost faith that their contributions really mattered in the East German society at large.[64]

Another inescapable conclusion is that the high degree of criminalization of subcultures in the GDR and elsewhere in the Eastern Bloc created a political and cultural climate far different than that in the West. It emphasizes that cultural identity and lifestyle choices had far deeper and more long-lasting repercussions for members of subcultures and frequently turned cultural rebellion into enduring political opposition. Closely related to this, the increasing lack of an appealing GDR popular music scene by the 1980s de-territorialized many young people in East Germany and permanently and significantly heightened their identification with transnational bands and cultural influences.

The inability to update and innovate its media infrastructure or to expand the technological equipment and know-how in East Germany ultimately robbed the GDR broadcasting industry as well as its musical artists of the opportunity to stay competitive or relevant on the international stage. A wide array of technologies and trends—cable and satellite broadcasting and the emerging digitalization of media as well as the increased commercialization and new cultural modes of expression—all combined to greatly transform the international media landscape. Coupled with the debilitating and often arbitrary meddling in music bands and their cultural creative process, GDR officials demoralized and ultimately suffocated potentially appealing cultural adaptations and expressions. The combined impact of these various developments highlights that East Germany was in the thralls of powerful challenges. It had to confront hostile and subversive Western radio stations as well as an alienated population, especially its own de-territorialized youth. In the 1980s in particular, it also came face-to-face with the accelerating impact of international media developments that ultimately forced it to abandon its socialist cultural vision, which significantly undermined the long-term political stability of the GDR.

Notes

1. For insightful overviews of GDR radio broadcasting, see Klaus Arnold and Christoph Classen, eds., *Zwischen Pop und Propaganda: Radio in der DDR* (Berlin: Christoph Links Verlag, 2004); and Stefan Zahlmann, ed., *Wie im Westen, nur anders: Medien in der DDR* (Berlin: Panama Verlag, 2010). For an excellent analysis of East German youth radio, see Edward Larkey, *Rotes Rockradio: Populäre Musik und die Kommerzialisierung des DDR Rundfunks* (Berlin: LITVerlag, 2007).
2. On the emergence and development of RIAS, see Bernd Stöver, "Radio mit kalkuliertem Risiko: Der RIAS als US-Sender für die DDR, 1946–1961," in *Zwischen Pop und Propaganda*, ed. Arnold and Classen, 209–28. On the radio reforms of the GDR in connection with international broadcasting in the early 1970s, see Klaus Arnold, "Musikbox mit Volkserziehungsauftrag: Radio in der DDR I. Radio zwischen Partei und Publikum," in *Wie im Westen, nur anders*, ed. Zahlmann, 307–22.

3. Stig Hjarvard, *The Mediatization of Culture and Society* (London and New York: Routledge, 2013), 25.
4. Two more recent anthologies provide particularly intriguing and insightful case studies of these highly varied developments: William Jay Risch, ed., *Youth and Rock in the Soviet Bloc: Youth Cultures, Music, and the State in Russia and Eastern Europe* (Lanham, MD: Lexington Books, 2015); and Ewa Mazierska, ed., *Popular Music in Eastern Europe: Breaking the Cold War Paradigm* (London: Palgrave Macmillan, 2016). These newer anthologies have significantly added to and complicated the assessments of earlier overviews, such as Timothy W. Ryback, *Rock around the Bloc: A History of Rock Music in Eastern Europe and the Soviet Union* (New York and Oxford: Oxford University Press, 1990); and Sabrina Petra Ramet, ed., *Rocking the State: Rock Music and Politics in Eastern Europe and Russia* (Boulder: Westview Press, 1994).
5. "Die Funktion der Massenmedien bei der kommunistischen Erziehung der Jugend," p. 82, June 1984, SAPMO-BArch, DC4 630.
6. Ibid., p. 83.
7. "Zu einigen Entwicklungsproblemen der populären Musik in der DDR," 30 September 1985, SAPMO-BArch, DR1 1983, pp. 1–10; the quote is on p. 9.
8. For the interview with Krahl, see Georg Maas and Hartmut Reszel, "Whatever Happened to . . . : The Decline and Renaissance of Rock in the Former GDR," *Popular Music* 17, no. 3 (October 1998): 267–77. For a discussion of GDR bands with international appeal that were allowed to travel abroad, including City, see Edward Larkey, "GDR Rock Goes West: Finding a Voice in the West German Market," *German Politics & Society* 23, no. 4 (Winter 2005): 45–68.
9. See Michael Rauhut, *Beat in der Grauzone: DDR-Rock 1964–1972: Politik und Alltag* (Berlin: BasisDruck, 1993), 253–56, 274–76; and Larkey, *Rotes Rockradio*, 138–40.
10. For a discussion of City's career in the late 1980s, see Michael Rauhut, *Schalmei und Lederjacke: Udo Lindenberg, BAP, Underground. Rock und Politik in den achziger Jahren* (Berlin: Schwarzkopf & Schwarzkopf, 1996), chapter 5.
11. Michael Rauhut and Thomas Kochan, eds., *Bye Bye Lübben City: Bluesfreaks, Tramps und Hippies in der DDR* (Berlin: Schwarzkopf & Schwarzkopf, 2013); the quote is on p. 8.
12. Christoph Dieckmann, "Küche, Kammer, Weite Welt: Mythen der Erinnerung," in *Bye Bye Lübben City*, ed. Rauhut and Kochan, 15.
13. On the symbolic meanings of jeans, see Rebecca Menzel, *Jeans in der DDR: Vom tieferen Sinn einer Freizeithose* (Berlin: Ch. Links Verlag, 2004), especially chapter 3. The increasing acceptance of US emblems is discussed in the document "Jugend im FDJ-Aufgebot DDR 30," p. 41, April 1978, SAPMO-BArch, DC4 323.
14. Paul Kaiser, "Heckenscheren gegen Feindfrisuren: Das Vokabular der Macht. Asozialität, Dekadenz und Untergrund," in *Bye Bye Lübben City*, ed. Rauhut

and Kochan, 328–48. As Detlef Siegfried points out in his article in the same volume, long hair was also an object of official condemnation in West Germany, but it did not possess even close to the same explosive symbolism as in the GDR: "White Negroes: Westdeutsche Faszination des Echten," in ibid., 408–19.
15. Bundesbeauftragter für die Unterlagen des Staatssicherheitsdienstes der ehemaligen DDR (hereafter BStU), BV Berlin 004070, July 1975; quote is on p. 6.
16. Rebecca Wenzel, "Wittstock vs. Woodstock: Hippies Ost und Hippies West," in *Bye Bye Lübben City*, ed. Rauhut and Kochan, 549. Very similar to this, Peter Wicke argues that it took far greater commitment and had far more severe and long-lasting consequences to become a musician in a GDR rock band: "Zwischen Förderung und Reglementierung: Rockmusik im System der DDR-Bürokratie," in *Rockmusik und Politik: Analysen, Interviews und Dokumente*, ed. Peter Wicke and Lothar Müller (Berlin: Ch. Links Verlag, 1996), 11–12.
17. See, for example, Thomas Kochan, "Da hilft kein Jammern: Zwischen Resignation und Aufbegehren. Die Szene lebt den Blues," in *Bye Bye Lübben City*, ed. Rauhut and Kochan, 84–102.
18. Bence Csatári and Béla Szilárd Jávorszky discuss the success story of Omega in their essay "Omega: Red Star from Hungary," in *Popular Music in Eastern Europe*, ed. Mazierska, 265–82. On the Polish rock music of the 1970s, see Ewa Mazierska, "Czeslaw Niemen: Between Enigma and Political Pragmatism," in ibid., 243–64; and Tom Junes, "Facing the Music: How the Foundations of Socialism Were Rocked in Communist Poland," in *Youth and Rock in the Soviet Bloc*, ed. Risch, 229–54. The mid-1970s Soviet rock scene, including its "Estonian Invasion," is discussed by Christopher J. Ward, "Rockin' Down the Mainline: Rock Music during the Construction of the Baikal-Amur Mainline Railway (BAM), 1974," in *Youth and Rock in the Soviet Bloc*, ed. Risch, 255–66; and Aimar Ventsel, "Estonian Invasion as Western Ersatz-Pop," in *Popular Music in Eastern Europe*, ed. Mazierska, 69–88. For a discussion of the connections between the Solidarity movement and the Polish rock scene, see Junes in the same anthology, "Facing the Music," 235–50. On the growth and influence of rock music in the Soviet Union, see Alexei Yurchak, *Everything Was Forever, Until It Was No More: The Last Soviet Generation* (Princeton and Oxford: Princeton University Press, 2005), chapters 5–6.
19. See the interviews with Luise Mirsch and Walter Chikan in *Rockmusik und Politik*, ed. Wicke and Müller, 73–85; and Larkey, *Rotes Rockradio*, chapter 2.
20. Interview with Jürgen Hagen, p. 174. For the clear preference of classical music as well as other examples of petty censorship, also see the interviews with Hansjürgen Schaefer, Eike Sturmhöfeland, and Dieter Gluschke; all interviews are printed in *Rockmusik und Politik*, ed. Wicke and Müller, 111–33. For an overview of GDR rock music and cultural policies in the 1960s

and early 1970s, see Rauhut, *Beat in der Grauzone*. For the early 1980s, see Rauhut, *Schalmei und Lederjacke*, chapter 1.
21. "Tendenzen der Beliebtheit von Formen der populären Musik aus dem Hitlistenvergleich 1979/1984/1985," November 1985, SAPMO-BArch, DC4 705, p. 5; and "Die Einwicklung musikkultureller Interessen und Verhaltensweisen Jugendlicher in der ersten Hälfte der 80er Jahre," p. 15, July 1985, SAPMO-BArch DC4 702.
22. "DDR- Rockmusik und DDR-Jugend," p. 30, December 1988, SAPMO-BArch, DC4 728.
23. "Standpunkt zur Entwicklung der Rockmusik in der DDR," pp. 2–4, 12 May 1984, SAPMO-BArch, DY30 27376. For an assessment on the rise and impact of the New German Wave, see Sabine von Dirke, "An Analysis of the Development of German Rock Music," *German Politics & Society* 18, no. 3 (Fall 1989): 64–81.
24. Rauhut, *Schalmei und Lederjacke*, chapter 3.
25. Gerhard Paleczny et al., eds., *Punk und Rock in der DDR: Musik als Rebellion einer überwachten Generation* (Norderstedt, Germany: Books on Demand GmbH, 2014), 50; German lyrics: "Nazis, Nazis, Nazis wieder in Ostberlin; Nazischweine, Nazischweine, Nazischweine in Ostberlin!"
26. For very informative overviews of the punk movement in the GDR, see the last three sections in Paleczny et al., *Punk und Rock in der DDR*, written by Alexander Thrum, Maria Hess, and Sebastian Wagner. The song is quoted on p. 179.
27. See Kate Gerrard, "Punk and the State of Youth in the GDR," in *Youth and Rock in the Soviet Bloc*, ed. Risch, 153–81; and Jeff Hayton, "Ignoring Dictatorship? Punk Rock, Subculture, and Entanglement in the GDR," in *Dropping Out of Socialism: The Creation of Alternative Spheres in the Soviet Bloc*, ed. Juliane Fürst and Josie McLellan (Lanham, MD, and London: Lexington Books, 2017), 207–32.
28. Katrin Wissentz, "Unabhängige Kulturszene ab Ende der 1970er Jahre: Die Punkbewegung in der DDR," in *Dropping out of Socialism*, ed. Fürst and McLellan, 37–45; the quote is on p. 45. See also Michael Horschig, "In der DDR hat es nie Punks gegeben," and Torsten Preuss, "Stasi, Spass und E-Gitarren: Die Geschichte der Berliner Punkband *Namenlos*," both in *Wir wollen immer artig sein . . . : Punk, New Wave, Hiphop, und Independent-Szene in der DDR von 1980 bis 1990*, ed. Roland Galenza and Heinz Havemeister (Berlin: Schwarzkopf & Schwarzkopf, 2013), 30–70, 71–89.
29. Klaus Michael, "Macht aus dem Staat Gurkensalat: Punk und die Exerzitien der Macht," in *Wir wollen immer artig sein . . .* , ed. Galenza and Havemeister, 136–37. For a discussion of the "Blues-Messen," see Friedrich Winter, "Die Ostberliner Bluesmessen: Ein Insider-Bericht über sieben Jahre Lernprozess," in *Bye Bye Lübben City*, ed. Rauhut and Kochan, 190–214.
30. An intriguing analysis of this phenomenon is provided in several essays in Fürst and McLellan, *Dropping Out of Socialism*. See especially their introduction, chapter 8, and the conclusion of this anthology.

31. See Hayton, "Ignoring Dictatorship?," in *Dropping Out of Socialism*, ed. Fürst and McLellan, 214–20.
32. Ronald Galenza, "Glatzen & Bombenjacken: Skinheads in der DDR," in *Wir wollen immer artif sein . . .* , ed. Galenza and Havemeister, 178–93. On hip-hop, see Mike Wagner's article in the same collection: "Rap Is in the House: Hiphop in der DDR," 601–22.
33. Susanne Binas, "Kassetten als Kassiber," in *Wir wollen immer artig sein . . .* , ed. Galenza and Havemeister, 455–71; and Alexander Thrum, "DDR Punker. Gefahr für Bürger und Staat? Analyse einer Jugendkultur, ihres Selbstverständnisses und ihrer Musik," in *Punk und Rock in der DDR*, ed. Paleczny et al., 180–87.
34. Quoted in Rauhut, *Schalmei und Lederjacke*, 62. For the discussion of the notion of "de-territorialized culture," see Andreas Hepp, *Cultures of Mediatization* (Cambridge and Malden, MA: Polity Press, 2013), chapter 5.
35. "Stand und Perspektive der Musikproduktion im Rundfunk," pp. 1–7, December 1979, SAPMO-BArch, DR6 730b.
36. For a detailed and insightful analysis of Soviet radio broadcasting, see Kristin Roth-Ey, *Moscow Prime Time: How the Soviet Union Built the Media Empire That Lost the Cultural Cold War* (Ithaca and London: Cornell University Press, 2011), chapter 3.
37. Andreas Ulrich and Kalle Neumann, "Der Anfang: Andreas Ulrich im Gespräch mit Kalle Neumann, dem ersten Moderator von DT 64," in *DT64: Das Buch zum Jugendradio, 1964–1993*, ed. Andreas Ulrich and Jörg Wagner (Leipzig: Thom Verlag, 1993), 17–27; and Heiner Stahl, "Agit-Pop: Das Jugendstudio DT 64 in den swingenden 60er Jahren," in *Zwischen Pop und Propaganda*, ed. Arnold and Classen, 229–242.
38. Larkey, *Rotes Rockradio*; the quote is on p. 139. For a good overview of youth radio programming in the GDR, see chapter 4.
39. "Vorschläge zur Erweiterung des Programmangebotes für jugendliche Rezipienten," pp. 9–20, 15 March 1977, SAPMO-BArch, DR6 723a.
40. For an overview of "Duett," see Larkey, *Rotes Rockradio*, 150–65. In terms of its importance in the lives of East German youth, see Alexander Osang's reminiscences: "Keinen Sender Mehr," in *DT64*, ed. Ulrich and Wagner, 54–61.
41. Larkey, *Rotes Rockradio*, 160–65. For the comments by Walter Bartel, see *Rockmusik und Politik*, ed. Wicke and Müller, 89–101.
42. For the first two exchanges, see DRA Historical Archive, Berliner Rundfunk, Jugendstudio DT 64, Listener Mail 1980, H004-02-04/0127, pp. 91–192 and H004-02-04/0129, pp. 285–88. For the harsher response in connection with KISS, see DRA Historical Archive, Listener Mail 1983, H004-02-04/0205, pp. 468–69.
43. DRA, Historical Archive, Listener Mail 1982, H004-02-04/0156, pp. 415–22.
44. DRA, Historical Archive, Listener Mail 1983, H004-02-04/0211, pp. 248–60.
45. See the collection of essays published by Ulrich and Wagner, *DT64*. For additional useful surveys and analyses of East German youth programming,

see Andreas Bauhaus, "Jugendpresse, -hörfunk und –fernsehen in der DDR. Ein Spagat zwischen FDJ-Interessen und Rezipientenbedürfnissen," dissertation, Universität Münster, 1994; and Aiva Yamac, "Jugendradio DT 64 zum Ende der DDR (1987–1991)," Diplomarbeit, Fachhochschule Mittweida, 2005.

46. The twenty competing radio stations are mentioned in "Die Funktion der Massenmedien bei der kommunistischen Erziehung der Jugend," p. 82, June 1984, SAPMO-BArch, DC4 630; for the quote, see "Tagesordnung für die Komiteesitzung vom 10.6.1980," p. 2, SAPMO-BArch, DR6 733b.

47. Yamac, "Jugendradio DT 64," introduction; on the impact of the RIAS decision, see Larkey, *Rotes Rockradio*, chapter 6. See also Larkey's article "Radio Reform in the 1980s: RIAS and DT-64 Respond to Private Radio," in *Cold War Cultures: Perspectives on Eastern and Western European Societies*, ed. Annette Vowinckel, Marcus M. Payk, and Thomas Lindenberger (New York and Oxford: Berghahn Books, 2012), 76–93.

48. For the quote, see "Jahresendstatistik der Hörerreaktionen für das Jahr 1987," 20 January 1988, SAPMO-BArch, DR6 967c; no page numbers provided. The financial and technical challenges are discussed in a letter to the head of the Staatliches Komitee für Rundfunk, 13 March 1987, DRA Historical Archive F000-03/0026, pp. 187–89.

49. "Hörerreaktionen von Jugendradio DT 64 (ab Dezember 1987): Meinungen junger Hörer zum Jugendradio-Programmangebot und zur Medienkooperation," 22 April 1988, SAPMO-BArch, DR6 967b; quote is on p. 5.

50. Lutz Schramm, "Sonderstufe mit Konzertberechtigung: Die DT64-Indie-Nische," in *DT64*, ed. Ulrich and Wagner, 74–91.

51. In addition to Schramm's recollection, see Thrum, "DDR Punker," on the attempted concession to the punk scene (pp. 184–86); Binas, "Kassetten als Kassiber" on the punk-LP (pp. 463–66); and Michael, "Macht aus dem Staat Gurkensalat" on the rather belated reforms (pp. 166–67); all in *Wir wollen immer artig sein...*, ed. Galenza and Havemeister. The same collection also includes an interview with Schramm, "Spule, Feedback und Zensur: Interview mit Lutz Schramm (DT 64)," 559–70.

52. The greater commitment of *DT 64* staff is discussed in the interview with Walter Bartel, the chief editor for music of the station, in *Rockmusik und Politik*, ed. Wicke und Müller, 99. The reference of the "middling courage" comes from Thomas Braune's article, "Gegen allerschärfste Anweisungen: DT 64 Journalismus zwischen 1985 und 1989," 65, and for the quote by Brasch, see her article, "Die kleine Renitenz," 108; both of the latter articles are in *DT64*, ed. Ulrich and Wagner. For its sometimes oppositional broadcasting and the resulting listener loyalty, see Jörg Wagner, "Das Ende: Der Rias-Coup," 8–17, and Harald Müller, "Zwischen Sputnik und Tienanmen: Der verordnete Sozialismus kippt," 98–105; both in *DT64*, ed. Ulrich and Wagner.

53. "Forschungsbericht '20 Stunden Jugendradio': Hauptergebnisse einer operativen Studie," July 1988, pp. 4–9, SAPMO-BArch, DC4 641; the quote is on

p. 28. On the overall lack of programming variety on GDR broadcasting, see for example "Weitere Profilierung der Rundfunksender der DDR," pp. 1–5, 9 September 1981, SAPMO-BArch, DR6 919. See also the introduction in *Zwischen Pop und Propaganda*, ed. Arnold and Classen; and Konrad Dussel, "Rundfunk in der Bundesrepublik und der DDR: Überlegungen zum systematischen Vergleich," in ibid., 301–22.

54. "Ausgewählte Ergebnisse zum Hören des erweiterten Programms von 'Jugendradio DT 64' bei Leipziger Schülern," pp. 17–18, January 1988, SAPMO-BArch, DC4 640.
55. Wicke, "Zwischen Förderung und Reglementierung," in *Rockmusik und Politik*, ed. Wicke and Müller, 27.
56. On the relative lack of young people in GDR broadcasting, see "Auswertungen der politischen, Alters- und Qualifikationsstruktur der Mitarbeiter des Staatlichen Komitees für Rundfunk," pp. 6–7, 2 November 1981, SAPMO-BArch, DR6 914. The qualities and superiority of Western DJs is discussed in the report cited earlier entitled "Forschungsbericht '20 Stunden Jugendradio," p. 9.
57. See Larkey, *Rotes Rockradio*, especially chapter 5.
58. "Information über die Ergebnisse von Empfangsbeobachtungen auf Längenwelle 185 kHz (Sender "Stimme der DDR") im Zeitraum 22.05–26.05.78," pp. 1–4, 30 May 1978, SAPMO-BArch, DR6 727a.
59. See "Beschlüsse des Ministerrates vom 30. Juni 1977," 8 July 1977, SAPMO-BArch, DR6 724; letter to Staatliches Komitee für Rundfunk, 31 December 1987, DRA Historical Archive F000-03/0026.
60. On the ownership of home electronics, see "Zusammenfassung wesentlicher Forschungsergebnisse als Zuarbeit für die Führungsvorgabe 1982," 12 May 1981, SAPMO-BArch, DR6 916; the deficits in stereo programming are discussed in "Bericht über die betriebswirtschaftliche Arbeit des Rundfunks, 1985," 24 March 1986, SAPMO-BArch, DR6 952a.
61. Quoted in Dussel, "Rundfunk in der Bundesrepublik und der DDR," in *Zwischen Pop und Propaganda*, ed. Arnold and Classen, 306.
62. "Einführung der Digitaltechnik im Rundfunk der DDR," 17 June 1986, SAPMO-BArch, DR 6 952c; and "Jahresplan 1987 für Staatliches Komitee für Rundfunk, HA Wissenschaft und Technik," 19 September 1986, DRA Historical Archive F000-03-00/0007, pp. 155–60.
63. "Problemmaterial für die Beratung über den komplexen Planentwurf des Volkswirtschaftsplanes 1982 sowie des Fünfjahresplanes 81/85 des Rundfunks der DDR," especially pp. 2–6, 22 October 1981, SAPMO-BArch, DR6 916.
64. For the survey of GDR youth, see "Zur Wirksamkeit des FDJ-Angebotes DDR 40," pp. 15–24, July 1989, SAPMO-BArch, DC4 346.

CHAPTER 5

Western Consumer Culture or Bust

Intershops and East German Consumption Policies in the 1970s and 1980s

> And in this context, let me also say another honest word about the Intershops. Naturally, these stores are not a continuous companion of socialism.
> —Erich Honecker, *Neues Deutschland*, 1977

In September of 1977, when Erich Honecker made this comment as part of a speech in Dresden, concurrently published in the party newspaper *Neues Deutschland*, he had an unusual moment of political clairvoyance. Intershops, the hard-currency stores where those with Western money could fulfill their long-delayed consumer desires among a cornucopia of Western products, indeed had no place in a socialist society. As Honecker well knew, these stores deeply divided his population between the haves and have-nots, or more accurately between those with "an aunt with a Western address," as the saying went, and those without. Moreover, Intershops wreaked havoc with the political vision of a socialist economy that would provide equally for all and in a manner that was roughly competitive with its capitalist arch-nemesis. Similar to the takeover of East German cinema and television by Western films and TV genres, as well as the dominance of Western popular music, Intershops were another visible and stinging admission on the part of GDR government officials that their system could not keep up with the West. In fact, it was a silent confession that they had run out of alternative ideas and were throwing in their lot with the ideological class enemy. It was symptomatic of larger trends in the late 1970s and 1980s, which increasingly relied on using Western culture and consumer products as crutches in order to support and maintain an ailing political and deteriorating economic system as long as possible—while still desperately hoping that the long-promised, elusive, and ultimately ephemeral innovation and productivity boost in East Germany would miraculously save the socialist system.

Intershops, and the policies related to them, are a good barometer of the economic and political development of East Germany as well as the consumerist aspirations of the government and its citizens in the last two decades of its existence. They highlight the unstoppable desire for Western consumer goods, register policy reversals as well as periods of intensified public protests, and speak to the desperate degree to which the SED leadership would go to buy legitimacy from a perennially disgruntled population. Just as importantly, against the best economic advice, the pursuit of living standards approaching those in the West would lead to continuous overspending, which mortgaged East Germany's future and led to what Jonathan Zatlin has aptly termed "the tyranny of debt" in the 1980s.[1]

As we know, Honecker's moment of political clarity was fleeting, quickly obfuscated by the next look at the GDR budget ledgers, which reminded him that his chosen consumption policies left him no other choice: the infusion of hard (Western) currency, no matter how it was produced or what political compromises or accommodations it entailed, was an economic necessity by the late 1970s. Not surprisingly, then, Intershops were continued and even further expanded in the 1980s. This search for Western currency would take the GDR in all conceivable directions: among others, it would lead to the deposing of West German and especially West Berlin garbage on East German soil, the selling of GDR art and antiques, as well as the freeing of political prisoners for raw materials. A few of these dealings were illegal and some morally questionable, but most of them were perfectly legal, although politically damaging and ideologically irreconcilable with a socialist vision. These business ventures ran separate from the regular state budget, and their hard-currency profits were invested as the SED leadership saw fit. They were carried out by an agency known as "Commercial Coordination" (Kommerzielle Koordinierung [KoKo]) under the leadership of Alexander Schalck-Golodkowski. Intershops, as part of the Forum, Inc. subsidiary, were an important part of KoKo and brought in about one-third of the total profits during its existence from 1966 to 1989. And as it turned out, 1978—the year after Honecker's speech—would be the most profitable year for Intershops up to that point in East Germany's history.[2]

Like all trends and reversals driven by the influences of Western culture, goods, or lifestyle, Intershop-like stores were not unique to East Germany. They existed under different names and in different configurations in most Eastern European countries, as Paulina Bren points out: Tuzex in Hungaria, Corecom in Bulgaria, Intertourist in Hungary, Pewex in Poland, and Comtourist in Romania. All of these foreign-currency stores were different, yet all of them played a similar function. They satiated at least some of the unquenchable desire for Western goods and luxuries, they represented the good life that lay beyond the borders of the communist economies of need and shortage, and they were attainable only to a select minority or for special occasions through the use of black-market currency exchanges. They embellished the appeal of the West, deepened class divisions and envy, and invited crime and corruption; yet almost every socialist country in the Eastern Bloc introduced them and maintained some form of hard-currency stores nevertheless. They became part of the social bargain, in which consumption and access to Western goods purchased political acquiescence and relative stability, reflecting the accelerated "consumerist turn" all Eastern European communist societies took, especially in the 1970s and 1980s.[3]

Because of the daily barrage of West German media and advertising, the consumer culture and consumption in the former East Germany were particularly exposed and politicized, just like competitions in sports and popular culture. As Ina Merkel has poignantly put it, "consumer culture was the Achilles' heel of the system," and the SED party leadership was painfully aware of the constant comparisons and public debate that it engendered. It was neither a theoretical nor necessarily an ideological debate, but a perennial part of everyday conversations in which everyone participated and everyone was an expert. It mattered greatly which products one could buy and which ones were out of reach. Likewise it mattered greatly how products tasted, looked, or felt because it was a daily reflection of the economic and political system that had produced them.[4] Viewed with the advantage of hindsight, it is hard to imagine a more effective way to promote Western products and consumer culture than the way shopping and consumption emerged in East Germany in the 1970s and 1980s.

To be fair, Honecker used his speech in Dresden to simultaneously announce the vast expansion of GDR specialty stores known as Exquisit and Delikat. He promised that even those without access to Western currency would be able to fulfill their consumer desires, including some imported goods, even though at prices that were about three to four times higher than in general stores. The goal for these

East German luxury chains was to blossom into strong competitors to Intershop stores. Part of this strategy temporarily succeeded in that a greater number of East German shoppers gained access to higher-quality products and greater choice in the late 1970s. However, this only added yet another layer to what had already become a two-tiered and two-currency consumer culture with the legalization of the Intershops for GDR citizens in 1974. With the expansion of the premium chains in the late 1970s, the GDR essentially became a three-class society as far as consumption was concerned: those who had hard currencies, primarily Deutschmarks, could splurge in Intershops; those who were high-income earners could primarily shop in the Delikat and Exquisit stores with Ostmarks (Mark der DDR); and finally those who were largely relegated to the general stores—generally known as HO (Handelsorganization) stores—with the lowest quality and least choice in products.[5] An internal report published in the mid-1980s admitted that the economic disparity in East Germany had greatly increased since 1970 and was causing particular hardships for the third of the population at the lower end of the income spectrum by the 1980s.[6]

Because of the ubiquitous nature of consumption, the competition with the West underlying the GDR consumer politics was even more fierce and vital than the athletic and cultural warfare discussed in previous chapters. What made this rivalry so much more significant and even existential was that the SED government had to engage in appeasement through consumption at an ever-faster pace. Perennially concerned about public protests or, worse yet, popular uprisings, especially those that were based on broad economic discontent related to food shortages or deep-seated consumer resentments, the East German leadership under Erich Honecker bent over backward to either forestall or quickly address such potential unrests. The ensuing consumer policy, which the East German government pursued in the 1970s and 1980s, was politically and economically ruinous, and it was one of the root causes for the repeated economic crises as well as the ultimate demise of the GDR in 1989.

Intershops, Social Stratification, and Appeasement through Consumption in Late Socialist East Germany

Honecker's 1977 speech came at a critical moment in the history of East Germany and his tenure as general secretary. His ebullient start in the early 1970s, when he had announced a new era for the country and promised the population "a unity of social and economic policy" with a strong focus on "consumer socialism" was more than half a decade in the past. This shift was a decisive one, because it prioritized consumption over production every step of the way under his leadership.[7]

After achieving international recognition on equal footing with the FRG in the early 1970s, the East German leadership set upon the task of significantly increasing the social safety net and living standards of its citizens. In addition, forbidden Western fruits, like watching West German television or shopping Western products in Intershop stores, were allowed in 1973 and 1974, respectively. But soon thereafter, the short cultural liberation of the early 1970s came to an end, and the expulsion of Wolf Biermann in 1976 and its contentious aftermath shook the confidence of the regime and left deep political marks for years to come. In 1977, against the backdrop of the worldwide economic crisis, economic troubles added to the sense of disillusionment with the Honecker government as a coffee crisis descended upon the country. An essential item of every German diet and daily routine, this seemingly innocuous crisis quickly ballooned into a political emergency. This crisis became especially urgent after a coffee mix substitute introduced by GDR industry officials was widely ridiculed and decidedly rejected by the population. East Germans joked that one of their favorite West German coffee brands, "Jacob's Crowning" (Jacobs Krönung) had been replaced with "Honecker's Crowning" (Honeckers Krönung), as the maligned coffee substitute had been dubbed in public parlance.[8] Since those with Western currency could still purchase roasted coffee as well as other restricted products in the always well-stocked Intershops, these stores became a lightning rod for the political and economic crisis that ensued. The paradox of separate hard-currency stores existing in a socialist society certainly had not gone unnoticed previously, but this coffee crisis forced the issue and created a significant wave of public discontent. It further laid bare what had long been a known fact: despite its egalitarian promises, East Germany was not a classless society.

From its inception, inequality and privilege were part and parcel of the socialist GDR society. Large cities, particularly Berlin, were first and most generously served, while county seats and the rural areas had to be content with the leftovers. Retired people and single-income earners, including single women with children, most frequently found themselves among the lower-income groups who struggled economically. And even though East Germany pursued progressive women's rights policies, especially in terms of access to work, the majority of women workers still found themselves relegated to lower-income jobs by the mid-1980s. As in every society, those in power and places of leadership enjoyed special rewards and privileges. In East Germany, the same was true for those who were lucky enough to have generous relatives in the West, since it gave them access to the highly valued Deutschmark currency, which granted entry to the Intershops. Finally, those with connections to salespeople and "under-the-counter wares" as well as those with high incomes could at least count on the steady supply of medium-quality products available in GDR stores.[9]

In fact, rather than erasing economic differences, the GDR society was becoming increasingly more stratified in the 1970s and 1980s, and shopping—and the consumer products one could afford—became one of the most visible expressions of this growing stratification. Those in charge of trade and commerce were certainly familiar with the popular dissatisfaction, because they heard about it from their citizens. "Only those with capitalist currency can afford scarce items," one letter writer opined in 1977, while another asked, "Are we not selling out our ideology this way and only increasing the desire for all things Western among our people?" To others, it seemed to confirm the widely circulating notion that one lived a better life with Western currency, and a parent worried in general that "ever more children were bringing FRG products to school and inadvertently advertising for them." Finally, even craftsmen were much easier to hire and quicker to complete repairs if the payments were offered in Deutschmarks.[10]

To make matters worse, the shopping experiences at a general GDR store and an Intershop could not have been more different. Instead of the general drudgery of shopping GDR-style, which involved standing in line for hours for rare products like fresh fruit or quality meat and cheese, going to the Intershop was a fun shopping experience, almost like the consumerist adventures portrayed in Western movies and TV shows. Though Intershops were not widely advertised in East Germany, everyone knew where they were located, and one smelled and saw the difference as soon as one entered. The aromas of imported roasted coffee as well as West German soaps and cosmetic items blended with the bright and playful packaging of West German and Swiss chocolate products, side by side with inviting labels of imported wine and hard liquors. Jeans—even Levi's jeans—as well as other priced articles were readily available, and hard-to-find electronic products like color televisions or cassette recorders were usually available in multiple brands. Moreover, one did not have to rush to an Intershop after work in the hope that something valuable and useful would still remain on the shelves, nor did one have to depend on salespeople who were friends

Figure 5.1. Queuing shoppers in front of a Leipzig grocery store. For most East Germans, shopping was a time-consuming chore. (Courtesy of Bundesarchiv Koblenz; Bild 226-001.)

or family members in order to reserve items from precious deliveries under the counter. For the shoppers' convenience, Intershops had extended evening hours and were even open for business on weekends, including Sundays. For families with Western connections, this became a unique and enjoyable Sunday excursion, especially before holidays or special family celebrations.[11]

Those responsible for Intershops were quick to point out the many advantages of the new development. They argued that these stores were a necessary solution for otherwise intractable problems and rightly pointed out that a certain amount of Western consumer products—just like Western films, television, and popular music—would have to be imported anyway or would find their way onto the always receptive black market. By selling these products for hard currency, East Germany was both saving expensive subsidies and undercutting the black market. In addition, Intershops benefited from visitors and border shoppers as well as siphoned off Western currency that had come into the possession of East German citizens, thereby benefiting the GDR economy and not capitalist banks. Of course, as even Intershop advocates realized, this economic arrangement came at a political price.[12]

Intershops had their origins in the mid-1950s and early 1960s. They first emerged in the mid-1950s as venues where Westerners delivering goods to East German harbors could purchase familiar products on a duty-free basis. In 1962, after the construction of the Berlin Wall a year prior, Intershops were officially started at segue points that West German travelers and visitors frequented, such as transit train and subway stations, but their uses remained officially prohibited for East German citizens. Recognizing their potential for garnering ever-scarce Western currencies, the SED expanded these stores in the 1960s to other hubs where foreigners gathered, such as the first Interhotels exclusively used by visitors and tourists in Berlin, Leipzig, and other desirable destinations. Already in 1966, some East German shoppers could partake in these shopping excursions, because the showing of identity cards was no longer required upon purchase. This change was only passed on verbally and not in the form of an officially written policy, which meant that it was handled unevenly in different stores. In February 1974, the prohibition against East German shoppers was finally lifted for Intershops, and now everyone with access to Western currency could use the stores. Even prior to this official reversal, Intershop stores had more than doubled their revenue and profits between 1970 and 1973.[13]

The other hard-currency retail option for East Germans at the time was a mail-order catalogue known as Genex (Geschenkdienst und Kleinexport GmbH), but it stagnated as a direct result of the expanded Intershop chain of stores in the 1970s and 1980s. It started in the late 1950s as an opportunity for Western relatives and friends to purchase luxury goods for East Germans with Western currency. Especially after the building of the Berlin Wall, the business expanded more briskly and the merchandise became more heavily dominated by imports from the capitalist West. The high point of Genex's sales came in the 1960s and early 1970s, when more than a million packages reached GDR households through its service annually. Yet the aggressive expansion of the Intershops in the second half of the 1970s severely cut into the appeal and usage of the Genex mail-order business, and its annual sales flatlined, especially in the 1980s.[14]

When Intershops gained the official party stamp of approval in 1974, their sales and profits skyrocketed in the next few years, tripling their sales volume by 1978. As usual, imported tobacco, liquor, and coffee as well as chocolate/cocoa products—almost all of them of Western origin—accounted for roughly two-thirds of all purchases. Imported clothing, cosmetics, and household items as well as electronic appliances from the West usually rounded out most of the remaining third. One of the biggest changes from the 1960s was that the majority of buyers, accounting for the majority of sales, in the rapidly expanding

Intershop network of the early to mid-1970s were East Germans. In 1977, 3.5 to 4 million East Germans visited Intershops, and they accounted for over 80 percent of that year's customers. These same East Germans also purchased the vast majority of products—more than 70 percent of the total sales volume that year.[15]

It is no coincidence then that public resentment was beginning to boil over in 1977. On the one hand, East Germany was in the grips of a serious economic crisis that significantly reduced the food and consumer products available to the general public, as highlighted in the coffee crisis discussed earlier. But clearly these shortages did not affect everyone to the same degree. This late 1970s crisis highlighted the shopping disparity in starker terms than usual, and Honecker's 1977 speech occurred in direct response to this consumption crisis. In fact, the SED leadership even debated going back to the more restrictive 1960s Intershop policy, which allowed only foreigners and visitors to purchase in the stores. But this would have cut profits at the Intershop stores—and the corresponding Western currencies they produced—by more than half. In addition, it would have created supply gaps for up to four million GDR shoppers, which would have to be filled through additional imports. Just to be more cautious, though, the officials agreed to significantly reduce the number of high-quality products manufactured in the GDR available in Intershops as well as to destroy all public signage for Intershops and Interhotels. Even inside their stores, GDR officials insisted, "Intershops are going to advertise with their products only."[16]

The other, far more substantial and impactful, response by the SED leadership in the wake of the 1977 economic crisis was to vastly expand the networks for GDR premium stores. Delikat, which was a chain of deluxe grocery stores that primarily carried quality GDR products as well as some Western imports, was supposed to grow its sales volume by roughly 250 percent in 1978, and the number of stores was projected to increase from just over twenty to seventy within one year's span. Likewise, the expenditures for the Exquisit chain, which supplied East Germans with superior fashion, leather, and cosmetic products, was to see an enormous influx of additional resources, totaling nearly 1 billion Ostmarks more for 1978 alone.[17] All of this amounted to another major plank of Honecker's consumerist offensive in the 1970s, which in this case was aimed at aggressively expanding East German luxury chains and bringing them up to competitive standards with Intershops.

The early evolution of the Exquisit stores mirrored that of Intershops. The first fashion boutiques emerged in the late 1950s, primarily in East

Berlin, as competitors to those in the western part of the city. By the time the Berlin Wall was completed, there were more than thirty stores in major East German cities. Unlike Intershops they were geared almost exclusively to GDR citizens who could afford the higher prices, but who paid in East German marks. The network of Exquisit stores increased only slightly in the 1960s, partly because increasing Intershop sales and offerings significantly cut into their appeal and profits. This trend is also reflected in the significant decrease of imported textiles and shoes available in Exquisit stores in the 1960s. While Western imports made up 90 percent of all products in these boutiques in the early 1960s, their share had decreased to 30 percent by the end of the decade. In general, Exquisit purchases remained a meager 1 to 2 percent of the overall fashion sales in East Germany throughout the 1960s.[18]

The food-based Delikat chains got a slightly later start than Exquisit, but it grew significantly faster initially. The first stores opened in 1966, and the large variety of Western as well as high-quality GDR products immediately attracted large crowds, even though prices were usually three times higher than in general stores. The network quickly expanded to over thirty stores in the late 1960s, but the GDR authorities found it difficult to meet the growing demand. The imported items were heavily subsidized and drained valuable Western currencies, which Honecker's predecessor, Walter Ulbricht, hoped to use for increases in production and innovation. For these reasons, the Delikat chains stagnated at the turn of the decade, facing a large gap between the willingness of many East Germans to pay for higher-quality products and the inability of the GDR economy to meet this demand.[19]

In light of these difficulties, and in the context of the mounting debt burden, the spectacular and largely unfunded expansion of the Exquisit and Delikat chains in the late 1970s amounted to an adventurist policy decision. The only sensible explanation is that the SED leadership was rattled by the public unrests and resentments at the time, fearing popular protests similar to those in the neighboring Poland or reminiscent of the June 1953 uprising in East Germany, when wage cuts and price increases created massive demonstrations that could only be subdued with violent intervention. This was a prospect that continually haunted the regime and unerringly guided the consumption policies of the GDR government in the late 1970s and 1980s, which continually superseded economic rationales or budget concerns. As André Steiner has argued, even though "the Politbüro regarded the population's consumption demands as the root cause of the [economic] problem," austerity plans were rejected and sound economic reasoning was discarded.[20]

This dynamic of a quickly increasing demand for consumer goods and luxury items was also a challenge with which other Eastern Bloc countries had to contend. After all, over time desirable and unattainable "luxuries" become part of most people's normal consumption habits. In Eastern European countries, just as in other modern societies, this meant that consumerist demand was always on the rise, creating situations where the majority of people became unsatisfied with economies of need and the limited access to desired goods. Whether this concerned the appeal of French high fashion in the Soviet Union or luxury products in Bulgaria, all Eastern Bloc societies faced dilemmas very similar to East Germany in connection with its Exquisit and Delikat stores: how should a socialist government respond to the upwardly spiraling effects of consumer demand, especially when previous luxuries became normalized and new ones consistently added to the comparative burden?[21]

The 1970s consumer expansion in East Germany is a perfect example of the gradually disempowering accommodations forced on the GDR leadership by this dynamic. In the latter part of the decade, the expenditures for both Exquisit and Delikat stores grew exponentially in

Figure 5.2. Customers at bakery counter in Berlin, 7 August 1985. While Western luxury items were unaffordable to many East Germans, most basic food items remained widely available and heavily subsidized by the government. (Courtesy of Bundesarchiv Koblenz; Bild 183-0807-300.)

East Germany. By 1979, the budget for Exquisit had more than doubled in comparison to 1976, increasing from 630 million to about 1.3 billion Ostmarks. The meager network of stores had been expanded to over two hundred shopping venues, although many of these were extensions of already established general stores. As always, major cities were serviced first, and Berliners alone enjoyed over thirty of these specialty clothing stores by the late 1970s. The consumption pecking order in East Germany held firm even during the expansion. Four major cities—Berlin, Leipzig, Dresden, and Halle—were serviced first and consumed half of all the high-priced clothing and shoe products. But the policy directive also insisted that the increase in quality products be felt in district cities and county seats.[22]

By more than doubling of the number of Delikat stores in the late 1970s, East German economic planners followed a very similar strategy. Priority was given to Berlin as "the display window of the GDR"; it was expected that 30 percent of all sales would transpire in the capital. Even more than in the case of Exquisit, this necessitated a significant expansion of Western imports in order to stock Delikat stores even halfway adequately. New, additional resources were made available to buy Western wine and liquor, tea, salad dressing, and chocolate, as well as cigarettes, fruit cocktails, olive oil, and "a thousand little things," as GDR officials liked to call it. Maybe not surprisingly, the assortment of offerings was frequently guided by what West German television had been advertising. As one policy directive pointed out, "in connection with the Western imports, there is a particular demand for quality brands—especially those that were recently advertised on West German television."[23]

Another integral part of the consumerist expansion at the end of the 1970s was a major concession of the GDR leadership in terms of fashion. While jeans, especially Western jeans, were still officially frowned upon, their import was increasingly condoned and actually subsidized by the East German authorities. In late 1978, in an attempt to appease especially East Germany's disaffected young people, the Commercial Coordination agency (KoKo) purchased one million Western jeans at the price of 25 million Valutamarks (VM) just in time for the Christmas holidays that year; 90 percent of the imported textiles were pants. GDR officials made sure that all of them were the brands most advertised by Western media and most highly prized by young people in East Germany, primarily Levi's and Wrangler. The suggested price per jeans would range between 150 and 200 Ostmarks, and it was agreed that they should be made available in stores close to universities as well as businesses and factories where young people were predominant. Berlin's privileged position again came through: four hundred thousand of the special imports were destined for the capital city. This special delivery was in addition to the well over one million jeans (90 percent of them pants) already sold in Intershops that year. Despite these sales, there was still an unmet demand for an estimated five to six million Western jeans in East Germany by the late 1970s. And while East Germany also produced three million jeans yearly, they were only worn as a substitute until the "real one" became available.[24]

One other potential flashpoint that was on the minds of the SED leaders right around this time was the upcoming thirtieth anniversary of East Germany in October 1979. Even though one might assume that this would be cause for joyful celebrations, this was decidedly not the case. Similar to special holidays like Christmas or Easter, which had to be supported by government largesse, GDR anniversaries called for similar special deliveries and were particularly stressful times for party officials. The main reason for this was that the regime and its accomplishments were usually put under the microscope. Simultaneously, comparisons to its West German counterpart frequently became an intensified focus of political coverage in the FRG media and an issue of public debate among the East German population. Therefore, every such occasion had to be properly arranged and planned, and without fail this included special orders for expensive Western imports that were to arrive just in time to cushion the celebrations. This made one thing very clear: consumption was privileged and seen as politically essential, even if it proved economically harmful.[25] Fearing the popular wrath, the tendency to prevent or quickly stanch public protests at any cost became even more pronounced in the late 1970s and into the 1980s, when the economic flexibility narrowed significantly and budget choices by SED planners became more dire and desperate.

In the meantime, both Delikat and Exquisit benefited from this dynamic in 1979 as their rapid expansion continued. The preparations for the thirtieth anniversary of the GDR were meant to provide a noticeable boost in the supply of high-quality consumer products in East Germany. The estimated budget for additional Western imports was close to 200 million VM. At the top of the list were luxury clothing items for women and men, fruit drinks for kids, and twenty thousand color TVs and fifty thousand radio cassette players delivered by Japanese companies. In addition, special wine and fish imports were ordered from Portugal. Officials insisted that at least 80 percent of all additional food deliveries had to be available for purchase prior to the anniversary celebrations in October, as well as 75 percent of the color televisions. This anniversary budget was approved despite the fact that 1979 was already on track to create the highest deficit of any year in East Germany's history. In fact, 1979 would set a new GDR deficit record due to more than 6 billion VM worth of imports from the capitalist West.[26]

Despite this worsening economic situation, East German leaders frequently comforted themselves with the fact that they were still doing well in international comparisons. A 1980 economic report rightly claimed that the GDR still had the highest average income as well as the highest consumption rate of any country in the Eastern Bloc. Less realistically, officials argued that East Germany's consumption rate was on par with Japan and that the country still placed tenth in terms of international GDP rankings. But the report also acknowledged that the gap in the standard of living between East and West Germany as well as the GDR and other capitalist countries had widened even further in the 1970s. East German families were far less likely to own freezers or dishwashers, for example, and 50 percent of West German households in 1978 had a color TV, compared to only 7 percent in the GDR. In addition, car ownership as well as average income was twice as high in the FRG compared to East Germany, and the average Western car had a four-cylinder and not a two-stroke engine like the much ridiculed Trabant.[27] As GDR officials knew, whether it pertained to popular culture or consumer culture, East Germans did not compare themselves to other Eastern Europeans, but firmly fixed their gaze across the Berlin Wall to the West. The one Eastern Bloc country that probably came closest in terms of the predominantly West-centered focus of its media and consumer culture as well as its citizens' preoccupations was Czechoslovakia, because of both its geographical location and its shared history and linguistic overlap with neighboring Austria and West Germany.[28]

In the wake of the 1977 decision to expand the Exquisit and Delikat networks, the consumer offerings and choices did in fact increase across East Germany for the next few years. Exquisit expanded its sales by over 300 percent between 1977 and 1984; these sales accounted for well over 20 percent of all clothing and shoe purchases in East Germany by the mid-1980s. In the same time period, the percent of imported goods sold in Exquisit stores declined from 50 percent in 1978 to about 35 percent in 1984. Moreover, the overall sales volume more than doubled for Exquisit stores from 1978 to 1984 and more than tripled for the Delikat over these same six years. Finally, by 1984 the Exquisit chain had more than doubled the numbers of its stores, and the Delikat network expanded more than tenfold—even though most of them consisted of special sections for high-quality goods established within general HO stores.[29]

As GDR planners soon realized, adding more shopping networks and further raising the consumer expectations of the East German public created at least as many problems as it solved. To start with, the expansion strategies for Delikat and Exquisit, like all economic planning in East Germany, over-promised and under-delivered. Already in 1978, internal reports emphasized that supply was inadequate to fill the shelves in the new stores; sometimes as much as one-third of promised products never arrived. Other times, deliveries from abroad, like imported shoes from Yugoslavia, were flawed and had to be sent back. Just as frequently, the supply chains broke down even earlier because the SED officials simply could not secure enough raw materials or partially finished imports necessary to complete domestic orders. Likewise, logistical jams, emphasis on quantity over quality in the East German production process, or poor judgment on the part of officials foiled ambitious expectations and economic directives.[30] Despite increased supplies, then, neither the Exquisit nor Delikat networks ever managed to satisfy the rising consumer demand in the GDR.

Simultaneously, officials in charge of trade and commerce wrestled mightily with other questions: how did one know which consumer

Figure 5.3. Delikat store in East Berlin in 1969. Responding to the ever-increasing demand for higher-quality goods and produce, the Delikat chain was significantly expanded in the 1970s and 1980s. (Courtesy of ullstein bild / Granger, NYC—All Rights Reserved, New York; Image ID 0642806.)

product belonged in which store, and what was the right mix of offerings for the expanded Exquisit and Delikat chains? Clearly, these stores worked only if they offered something that the general HO stores were not carrying. Without a functioning supply-and-demand system or a realistic pricing structure, it was often left up to district personnel to make the final calls. In the late 1970s, local officials in turn complained that they had no clear instructions on how to answer these questions and how to justify their choices to grumbling customers. They desperately requested guidance on which materials and styles should be targeted at Exquisit and Delikat consumers as well as how long they were expected to withhold specific products from the general HO stores. Likewise, at the other end of the spectrum, sales managers inquired which Western imports should be moved from the Intershop to the Delikat and Exquisit chains and which consumer products were most in demand.[31] With tens of thousands of individual items for sale and constantly fluctuating styles and consumer demands, the East German authorities can be forgiven if they never developed clear answers and directives in response to these questions. Their inability to manage distinct chains and levels of merchandise was but one of a number of symptoms that exposed the limits and weaknesses of a centrally planned economy.[32]

Another troublesome trend also emerged parallel to this expansion: Intershops suffered as a direct result of the multiplying GDR premium stores in the late 1970s, cutting into an important source of Western currency for the SED government. In 1979, the year after the Exquisit and Delikat chains had been significantly expanded, the Intershop sales volume dropped by roughly 14 percent compared to the previous year—despite an overall increase in sales by visitors and transit travelers. Frugal GDR shoppers clearly were taking advantage of the new Exquisit and Delikat stores and grazed these offerings before they spent their valuable Western currency on items unattainable anywhere else. The second factor that slowed Intershop sales by GDR citizens that year was the introduction of "Forum-checks," which GDR authorities introduced as the mandatory domestic payment method for Intershop purchases. The main goal of these checks, which could only be acquired at GDR banks by those with checking accounts containing Western currency, was to cut back on the black-market exchange of Ostmarks versus Deutschmarks and the criminality this engendered. By the late 1970s, the black-market value of the Deutschmark had already climbed to four times the value of the Ostmark. The overall outcome of these combined trends was that the purchases by GDR citizens in Intershops dropped below 50 percent of total volume in 1979—compared to roughly 75 percent two years prior. In addition, the slump in overall Intershop purchases continued; the yearly sales volume did not return to its 1978 level until 1982.[33]

The final question posed by all of this was of course: how would East Germany pay for this vast consumerist expansion? As discussed in earlier chapters, economic planners were not blind to what was happening. They recognized the increasing danger of insolvency as Honecker's insistence on social and consumer policies piled debt upon debt. When Günter Mittag pushed back against Honecker's insistence on consumption over production in 1978 and 1979, he was told in no uncertain terms that nothing could change the general secretary's desire to increase the standard of living in the GDR. According to his own account, when Mittag finally saw the full expenditures connected to these manifold expansions, his response was unequivocal: "This [was] a path into catastrophe."[34]

By the late 1970s, East Germany was increasingly caught in an economic vicious cycle, which worsened significantly as the 1980s progressed. But a lack of transparency and clear insight into the real economic situation in East Germany on the part of Western banks and governments allowed the GDR continued access to financial markets as well as extensive loans, which came back to haunt the country. Domestically East Germany had committed itself to an unprecedented expansion of its services and its consumption policies under Honecker's "Main Task," trusting that production increases would follow as long as the population saw tangible rewards tied to an increasing standard of living. The combined outcome was a devastating debt crisis, which increased deficits tenfold over the course of the 1970s, from roughly 2 billion VM to well over 23 billion VM in 1980—with little to show for in terms of innovation or productivity increases.[35]

Moreover, the corrosive social and political implications of these consumer policies were just as damaging as the economic malpractice. By the late 1970s at the latest, the Deutschmark was the unrivaled king in East Germany's consumption hierarchy. Starting in 1976, prices in Intershops were no longer listed in multiple Western currencies, but exclusively in Deutschmarks, largely in order to avoid confusion and sales complications. Yet it also had a larger symbolic impact. Only the West German currency unlocked the doors to the GDR luxury palaces. It made shopping fun, fulfilled material fantasies, and elevated one's social and cultural status through ownership of the priced wares. And by increasing "the fetishization of West German money,"[36] it rooted the attraction and superiority of the Deutschmark and all it stood for even more firmly in the collective consciousness of the East German public.

The 1980s: Blossoming Intershops amidst a Wilting GDR Economy

In the 1980s, the public mood soured precariously in East Germany. Two deep economic crises—one in the early 1980s and the other toward the end of the decade—caused by high indebtedness combined with lack of innovation and productivity, brought the country close to financial insolvency and led to significant cutbacks in consumer goods and painful belt-tightening. The causes for the first GDR economic crisis, which peaked in 1982 and 1983, were to a large part self-inflicted. The main culprit was Honecker's reckless spending on social programs and consumption. After Honecker's takeover of power in 1971, the trading deficits with Western countries worsened every year, and the debt burden increased tenfold by the end the decade. The global recession and oil crisis of the 1970s added to this ominous trajectory, especially after the Soviet Union drastically cut back on deliveries of subsidized oil in 1981. By 1981–82, the GDR approached financial bankruptcy, and only two separate billion-dollar loans by West Germany and the renewal of oil-based subsidies by the Soviet Union restored its credit worthiness. But the near collapse also forced Honecker and his government to severely curtail domestic budgets, including his excessive consumer spending.[37]

The East German budget crisis in the late 1980s was equally severe. But since it came after a string of repeated economic downturns, broken promises, lowered expectations, and crumbling socialist states in the Eastern Bloc, it was politically even more debilitating than the first. Continued overspending combined with missed export targets once again burdened an already ailing economy in the mid-1980s, while the productivity rates and the innovation gap widened. In terms of developing new industries in sectors such as electronic data processing or digital technology, the GDR lagged about eight to ten years behind most Western countries. And the renewed cutback in Soviet support, especially in the form of cheap, subsidized oil imports in the mid-1980s, exposed the hopeless economic situation of East Germany even more dramatically than before.[38]

There are several indicators that reflect the plummeting public morale and the growing realization that grudging endurance as well as hope for possible improvements had worn out by the late 1980s. One source, which exposed the decline of the East German public mood clearly, was the secret reports of the West German Federal Intelligence Agency (Bundesnachrichtendienst [BND]), which was as well informed as its more infamous counterpart in the GDR, the Stasi. At the height of the first economic crisis in East Germany in 1983, the FRG government agency reported that things were turning dire in the socialist state. The bleak public mood was turning "from miserable to explosive," as even SED officials acknowledged, according to well-placed sources. An increasing number of East Germans compared their situation to Poland, where spontaneous strikes in the early 1980s had upended the socialist government and had led to ongoing protests as well as the creation of the independent workers' union Solidarity (Solidarność). The West German intelligence agency noted an increasing number of petty thefts and break-ins by desperate or simply frustrated East Germans, many of them young people. Even more ominous, there had been a number of spontaneous protests or work stoppages, which was exactly what GDR leaders dreaded the most. In several instances, this related to East German meat-packing workers who refused to load GDR choice meat because they knew that it was destined for export to Western countries in exchange for hard currency at the same time that their own store shelves laid bare. But faced with insolvency in 1982, the SED economic planners were forced to further increase such unpopular exports in order to meet their financial obligations and preserve their ability to borrow money.[39]

Another rough gauge of public morale was the jokes circulating in East Germany all through its existence. They were certainly nothing new in the 1980s, but their tenor became darker and took on a sharper edge, veering increasingly toward gallows humor as the decade progressed. In connection with the Polish political and economic crisis, for example, East Germans joked that their travel agencies had started to hand out free passes for day trips to the neighboring country so that GDR citizens could see for themselves what their lives would look like by the next year. Likewise, the "SED" abbreviation became the basis of yet another critical commentary. In the early 1980s, it morphed into "Selten Etwas Da"—"rarely anything available." Similarly, since they celebrated the one-hundred-year anniversary of Karl Marx's death in 1983, East Germans wondered aloud if his inheritance had been divided fairly: West Germans had inherited "the capital" (the title of Marx's classic book), they quipped, while East Germans were left with socialism. In reference to the re-emerging terrorist threats by the Red Army Faction in West Germany, East Germans asked, "Why are there no terrorists in

East Germany?" The answer: "Because they would have to wait for their escape car for thirteen years."⁴⁰

As mentioned, during the ensuing years and especially toward the end of the decade, the jokes took on an even edgier tone. Why did their country win almost all international competitions in bobsledding? one pun inquired around the mid-1980s. "Because we have home-field advantage: a wall to the left, a wall to the right, and downhill all the way at full speed!" At the end of the decade, GDR citizens coined a new term: "How do you define 'socialist forgetfulness'?" they asked. The answer: "When you're standing with an empty shopping cart in the middle of the grocery store and you forget if you have already shopped or not." As things got even more dire, a joke circulating in 1989 insinuated that all East Germans were finally going to get a free transistor radio because "after all, the *Titanic* too sank while the music was still playing."⁴¹

Another indicator that traces this deteriorating public mood in the 1980s is preserved in secret surveys conducted by a West German public opinion institute that worked on behalf of the FRG government. Its method consisted of surveying West German visitors after their return from the GDR and inquired about the visitors' general impressions and conversations with East German friends, relatives, and acquaintances. In the period from 1968 to 1989, roughly twenty-seven thousand such surveys were conducted, providing a rough barometer of the changing public opinion in East Germany. Early polls reflected the more positive and at times even hopeful atmosphere from the late 1960s to the mid-1970s. Most East Germans had developed a workable arrangement with their government at that time—neither embracing it nor fully rejecting it. Most importantly, GDR citizens seemed optimistic that the material conditions and living standards would further improve, and based on this perception they expressed a grudging acceptance of the SED leadership.⁴²

Starting in 1976, however, the impressions of West German visitors signaled a change in attitude in the GDR. More and more of them reported that East Germans felt that the economic progress in their country was slowing and perhaps even being reversed. These critical comments were getting louder, as the surveys indicated, even among those who had previously more strongly identified with the political system and its leadership. By the mid-1980s, visitors from the West reported a deep drop in public sentiment in East Germany. Material conditions had deteriorated, and the trend to withhold support from the government and to withdraw from politics altogether was escalating. While still expressing appreciation for their social safety network and the

GDR's educational system, only 15 percent of East Germans, according to the 1985 replies, still identified with their socialist government or saw it as a preferable alternative to West Germany. Similar to the bobsledding joke mentioned above, most East Germans felt that they were on a continued downhill slide as far as the economy and their living conditions were concerned. By the time the fortieth anniversary of the GDR rolled around in 1989, the prospects for any turnaround or significant improvement further dimmed, and the overwhelming majority of East Germans saw economic and political conditions in West Germany as far superior to those in their own country.[43]

Similar intriguing insights into the public mood and opinions of the East German population are provided by the unique petition system of the GDR. The right to petition government authorities had been ensured by a law passed in 1953. It was meant to reflect the notion that the SED was the people's party and that East Germany was truly a "worker and farmer state," as the slogan implied. Generally speaking, petitions were taken seriously by officials and usually received an individual response. They addressed taboo topics such as inequality and poverty among its citizens, corruption and callousness on the part of government officials or superiors, as well as inadequate working, living, and shopping conditions. Naturally, the petitions also had the advantage of alerting the SED authorities to potential trouble spots and bottlenecks that most upset East Germans at various periods of time.[44]

By the late 1980s, many petitioners who wrote to the officials in charge of trade expressed their concerns that things were moving backward in East Germany. "Forty-two years after the end of the war, will we ever arrive at a point where one does not have to search for months for certain articles and especially spare parts?" inquired one frustrated writer in 1987 and added, "Other countries seem to have figured this out." Even twenty years ago, supplies had generally been more plentiful, many writers insisted. Officials in the Ministry for Trade and Commerce acknowledged with deep concern that each consecutive year in the late 1980s set a new record in terms of the sheer number of critical petitions, and all surpassed the previous high point of complaints from 1983. The increase of roughly four hundred letters per year, which a 1988 report highlighted, "represented the highest rate of increase since 1981," and the author noted that "this continues a trend that has been ongoing for about five years." The fortieth anniversary of the GDR's existence became a particular flashpoint for people's anger and frustration. The tenor frequently was: "Forty years and nothing to show for it." On the eve of the upcoming celebrations, petitioners inquired what they should be proud of, especially when the most basic items of everyday life were periodically unavailable. Even more importantly, what were they supposed to tell their children as things were progressively getting worse: "We simply have no convincing arguments left to demonstrate to our kids that things are getting any better."[45]

The overall developments in East Germany reflected those in most other Eastern Bloc countries in the 1980s. As several historians have pointed out, the 1970s reflected a significant watershed decade for Eastern European nations. The delicate though contradictory mix of cultural influences, which included both acceptance and rejection of Western ideas and models in the decades leading up to and including the 1970s, decidedly tipped in favor of the capitalist West, especially in the 1980s. The significant shift toward a market-based consumer culture was part and parcel of this larger trajectory. In the process, what Alexei Yurchak has termed the "Imaginary West" only grew larger and more seductive in the minds of people in all socialist countries. While the anti-capitalist rhetoric and slogans employed in the GDR and elsewhere in the Eastern Bloc changed little, the realities on the ground shifted decisively and further estranged large segments of the population from the ideals and vision of what had been advertised as an alternative socialist modernity.[46]

One aspect of this trajectory in East Germany was that remarkable opulence and consumer choices stood side by side with stark scarcity in the sparse GDR consumer landscape of the 1980s. Intershops stood like glittering oases of plenty, and their lights shone more brightly than ever before. They became lightning rods for public anger and outrage, while their reputation as mythical places where material dreams could come true was further on the rise. Apparently, a rumor started circulating in parts of East Germany that the SED government had established two new Intershops in the mid-1980s where even those who only had Ostmarks could shop as well. In a petition from 1987, a woman from a small town in Thuringia referred to this rumor, which she had heard about for some time. She politely asked the officials in charge if they could please send her the exact addresses of the locations of the two stores. The letter writer had no Western currency, as she highlighted, but "it would be really nice to be able to shop there with our own money."[47] Unfortunately, such Intershops did not exist, and this petitioner as well as the majority of East Germans had to be content with simply visiting the stores, without the opportunity to buy any of the desired wares, however.

But Intershops did not only shine brighter as the 1980s progressed; there were also a lot more of them. Between 1983 and 1986 alone, an-

Figure 5.4. This Intershop in Magdeburg (1984) was a smaller store that mainly carried cosmetics. (Courtesy of ullstein bild / Granger, NYC—All Rights Reserved, New York; Image ID 06422812.)

other hundred new Intershop stores were added for the convenience of well-connected East German shoppers as well as international visitors and West Germans traveling to West Berlin. Moreover, starting in 1983, Intershops added fourteen hundred new Western imports to their assortments, so that they were even more fully stocked than before. And in 1984 prices were increased by an average 5–8 percent, especially in transit stores on popular items such as tobacco and liquor products. The outcome was that Intershops posted new record profits every year after 1982, including the short year of 1989.[48] The reason for this expansion and increased choice was neither callousness nor miscalculation on the part of the SED leadership, but sheer economic necessity. Intershops were some of the most significant sources of desperately needed Western currency both in the 1970s and 1980s. By the mid-1980s, their revenue was absolutely vital to fulfill East Germany's payment obligations. As Matthias Judt argued convincingly, "The Western currency earned by Intershops was ultimately needed to ensure the credit worthiness of the GDR vis-à-vis Western lenders all the way up to the fall of 1989."[49]

Another noticeable trend did not sit well with East Germans either. In pursuit of ever-increasing Intershop revenue, SED officials expanded the network of stores not with their own citizens in mind but mainly to increase sales to visitors. This hard-currency strategy ran in tandem with the increasing recruitment of Western tourists and group travel, primarily from West Germany, in the late 1970s and through the 1980s. In 1978, for example, roughly one hundred thousand FRG tourists came to East Germany, which yielded approximately 6 million Valutamarks for the GDR government. By 1987, that number had more than doubled, and the profits in Western currency, which included higher Intershop sales by Western visitors, had increased more than threefold.[50]

By contrast, the Intershop sales by GDR citizens dropped precipitously throughout the 1980s. The number of GDR shoppers in Intershops had peaked in 1976 at about 75 percent; the same year, East Germans had purchased the majority of the items in the hard-currency stores, accounting for close to 75 percent of the sales. In 1981 and 1982, domestic shoppers still accounted for the majority of all sales, but barely, with just slightly over 50 percent. By 1986, the sales volume of those who purchased with Forum-checks further decreased to about 43 percent. This steady decline could only spell trouble for the GDR leadership: ever more Western consumer paradises arose within their country and were open for entry to all, but most of the desired goods went to those who were visiting or traveling through. By 1987, the overall purchases of East Germans had taken another nosedive: the percentage of sales by domestic shoppers had declined to 38 percent. In addition, an internal report of that year's Intershop sales emphasized that there is "a uniform tendency of an increasing number of visitors but declining sales by shoppers."[51] It is quite possible that more East Germans came to see the plentiful choices firsthand but left with fewer Western goods or empty-handed altogether. Intershops thus were tantalizingly close and real, yet the desired products that they advertised and sold remained out of reach for most citizens living in East Germany.

The pursuit especially of foreign shoppers was quite apparent in several other proposals that emerged in the mid- to late 1980s. In 1984, KoKo explored yet another expansion for Intershops—this time through special cars in trains, especially trains that crossed the border into the West. Ultimately the proposal was dropped because the purchase of specially equipped wagons and the logistics of transporting goods as well as their secure storage were deemed too expensive and cumbersome. Instead the shopping networks along the border and at transit points were upgraded more than ever before. One final change in 1986 highlighted that advertising for Intershops and its special sales promotions were not just back but were further expanded. Economic planners encouraged the rather blatant copying of Western marketing strategies, highlighting campaigns such as using certain themes and seasons as well as stimulating sales by creating targeted campaigns for specific products.[52]

In the 1980s, East Germans inhabited a starkly polarized consumer landscape. On the one hand, they saw the rapid increase of Intershops with plentiful offerings of Western luxury items, which remained out of reach for most. On the other, they were faced with escalating periodic food shortages as well as the declining quality of many East German products. Both of these developments meant that the Delikat and Exquisit chains came under even more pressure than before. After all, the expansion of these shopping networks in the late 1970s had been touted by government officials as an attempt to create relatively equal competitors to Intershops. The majority of GDR citizens had enough money to purchase their products and were willing to pay prices that were three to four times higher than the lower-grade products available in the general HO stores, as long as they felt that they were getting their money's worth. To a limited degree, SED officials were able to deliver on this promise in the late 1970s. Despite ongoing criticisms about the high prices of some items, the lack of quality of certain GDR products, and the continuous undersupply of highly desirable Western imports, customers generally welcomed the new initiative and rated their initial shopping experiences in the late 1970s as satisfactory. It is also noteworthy that the early reports indicated that the vast majority of East Germans were taking advantage of the expanded assortments, with significant differences in the number and volume of their purchases, of course. But even those with limited incomes could at least occasionally fulfill their consumer desires by bringing home a special treat.[53]

But what is also apparent is that the expansion of the Delikat and Exquisit stores from 1978 to 1981 came at the expense of Intershops. The luxury stores had their best year in 1978, before their sales and revenues plummeted for several years. Only in 1982 did the sales volume of Intershops return to the 1978 level, and yearly revenue rose steadily for the rest of the decade. Exquisit's and Delikat's fortune ran exactly reverse to this. They expanded rapidly from 1978 through 1980, offering increasing amounts of Western imports in their multiplying stores. Their worst years came in 1982 and 1983, the exact same years when Intershops staged a comeback, spurred by the fact that the GDR was in desperate need for Western currency in order to avert financial insolvency. In the late 1970s and early 1980s, then, the highs and lows of Intershops and the Delikat and Exquisit chains were intricately connected with each other: in the late 1970s, SED economic planners shifted supplies from

Intershops to the domestic premium chains to satisfy at least some of the pent-up demand for Western imports and appease the general public through consumption. By the early 1980s, when the social welfare and consumerist policies of the Honecker administration had brought the country close to bankruptcy, this move was reversed and led to a severe crisis especially for the Delikat stores from 1982 to 1983—while Intershop sales soared again.[54]

The Exquisit chain went through a very similar up-and-down cycle, inversely related to the Intershop sales. Both its network of stores as well as its sales rapidly increased in the late 1970s, with the sales volume more than doubling between 1977 and 1980. In the two ensuing years, however, revenue stalled as imports were redirected to Intershops and the budget for imported items was reduced. In 1983, increasingly relying on high-quality domestic products, steady revenue increases returned to the Exquisit stores, but that did not mean that customers always left happy. As sales increased to almost 25 percent of overall clothing purchases in 1984, many customers voiced criticisms that they were paying more than previously for general-store merchandise. And especially in large GDR cities, Exquisit stores became the new normal for clothing and shoe purchases, as nearly two-thirds of all such sales were Exquisit transactions.[55]

Through this strategy of shifting products and resources from one shopping network to another, the SED leadership bought itself some time during the late 1970s and early 1980s. But during the next economic crisis in the second half of the 1980s, even this option was exhausted. The reason was that it had been made possible through rapidly ballooning credits from Western lenders, and this option was decidedly more limited by the latter 1980s. But how were the Delikat and Exquisit stores supposed to stage their own comeback in the mid-1980s when they could no longer siphon off subsidized imports from Intershops? The answer came in the only way that was still feasible in the mid-1980s: in order to enhance their appeal and revenue as well as to distinguish themselves clearly from the general stores, economic planners turned the Delikat and Exquisit chains against the HO network. This meant that the highest-quality as well as most popular items from the general stores migrated to the premium chains; this was especially prevalent for the Delikat stores. This solved two problems at once for the SED government: it brought in more revenue and at the same time stabilized the East German currency by siphoning off surplus buying power on the part of the GDR population. Two parallel trends in 1984 confirm this dynamic: the significantly rebounding sales of the Delikat network, and the increasing complaints against the declining quality in the general stores. Not surprisingly, the shift did not sit well with the public, especially the millions of customers who relied primarily on the HO stores for their daily purchases.

Delikat stores posted a 40 percent increase in sales volume in 1984. Per-person spending by East Germans in the premium stores increased from 150 to 210 Ostmarks that same year. In addition, the tendency to significantly expand higher-quality GDR products in the Delikat offerings, which had started in 1981, reached a new peak in 1984, as over three hundred new or enhanced domestic products were added to the assortment. Simultaneously, all GDR districts reported an increasing number of East Germans who were complaining about the declining quality of products offered to general HO store customers. As several districts reported, customers were voicing their distinct displeasure about the declining availability of quality cheese and meat products in HO stores and expressed their frustration "that they were forced to revert to the Delikat assortment." And if they felt that the sausage bought in general stores tasted different, they were in fact right. In 1984, sausage factories supplying HO stores were adding 2 percent substitutes, in the form of potato starch or blood plasma among others, to the production of general-store meat products, while the Delikat-bound ware did not include any substitutes. In addition, the shifting of quality products from HO stores to Delikat stores was handled very unevenly across the country. While roughly 20 percent of all bacon products produced in East Germany were targeted for the Delikat network, officials in Karl-Marx-Stadt sold over 30 percent of their allotted bacon through these stores, while those in Halle distributed less than 20 percent through the premium stores.[56]

GDR citizens relayed their discontent rather freely to Western friends and families as well, and the growing resentment against shifting quality supplies to the premium stores was noted in one of the secret opinion surveys conducted with returning West German visitors in 1986. The responses highlighted that while the Exquisit and Delikat chains had slightly improved the supply with higher-quality goods, many East Germans viewed the SED strategy as a form of government extortion: numerous products had been shifted from general stores to Delikat and Exquisit venues and were now for sale at higher prices. In turn, this placed formerly affordable products out of reach for many citizens who lived on limited incomes. When "Delikat-butter" was introduced in 1988, one frustrated retiree probably spoke for many when he criticized this new development in a petition to the government. The new, higher-quality "Delikat-butter" cost 6,80 Ostmarks, whereas the regular butter in general stores cost 2,40 Ostmarks. What kind of butter were the regular people eating then, the petitioner wondered? And what about all the hard work he and others had put in over all those years and the values for which they sacrificed so much? For the third of the population primarily reliant on general stores, which included most retired people in East Germany, the future prospects looked particularly grim.[57]

In the late 1980s, officials in charge of the Delikat and Exquisit networks struggled mightily to navigate these treacherous waters. They insisted that they had made tremendous progress in terms of expanding both premium networks. By 1988, both chains had grown their sales five- to six-fold compared to their sales volume ten years earlier. And especially in the mid-1980s, additional resources had been provided in an attempt to close the gap between supply and demand for higher-quality products. But instead of narrowing the social divide in the country, the gap widened even further in the second half of the 1980s, just as the return of a severe economic crisis made it even more difficult to keep the consumption pace afloat. Officials were aware that they were able to meet only about two-thirds of the demand for Delikat and Exquisit products. Still, the available assortment was criticized more harshly than ever before for lacking healthy alternatives, for poor and unattractive packaging, and for not providing the right atmosphere to ensure a pleasant shopping experience (Einkaufserlebnis).[58]

By 1988 and 1989, economic planners could not even maintain the modest improvements made during the previous years. Both Delikat and Exquisit sales began to decline. Delikat stores were missing previously available products such as quality meat, cheese, and chocolate items as well as specialty beer. The Exquisit chain needed more money just to purchase specialty wool and fabric in order to manufacture higher-quality GDR textiles. But instead of increased budgets and imports, both were asked to do with less. Simultaneously, consumer expectations of East German customers had risen and were oriented toward international standards mediated by West German television and Western media. When GDR officials undertook detailed studies on the comparative assortments in East and West German stores in the late 1980s, the findings were both predictable and bleak. In a typical 10,000-square-foot store, the FRG version offered over four thousand items for sale, while the same-sized store in East Germany featured less than eight hundred products. Even more disappointingly, as this 1989 report emphasized, "studies in [GDR] shopping centers demonstrated that the average assortment either stagnated or shrank in the 1980s." Only the selection of

Figure 5.5. HO Store in Berlin, 25 November 1973. The regular HO network remained the backbone of the shopping experience for most people in East Germany through the 1970s and 1980s. (Courtesy of Bundesarchiv Koblenz; Bild 183-M1125-017.)

hard liquor was an exception; its assortment increased by 250 percent between 1983 and 1988.[59]

Other international comparisons were no less unsettling for the GDR government. When the East German Institute for Market Research compared radios and TV sets produced in the GDR with those of its international Western competitors, the researchers had to concede that East German products simply could not compete. None of the domestically produced radios could match the international standards, as one of these reports emphasized, adding, "The gap between two comparable products on the international market has further widened." For television sets, the news was even worse: only about 50 percent of East German households owned a color TV by 1989, even though acquiring one remained a top priority for GDR citizens at the time. But the East German economy could not produce even close to enough sets to meet demand, and the ones for sale were hopelessly behind the international competition. Most GDR TVs still lacked stereo sound and came without a remote. And none of them were set up for cable or satellite technology or video text capability—all of which were rather standard features of color TVs produced in the West or in Japan by the 1980s.[60]

What was particularly troublesome for economic ministry officials was that they found themselves confronted with an angry and frustrated public despite the fact that subsidies had increased tremendously over the years. In the early 1970s, government subsidies for food and rent accounted for less than 10 percent of the GDP in East Germany, whereas by the late 1980s it had soared to nearly 25 percent. During the same time span, the buying power of the Ostmark slipped, as did the economic productivity of the country. By 1988, it took at least 8 Ostmarks to buy 1 Deutschmark on the black market. And since East German citizens did not see any improvements in their living standards, their willingness to lend even grudging support to the government declined accordingly.[61]

In fact, the resentment against the SED authorities and the willingness to defy them rather publicly became more widespread. One such example was the "antenna communities" that were sprouting like mushrooms in the Dresden region in 1988, according to a West German intelligence report. Commonly known as the "valley of the clueless" because of their lack of reception for West German television, citizens in and around Dresden finally took matters into their own hands in the late 1980s and transformed their area into what now became known as the "valley of the dishes." As the report highlighted, neighbors came together all over the region and in rather frantic fashion erected community antennas and dishes that finally allowed them, too, to enjoy Western television and culture firsthand. The individual financial contribution usually came to 1,000 Ostmarks per household, but even retired people were willing to spend the equivalent of three months' rent to partake in the cultural expansion. Because of the overwhelming popular support behind the ad hoc community movement, there was little for the SED authorities to do but to approve the development retroactively. Less public but even more emphatic, as an earlier intelligence account asserted, was the mood among young people in East Germany: GDR youth had mentally and politically left East German politics and media behind them by the second half of the 1980s. By 1988, 80 percent had turned their back on the politics of their country, and close to 85 percent of young people in East Germany were now consuming almost exclusively Western media.[62]

Conclusion

By 1989, the SED government could no longer buy off its population through compensatory consumer policies. Appeasement through consumption had run its course and had run out of options. The Honecker regime had come to the end of the rope, left with no more consumption-based accommodations and no more hope for any meaningful reforms or an economic turnaround. Honecker's "Main Task," which had promised to bring about a "unity of social and economic policy," had failed—and in fact backfired. Western consumer goods—and especially the vastly expanded Intershop network—had turned the country inside out. Private consumerist fantasies had become government-subsidized advertisements of the "golden West." Western consumer culture in turn seduced and frustrated East Germans—ever present, tantalizingly close, and yet elusive for most. Raiding the general stores to supply its own premium chains of Delikat and Exquisit and building new Intershops primarily for visitors and foreigners in the mid-1980s were further betrayals in a long list of broken promises.

The SED elite, too, knew that the competition between the two systems was over. In fact, their own reality and preferences had long betrayed their true sentiments, even though they became fully public knowledge only after the collapse of the Berlin Wall. Secluded in the forest compound known as Wandlitz outside Berlin, the senior political elite, including the Honecker family, had long enjoyed a fully Western lifestyle. Only Western electronics, and only the best of them, satisfied their refined taste. Although Honecker himself reportedly shunned the plentiful fresh fruit brought in from West Berlin and preferred relatively simple German meals, others in the SED leadership enjoyed gourmet cuisine, complete with international wines. While the private dinners at Wandlitz as well as the state banquets at the Palais Unter den Linden generally reflected "a cautious sophistication," as Paul Freedman has called it, everything was available. Ever the hardline party official, Margot Honecker allegedly liked to eschew Western imports. But once the labels had been exchanged prior to delivery, she liked both the style and the fit of her thinly disguised wardrobe just fine.[63]

By 1989, their betrayal of every strand of socialist ideals and culture, both private and public, was complete. Hoping to become respected and maybe even loved by his people, Honecker's leadership of the GDR in the 1970s and 1980s had accomplished the opposite. A popular joke from 1989 captured the popular wrath that had accumulated against him rather aptly: As Honecker walks into his office for the last time, he looks at his picture on the wall and asks it what might become of them. To his surprise, his picture answers him: "Erich, I know the answer. I will be taken down, and you will be strung up."[64]

The de facto establishment of a three-class shopping and consumer culture in East Germany became even more firmly consolidated and more acutely felt than before in the second half of the 1980s. The ever-increasing number of Intershops certainly led the way in this development, but the poaching of the HO stores for the benefit of the Delikat and Exquisit chains further exacerbated this trend and drove yet another economic and social wedge between different segments of the GDR population. What had started out as an attempt to offer East Germans socialist alternatives to the seductive Intershops by guaranteeing Ostmark access to imports and luxury items in the late 1970s had turned into an exploitative tool under the tutelage of SED central planning by the 1980s. Not only did this further deepen the divisions among an already stratified population, but it unmistakably demonstrated to most of its citizens that East Germany was on an economic downhill slide without any chance for significant reforms or meaningful recovery.

Notes

1. Jonathan Zatlin, *The Currency of Socialism: Money and Political Culture in East Germany* (Washington, DC: Cambridge University Press, 2007), 92–103; see chapter 6 for an excellent analysis of Intershops in the GDR. See also Milena Veenis, *Material Fantasies: Expectations of the Western Consumer World among East Germans* (Amsterdam: Amsterdam University Press, 2012), especially chapter 7.
2. Matthias Judt, *Koko—Mythos und Realität: Das Imperium des Alexander Schalck-Golodkowski* (Berlin: Edition Berolina, 2015), provides a detailed discussion of the broad range of businesses and ventures through which the GDR earned hard currency. Intershops' overall profits are discussed on p. 259, and table 16 (p. 83) highlights 1978 as the most profitable year for Intershops up to the late 1970s. See also Peter Krewer, *Geschäfte mit dem Klassenfeind: Die DDR im innerdeutschen Handel, 1949–1989* (Trier: Kliomedia, 2007), chapter 3.
3. Paulina Bren, "Tuzex and the Hustler: Living It Up in Czechoslovakia," in *Communism Unwrapped: Consumption in Cold War Eastern Europe*, ed. Paulina Bren and Mary Neuberger (Oxford and New York: Oxford University Press, 2012), 27–48. The term "consumer turn" is used by Patrick Hyder Patterson in his essay in the same volume: "Risky Business: What Was Really Being Sold in the Department Stores of Socialist Eastern Europe?," 116–39. He and several other contributors of the volume also employ the concept

of a socialist consumerist bargain. See also Rossitza Guenrcheva, "Material Harmony: The Quest for Quality in Bulgaria, 1960s–1980s," 141–63; and Jill Massino, "From Black Caviar to Blackouts: Gender, Consumption, and the Lifestyle in Ceausescu's Romania," 226–49.

4. Ina Merkel, "Alternative Rationalities, Strange Dreams, Absurd Utopias: On Social Advertising and Market Research," in *Socialist Modern: East German Everyday Culture and Politics*, ed. Katherine Pence and Paul Betts (Ann Arbor: University of Michigan Press, 2008), 327. See also Merkel's excellent earlier book *Utopie und Bedürfnis: Die Geschichte der Konsumpolitik in der DDR* (Cologne: Böhlau Verlag, 1999).

5. Both Merkel in *Utopie und Bedürfnis* (pp. 274–77) and Zatlin in *The Currency of Socialism* (chapter 6) highlight this increased stratification, though primarily as a two-tiered one.

6. See the report by the Institut für Marktgeschichte, "Berechnungen zur gegenwärtigen Struktur der Haushalte nach Klassen und Schichten und Schätzung der Verteilung der Haushalte aud Einkommensgruppen bis 1990," 30 March 1984, SAPMO-BArch, DL 102/1637. Günter Manz argues that roughly 20 percent of all sales in the GDR in the 1980s consisted of Western products; see his *Armut in der "DDR"-Bevölkerung: Lebensstandard und Konsumniveau vor und nach der Wende* (Augsburg: MaroVerlag, 1992), 90.

7. See André Steiner, *The Plans That Failed: An Economic History of the GDR* (New York and Oxford: Berghahn Books, 2010), 143–50; and Zatlin, *The Currency of Socialism*, 66–78.

8. On the coffee crisis, see Katherine Pence, "Grounds for Discontent? Coffee from the Black Market to the Kaffeeklatsch in the GDR," in *Communism Unwrapped*, ed. Bren and Neuburger, 197–225.

9. For a discussion of most of these inequalities, see Annette Kaminsky, "Ungleichheiten in der SBZ/DDR am Beispiel des Konsums: Versandhandel, Intershop und Delikat," 57–80 (especially p. 61). The income inequality of women is highlighted in Lothar Mertens, "'Was die Partei wusste, aber nicht sagte ...' Empirische Befunde sozialer Ungleichheit in der DDR-Gesellschaft," 138–42. Both articles are published in Lothar Mertens, ed., *Soziale Ungleichheit in der DDR: Zu einem tabuisierten Strukturmerkmal der SED-Diktatur* (Berlin: Duncker & Humblot, 2002).

10. "Information über Meinungen zur Erweiterung des Angebots in Intershop-Läden," 17 January 1977, SAPMO-BArch, DL 226/894.

11. For excellent and detailed analyses, see Merkel, *Utopie und Bedürfnis*, especially part 2, "Handeln und Verteilen"; and Veenis, *Material Fantasies*, especially chapter 4.

12. "Argumentation zum Intershophandel," February 1977, SAPMO-BArch, DL 226/894.

13. "Bericht an das Zentralkomitee der Sozialistischen Einheitspartei Deutschlands," 12 February 1973, SAPMO-BArch, DL 226/893. See also Zatlin, *The Currency of Socialism*, 78–80; and Merkel, *Utopie und Bedürfnis*, 244–45.

14. Judt, *Mythos und Realität*, 83–85, 208–10; his tables for the yearly revenues of Genex on pp. 85 and 209 are particularly instructive. See also Zatlin, *The Currency of Socialism*, 270–78; and Merkel, *Utopie und Bedürfnis*, 246–47.
15. See two related documents from 1977: "Wesentliche Gesichtspunkte zur Charakterisierung der Bedeutung des Intershophandels" and "Information über die Umsätze und Ergebnisse aus dem Intershophandel 1977," no specific dates, both in SAPMO-BArch, DL 226/1231.
16. "Einschätzbare Auswirkungen bei Einstellung des Intershopverkaufs auf DDR-Bürger," n.d., and letter by Schalck to Mittag, 8 December 1977, both in SAPMO-BArch, DL226/1231. On the reduction of high-quality GDR products in Intershops, see "Vermerk für Gen. Dr. Schalck," 27 September 1977, SAPMO-BArch, DL 226/894.
17. "Zwischenbericht über den Stand der Durchführung des Beschlusses des PMR vom 20.10. 1977 zur Versorgung mit Delikaterzeugnissen," 23 February 1978, and "Information zu den bisher eingeleiteten Massnahmen zur Verwirklichung des Beschlusses des Präsidiums des Ministerrates vom 20.10. 1977," n.d., both in SAPMO-BArch, DL 1/23487 (4/601).
18. Judd Stitziel, *Fashioning Socialism: Clothing, Politics, and Consumer Culture in East Germany* (Oxford and New York: Berghahn Books, 2005), chapter 6; and Philipp Heldmann, *Herrschaft, Wirtschaft, Anoraks: Konsumpolitik in der DDR der Sechziger Jahre* (Göttingen: Vandenhoeck & Ruprecht, 2004), 285–90.
19. See Merkel, *Utopie und Bedürfnis*, 270–72; and Heldmann, *Herrschaft, Wirtschaft, Anoraks*, 290–93.
20. Steiner, *The Plans That Failed*, 190.
21. For intriguing discussions of these challenging dilemmas, see several essays in the anthology edited by David Crowley and Susan E. Reid, *Pleasures in Socialism: Leisure and Luxury in the Eastern Bloc* (Evanston, IL: Northwestern University Press, 2010): Ina Merkel, "Luxury in Socialism: An Absurd Proposition?," 53–70; Larissa Zakharova, "Dior in Moscow: A Taste for Luxury in Soviet Fashion under Khrushchev," 95–119; and Mary Neuberger, "Inhaling Luxury: Smoking and Anti-Smoking in Socialist Bulgaria, 1947–1989," 239–58.
22. "Geschäftsbericht des Volkseigenen Handelsbetrieb "Exquisit" zum Planablauf 1979," n.d., SAPMO-BArch, DL 1/2638 (5 v.5).
23. "Massnahmen zur Verwirklichung des Exquisit- und Delikatprogramms," 24 October 1977; "Vorschläge für Importe zur Sicherung des Warenfonds Delikat 1977," n.d.; and "Sortiments- und Preisstruktur-Erwartungen der Bevölkerung an das Delikatsortiment," 2 February 1978; all in SAPMO-BArch, DL 1/23487 (4/601). The quote is from the last document.
24. "Vorschlag zur Befriedigung des dringendsten Nachholbedarfes der Jugend der DDR an Jeans-Bekleidung," 28 October 1978, SAPMO-BArch, DL 226/1341; and "Information zur Durchführung des Verkaufs von Jeanshosen," n.d., and "Information über den Vergleich von Jeans aus der amerika-

nischen Produktion und in der DDR hergestellten Jeanshosen," 1 December 1978, both in SAPMO-BArch, DL 226/1720. For a broader discussion of the cultural and political role of jeans in the GDR, see Rebecca Menzel, *Jeans in der DDR: Vom tieferen Sinn einer Freizeithose* (Berlin: Ch. Links Verlag, 2004), especially chapters 3 and 4.

25. Heldmann, *Herrschaft, Wirschaft, Anoraks*, especially 123–29, 295–316.
26. "Information über den Stand der Vorbereitung und Durchführung von Sonderimporten," n.d., SAPMO-BArch, DL 226/1720. For a great overview of the GDR trading deficits with Western countries in the 1970s, see Judt, *KoKo—Mythos und Realität*, table on p. 51.
27. Institut für Marktforschung, "Die Konsumtion der DDR aus internationaler Sicht," 31 December 1980, pp. 7, 28, and 43, SAPMO-BArch, DL 102/1435.
28. This dynamic is particularly clearly analyzed in Paulina Bren's article, "Mirror, Mirror, on the Wall . . . Is the West the Fairest of Them All? Czechoslovakian Normalization and Its (Dis)Contents," in *Imagining the West in Eastern Europe and the Soviet Union*, ed. György Péteri (Pittsburgh: University of Pittsburgh Press, 2010), 172–93.
29. "Geschäftsbericht des Volkseigenen Handelsbetriebes Exquisit zum Planjahr 1984," March 1985, pp. 2–6, SAPMO-BArch, DL 1/26384; and "Information zur materiellen Stimulierung der Bezirksdirektoren des volkseigenen Einzelhandels (HO) und Direktoren der Handelsbetriebe mit Exquisit- und Delikatverkaufseinrichtungen," n.d., SAPMO-BArch, DL 1/2638 (5 v.5).
30. See, for example, "Bericht über die Bereitstellung von Geweben für die Produktion von Exquisiterzeugnissen im 2. Halbjahr 1978," March 1978, SAPMO-BArch, DL 226/893; and "Vorschläge zur Erschliessung volkswirtschaftlicher Reserven durch die Erhöhung der Warenbereitstellung bei Exquisiterzeugnissen," n.d., SAPMO-BArch, DL 226/1219.
31. "Kurzinformation zur Neueröffnung von Exquisitverkaufseinrichtungen," 21 June 1978, SAPMO-BArch, DL226/893; and "Massnahmen zur Verwirklichung des Exquisit- und Delikatprogramms," 10 October 1977, SAPMO-BArch, DL 1/23487 (4/601).
32. Gerhard Schürer himself made this point very convincingly in his article "Planung und Lenkung der Volkswirtschaft—Ein Zeitzeugenbericht aus dem Zentrum der DDR-Wirtschaftslenkung," in *Die Endzeit der DDR-Wirtschaft—Analysen zur Wirtschafts-, Sozial- und Umweltpolitik*, ed. Eberhard Kuhrt et al. (Opladen: Leske + Budrich, 1999), 67–97.
33. "Analyse des Intershophandels 1979," 4 January 1980, SAPMO-BArch, DL 226/1077. On the overall development of the Intershop sales volumes, see Zatlin, *The Currency of Socialism*, 253, 279.
34. Quoted in Burghard Ciesla, "Hinter den Zahlen: Zur Wirtschaftsstatistik und Wirtschaftsberichterstattung in der DDR," in *Akten. Eingaben. Schaufenster: Die DDR und ihre Texte; Erkundungen zu Herrschaft und Alltag*, ed. Alf Lüdtke and Peter Becker (Berlin: Akademie Verlag, 1997), 23. For a general discussion, see Gernot Gutmann and Hannsjörg F. Buck, "Die Zentralplan-

wirtschaft der DDR—Funktionsweise, Funktionsschwächen und Konkursbilanz," in *Die wirtschaftliche und ökologische Situation der DDR in den 80er Jahren*, ed. Eberhard Kuhrt (Opladen: Leske + Budrich, 1996), 7–51.
35. Among others, see Steiner, *The Plans That Failed*, chapters 5–6; Judt, *KoKo—Mythos und Realität*, chapter 1; and Armin Volze, "Zur Devisenverschuldung der DDR—Entstehung, Bewältigung und Folgen," in *Die Endzeit der DDR-Wirtschaft*, ed. Kuhrt et al., 151–88.
36. The change in the pricing policy is discussed in Schalck's letter to Böhm, 29 September 1976, SAPMO-BArch, DL 226/894. The quote is from Zatlin, *The Currency of Socialism*, 244.
37. Among others, see Volze, "Zur Devisenverschuldung der DDR—Entstehung, Bewältigung und Folgen," in *Endzeit der DDR-Wirtschaft*, ed. Kuhrt et al., 151–8; Ray Stokes, "From Schadenfreude to Going-Out-of-Business Sale: East Germany and the Oil Crises of the 1970s," in *The East German Economy, 1945–2010: Falling Behind or Catching Up?*, ed. Hartmut Berghoff and Uta Andrea Balbier (New York: Cambridge University Press, 2013), 131–44; and Steiner, *The Plans That Failed*, chapter 5.
38. See several articles in the anthology edited by Eberhard Kuhrt, *Die wirtschaftliche und ökologische Situation der DDR in den 80er Jahren* (Opladen: Leske + Budrich, 1996), especially the ones published by Marta Haendcke-Hoppe-Arndt, Gernot Schneider, and Klaus Karat. See also Ralf Ahrens, "Debt, Cooperation and Collapse: East German Foreign Trade in the Honecker Years," in *The East German Economy, 1945–2010*, ed. Berghoff and Balbier, 161–76; and Steiner, *The Plans That Failed*, chapter 6.
39. "Reaktionen aus der DDR-Bevölkerung auf die aktuelle Wirtschaftsituation in der DDR," 1 February 1982, BAK, B 206/576 (DDR 34-05-20/34-90, POL A 0013/83).
40. "Politische Witze, Parolen und andere Fundsachen aus der DDR," February 1983, BAK, B 206/576. For additional jokes as well as a discussion of their role in East German culture, see Kerry Kathleen Riley, *Everyday Subversion: From Joking to Revolting in the German Democratic Republic* (East Lansing: Michigan State University Press, 2008), chapter 3.
41. "Politische Witze, Parolen und andere Fundsachen aus der DDR," February 1990, BAK, B 206/576.
42. Everhard Holtmann and Anne Köhler, *Wiedervereinigung vor dem Mauerfall: Einstellungen der Bevölkerung der DDR im Spiegel geheimer westlicher Meinungsumfragen* (Frankfurt and New York: Campus Verlag, 2015), chapters 1–2.
43. Ibid. For the respective surveys, see pp. 106–7, 167, 190, and 242.
44. See Ina Merkel, ed., *"Wir sind doch nicht die Mecker-Ecke der Nation": Briefe an das DDR-Fernsehen* (Cologne: Böhlau Verlag, 1998), chapter 1; and Zatlin, *The Currency of Socialism*, chapter 7.
45. Letter to Minister für Handel und Versorgung, 14 December 1987, SAPMO-BArch, DL 1/26053 (1v.3); "Bericht über die Schwerpunkte und die Arbeit mit

den im Jahre 1988 an das MHV gerichteten Eingaben," n.d., and "Stimmungen und Meinungen der Bevölkerung aus den im Jahre 1989 an das MHV gerichteten Eingaben," n.d., both in SAPMO-BArch, DL 1/26336.
46. On a discussion of the 1970s as a watershed period, see Bren and Neuberger, *Communism Unwrapped*, especially the introduction and essays of part 2. Alexei Yurchak analyzes the concept of the "Imaginary West" especially in chapters 5–6 of his study *Everything Was Forever, Until It Was No More: The Last Soviet Generation* (Princeton, NJ, and Oxford: Princeton University Press, 2005). The notion of an alternative socialist modernity is highlighted in both of these discussions; it is also more directly discussed by György Péteri in the introduction to his edited anthology of essays *Imagining the West in Eastern Europe and the Soviet Union* (Pittsburgh: University of Pittsburgh Press, 2010).
47. Quoted in Merkel, *"Wir sind doch nicht die Mecker-Ecke der Nation,"* 117.
48. On the expanded offerings and increased prices, see "Information zur Realisierung der Anlage 3 der Festlegungen zur Entwicklung des Intershophandels vom 21.11.1983," n.d., and "Vorschäge zur Erhöhung der Umsatzleistung in Transit und GÜST-Bereich," 11 November 1983, both in SAPMO-BArch, DL 226/1054. On the increase of the stores, see Zatlin, *The Currency of Socialism*, 265.
49. Judt, *KoKo—Mythos und Realität*, 206.
50. "Kurzanalyse über die Durchführung des organisierten Tourismus aus der BRD und Westberlin im Jahre 1980," n.d., SAPMO-BArch, DL 226/1347; and letter by Schalck to Mittag, 10 August 1988, SAPMO-BArch, DL 226/1613.
51. For the years 1982 and 1986, see "Analyse zu ausgewählten Problemen des Intershophandels für das Jahr 1982," p. 10, 11 February 1982, and "Analyse zu ausgewählten Problemen des Intershophandels für den Zeitraum 1.1.-31.12.1986," p. 13, 22 January 1987, both in SAPMO-BArch, DL 226/1076. For 1987, see "Information zu den Ergebnissen des Intershophandels 1987," 9 December 1987, SAPMO-BArch, DL 226/1231. Even if some East Germans snuck through and paid with cash either by impersonating Westerners or simply without having to show ID cards at the time of purchase, these percentages highlight an important overall trend.
52. For the proposed train cars, see "Zum Schreiben des Genossen Otto Arndt vom 15.6.1984 über den Einsatz von speziellen Verkaufswagen in Reisezügen des grenzüberschreitenden Verkehrs mit der BRD," p. 3, SAPMO-BArch, DL 226/1055. The advertising and marketing strategies are discussed in "Analyse zu ausgewählten Problemen des Intershophandels für den Zeitraum 1.1.-31.12.1986," pp. 11–12, SAPMO-BArch, DL 226/1076.
53. "Information über operative Untersuchungen zum Angebot von Delikaterzeugnissen in der Hauptstadt der DDR, Berlin sowie in den Bezirksstädten Leipzig, Halle, Magdeburg und Cottbus," 2 February 1978, SAPMO-BArch, DL 226/893.

54. On the slump in Intershop sales and revenue and their ensuing rise in 1982, see "Planverteilung 1981—AHB Forum," 15 October 1980, SAPMO-BArch, DL 226/890; and "Analyse zu ausgewählten Problemen des Intershophandels für das Jahr 1982," 11 February 1983, SAPMO-BArch, DL 226/1076. For the declining revenues of Delikat especially in 1982 and 1983, see "Analyse des Verbrauchs bei hochwertigen Nahrungs- und Genussmitteln im Delikathandel, 1984," 31 January 1985; see especially the graph titled "Die Umsatzentwicklung Delikat 1980–1984 nach Quartalen," no page number, SAPMO-BArch, DL 102/1690.
55. See "Geschäftsbericht des Volkseigenen Handelsbetriebes Exquisit zum Planjahr 1984," n.d., SAPMO-BArch, DL 1/26384; and Merkel, *Utopie und Bedürfnis*, 266–67.
56. For the increase in overall sales, see "Analyse des Verbrauchs bei hochwertigen Nahrungs- und Genussmitteln im Delikathandel im Jahre 1984," 31 January 1985, SAPMO-BArch, DL 102/1690. The quote and specific examples are discussed in "Probleme und Entscheidungsvorschläge für die weitere Verwirklichung der Beschlüse über die Entwicklung der Versorgung mit Delikaterzeugnissen," 6 December 1984, SAPMO-BArch, DL 1/25509 (2 v. 4).
57. For the secret survey, see Holtmann and Köhler, *Wiedervereinigung vor dem Mauerfall*, 211; the petition is published in Merkel, "Wir sind doch nicht die Mecker-Ecke der Nation," 133–34. For a mid-1980s analysis of East Germany's increasing economic stratification, see "Unterschiede im Konsumverhalten der Haushalte nach Einkommensgruppen," 11 November 1984, SAPMO-BArch, DL 102/1675.
58. "Konzeption zur Entwicklung der Versorgung mit Delikaterzeugnissen bis 1995," May 1988, SAPMO-BArch, DL 226/1219.
59. "Vorschläge zur weiteren Erschliessung volkswirtschaftlicher Reserven durch Erhöhung der Bereitstellung von Delikaterzeugnissen" and "Vorschläge zur Erschliessung volkswirtschaftlicher Reserven durch die Erhöhung der Warenbereitstellung bei Exquisiterzeugnissen," both December 1988, both in SAPMO-BArch, DL 226/1692. For the FRG-GDR comparison as well as the increased alcohol consumption, see "Analyse des Lebensmittelverbrauchs im Zeitraum 1970–1988," 15 July 1989, especially p. 27, SAPMO-BArch, DL 102/2120.
60. For these two surveys, see "Der Markt für Rundfunkgeräte in der DDR—Analyse der 80er Jahre," March 1990, SAPMO-BArch, DL 102/2198; and "Fernsehgeräte in der DDR—Analyse der 80er Jahre," March 1990, SAPMO-BArch, DL 102/2210.
61. "Analyse über die Entwicklung der Stabilität der Währung der DDR—insbesondere im Zusammenhang mit den ausserwirtschaftlichen Prozessen," 3 October 1988, SAPMO-BArch, DL 226/1142.
62. On the "antenna communities," see "Psychologische Lage in der DDR (Berichtzeitraum: Sept. 1988–Mai 1989)," DDR 3405 POL A 0125/89, and

for the report on the GDR youth, see "Psychologische Lage in der DDR (Berichtszeitraum Januar-August 1988)," both in BAK B 206/570.

63. For a discussion of the Western lifestyle as well as the preferences of Honecker, his wife, and the senior SED leadership, see Krewer, *Geschäfte mit dem Klassenfeind*, 271–79. On the culinary preferences of Honecker and other leaders, see Jutta Voigt, *Der Geschmack des Ostens: Vom Essen, Trinken und Leben in der DDR* (Berlin: Gustav Keipenheuer Verlag, 2006), 17–19; and Paul Freedman, "Luxury Dining in the Later Years of the German Democratic Republic," in *Becoming East German: Socialist Structures and Sensibilities after Hitler*, ed. Mary Fulbrook and Andrew I. Port (New York and Oxford: Berghahn Books, 2013); the quote is on p. 184.

64. "Politische Witze, Parolen und andere 'Fundsachen' aus der DDR," 22 February 1990, BAK, B 206/576.

EPILOGUE
Out with the Old— in with the New?
Wende, Ostalgie, and the Serpentine Unification

> *Wende* (turn or turnaround): German term used to describe the political events in the GDR from the fall 1989 to the reunification of Germany in October 1990; sometimes referred to as *Wendejahr* (*Wende*-year).[1]

> *Ostalgie* (nostalgia for the East; longing for the former GDR): Neologism merging the German words *Nostalgie* (nostalgia) and *Osten* (East) during the 1990s and beyond.

The reason the Berlin Wall fell so fast in 1989 was that it had been crumbling for so long. It crumbled for a number of reasons, which merged, intersected, and amplified each other in the 1970s and 1980s. While this study focused on cultural and consumption-based dynamics in East Germany, it also demonstrates that these developments were intertwined with political, social, economic, technological, and international transformations and events. The lack of adequate resources deeply influenced every aspect of East Germany's media and consumer culture. Especially as repeated economic crises threatened the very existence of the SED regime, its leadership was forced to do with less, which ultimately created technological and material gaps that seriously hampered the competitiveness of East German rock music or the viability of sustained TV series with a popular appeal, for example. The increasing debt and funding shortages also forced cultural officials to embrace more Western import films, which helped to keep the struggling GDR film industry and infrastructure afloat both in terms of production and exhibition. International factors, such as the gradual opening of the Soviet Union and other Eastern Bloc countries in the 1980s, further limited the options for East German officials who resisted such changes, which made the importation of Eastern European cultural products at least as toxic as its Western counterparts and made cautious and bland East German films and TV series unappealing even to its socialist neighbors. Broader international cultural developments, such as the increasing tendencies toward entertainment and commercialization of the Western media in the postwar decades, extended their reach across the Berlin Wall and increasingly forced the hands of the SED leadership. Political tensions and fears, finally, gradually drained the vitality of the East German culture and media expressions. The initial cultural liberalization under Honecker in the early to mid-1970s dissipated with the Biermann crisis in 1976 and the invariable tightening of the leash, repeating a familiar cycle of tepid cultural openness followed by the strict reimposition of ideological priorities over the course of GDR history.[2]

This analysis also highlights how the SED leadership was forced to respond to the cultural and consumerist demands of its people with a series of retreats, grudging concessions, and reluctant accommodations. It was both the demand for and the influence of Western media and consumer culture that played such a vital role in the disempowering of the East German regime and dictatorship in the 1970s and 1980s. The standards of Western consumption and the products that symbolized the good life deeply imprinted themselves on the minds and desires of the East German people. This consumerist desire, which expressed itself in the fetishization of Western products as well as the Deutschmark and was fueled by Western media and the GDR's elusive Intershops, became one of the key factors that forced these policy decisions by the SED Politburo. Its inability to satisfy the growing consumerist demands further accelerated the delegitimization and disempowerment of the SED leadership. In this context, Honecker's "Main Task" of the early 1970s and his turn toward "consumer socialism," initiated to go toe-to-toe with its capitalist enemies, constituted a daring policy change built on overconfidence and hubris. To be sure, it spawned a short-lived period of increased legitimacy and respect for the often maligned GDR as well as more widespread popular support from the early to mid-1970s. Honecker's policy decisions were, to some degree, built on significant early improvements and successes, such as East Germany's enhanced international status after its effective anti–Vietnam War campaign as well as its unprecedented athletic successes at the 1972 and 1976 Olympics, which coincided with the longed-for acceptance into the international community at large. The deep crisis of the West in the early 1970s, fueled by America's loss in Vietnam and Watergate, Brandt's forced resignation in 1974, and the deep and painful oil shocks and economic crisis that enveloped the United States and all of Western Europe, further seemed to confirm Honecker's expansive course at the time. But it would not last, and it did not prove sustainable.

Analyzing East German media and consumer culture side by side and in a comparative manner, this study emphasizes the series of ultimately debilitating policy accommodations following Honecker's embrace of "consumer socialism" announced through his "policy of political and economic unity" in 1971. In 1973 and 1974, respectively, the East German government allowed the unhindered viewing of West German television and opened Intershops to East German customers as well. When political and economic crises threatened the regime's hold on power in 1977 and 1978, the SED leadership approved the aggressive expansion of the Delikat and Exquisit chains in order to appease the public, despite a budget that was already saturated in red ink. As the economic crisis worsened and budgets had to be tightened further toward the end of the 1970s, there was a significant loosening of film restrictions, especially when it came to imported Western films. Ideological considerations were retreating further into the background, and the decisive factors for imported movies were based on the popular appeal of these films and the potential revenue they might garner. This was closely followed by the second major television reform in the GDR in 1982 and 1983. Already far behind West German television in the early 1980s, which broadcast over three fully resourced channels, East German planners embarked on a desperate attempt to install at least a second all-day television channel. Like so many attempted media reforms, the "alternative television programming" of the early 1980s was underfunded and proved overly ambitious. In the second half of the 1980s, the SED leadership embarked on two more initiatives specifically targeted at regaining some ground with its alienated young people. In 1986, it launched Jugendradio DT 64, an all-day youth radio station in the midst of trying economic times in the GDR, which achieved some temporary and limited successes. Likewise, popular Western rock bands were invited for multiday open-air concerts in the late 1980s to the delight of their East German fans. Yet what most of these policy reversals have in common is that they no longer simply condoned Western media and consumer culture. Instead they actually embraced and privileged Western capitalist culture over the socialist vision and expressions. These cumulative shifts and accommodations symbolized a gradual capitulation in the face of the dominance and seeming superiority of the Western media and culture as well as the capitalist consumer products and Western way of life.

By the end of the 1980s, most East Germans felt that their country was sliding backward—with no hope for future improvements—and every survey confirmed that they saw the Western model as superior to their own. They felt demoralized and deprived, and many eagerly joined the peaceful demonstrations in the final years of the GDR regime. For their part, the SED leadership felt equally deflated and defeated, unable to pursue business as usual and just as incapable of projecting a feasible way forward toward meaningful reforms. By October 1989, the GDR regime and the Berlin Wall, which had kept it intact, collapsed with a whimper rather than a bang. With uncertain border guards looking on in stunned amazement, jubilant East and West Germans danced on top of the Berlin Wall drinking champagne or using sledgehammers to break through the hated symbol of the Cold War, creating some of the most iconic images of the twentieth century. One chant, which reverberated through all of these celebrations, summarized the mutual excitement of this historic moment: "We are one people!"—"Wir sind ein Volk!" At least as important, secluded behind the Berlin Wall and rooted in a socialist welfare state, East Germans had created a magical West for themselves over the past decades. It was a mirage so pure, perfect, and powerful

Figure 6.1. "Marxismus to Markismus," 1990. This Schoenfeld cartoon succinctly captures the ever-increasing fetishization of the West German Deutschmark—and Western consumer culture—in the GDR. (Courtesy of Karl-Heinz Schoenfeld.)

that no Western advertising agency could have conjured it up. And now they were ready to meet this fantasy land face-to-face for the first time. It was a momentous historic and personal moment.

Once the champagne stopped flowing, the fall of the Berlin Wall and the opening of the border unleashed an utterly predictable response. Enticed by the Western consumer paradise and 100 Deutschmarks as "welcome money" on their first trip to the FRG, East Germans flooded across the border, creating long Trabi traffic jams, especially on weekends, as they embarked on a veritable consumption frenzy. Eager to "test the West," as an opportunistic slogan of a West German tobacco company advertised its product after 1989, East Germans lined up at the closest cross-border supermarkets and shopping centers long before they opened. These highly anticipated shopping excursions were accompanied by a mixture of excitement and anxiety. The cornucopia of everything the West had to offer was finally available to them, but what should one buy and how should one choose with the limited resources at hand? To be on the safe side, most East Germans initially focused on smaller purchases of food items, cigarettes, candy, and alcohol of well-known brand names, the ones with which they were familiar through Western television advertising, catalogs, or strolls through the Intershops. They preferred to pay a bit more to make sure that they bought quality products instead of squandering their precious Western currency on cheaper, generic items with blander packaging. But they soon grew bolder and eventually were ready for larger purchases, redoing their home décor and replacing their antiquated household appliances and electronics, as money allowed. As a sign of the times, East German households produced on average three times as much garbage as their West German counterparts throughout 1990, indeed abiding by the adage "Out with the old—in with the new."[3]

But these continuing excursions were also fraught with uncertainty and anxiety. At times, East Germans could not shake their habit of asking store clerks if certain items like fresh fruit or fresh vegetables were available rather than asking what brands and what kinds their store was carrying. And despite the tutoring by the Western media during the socialist days, former GDR citizens often lacked the language or precise labels to identify the products of their choice. As anthropologist Daphne Berdahl observed in her conversations and travels with East Germans during these early days after the opening of the border, they often castigated themselves for their lack of cultural competency in the West. They did not know that "Tempo," though a brand name, was how their West German compatriots asked for tissues or that "Uhu" likewise referred to glue sticks. Pointing at articles rather than being able to name them regularly exposed East Germans as the cultural newcomers they were. But it also left a stinging sense of inadequacy, uncertainty, and inferiority. As a woman confessed to Berdahl after a trip to the West and her inability to name the kind of bread she purchased, "Now she probably knows I'm an *Ossi* ... I didn't know what the bread was called."[4]

Ossi, in fact, quickly emerged as the generic and generally derogatory term that West Germans used to describe these "newcomers" and their curious habits. Jokes started to circulate about GDR families on their first trip to a McDonalds, who sat down at their table and patiently waited for the waiter or waitress to arrive to serve them. East Germans, after all, were used to waiting, and service at their own GDR restaurants had always been slow and subpar. Rather predictably, Trabi jokes made the rounds as well: "How many workers does it take to make a Trabi?" Answer: "Two: One folds and one pastes." Or "what has happened if a Trabi doesn't go when the light turns green?" "It has gotten stuck in [chewing] gum." While this lighthearted humor had been a trademark of East German culture that created conspiratorial delight before the Berlin Wall came down, it took on a different tenor and connotation when the jokes were told by West German outsiders. In fact, they projected a decidedly more biting tone, especially in light of the outright degrading commentaries about *Ossis* that soon accompanied them, even in respectable mainstream journals like *Der Spiegel:* "They patiently line up in front of the Aldi [German supermarket chain] store before 9 a.m. Pale face, greasy hair, gaze directed downward, dressed in a short quilted jacket, washed-out, formless jeans, and beige-gray shoes, with rumpled plastic bags in their hands. ... Some smell, and others steal like magpies." East Germans of course returned the favor, and in response to the *Ossi* caricature they created their own cardboard *Wessi*, adding two more neologisms to the German lexicon. When the mutual resentments hardened even further during the early 1990s, two additional variations on the same words followed: *Jammerossi* (whining *Ossi*) and *Besserwessi* (arrogant, know-it-all *Wessi*).[5]

Although these cross-border tensions and notes of discord were beginning to emerge soon after the fall of the Berlin Wall (*Mauerfall*), the desire for German unity still reigned utmost in the minds of the majority of people in both east and west. East Germans initially voted for the West with their feet as hundreds of thousands permanently relocated to the former FRG in the immediate months after the *Mauerfall*. In March of 1990, by a vast margin and with over 90 percent participation, they officially voted in favor of rapid reunification, with the expectation that the introduction of the Deutschmark would not be far behind. It indeed followed in July 1990, when East Germans started to receive their salaries in the preferred Western currency and could exchange their savings of Ostmarks on a 2:1 basis. By 3 October 1990, with the strong support of both sides as well as that of West Germany's international allies and the Soviet Union's blessing, German reunification was complete. In less than a year, the remnants of the GDR political state disappeared and quickly reemerged as five new states (Bundesländer) added to the eleven already in existence in federalist West Germany. As so much in the hastily reunified Germany, it amounted to an absorption and incorporation of the former East Germany, leaving few traces of the previously independent GDR state. A new chapter in German history had begun—one that historians refer to as "the Berlin Republic."[6]

The task at hand would be more challenging than the celebratory speeches promising "blossoming landscapes" in the former GDR led everyone to believe. Economically, east Germany was in far worse shape than expected.[7] Regularly celebrated as an Eastern Bloc success story and the tenth-strongest economy in the world, its status was rather quickly downgraded to that of an emerging economy after west German auditors got hold of the real budget numbers and statistics. Weighed down by an aging infrastructure, lacking technological investments, and burdened by largely unchecked pollution, East German productivity levels had been less than 30 percent compared to those in the FRG, according to estimates by west German economists after the fall of the Berlin Wall. Only through massive subsidies and transfer payments did the east German economy stand a chance to catch up with the west German states in the 1990s and beyond. In the immediate years after unification, these cash transfers amounted to about 7,000 to 8,000 Deutschmarks for every east German; by 2006, subtracting east German tax payments and social insurance contributions, the net transfer amounted to roughly 1.2 trillion euros, equaling about 4–5 percent of Germany's yearly GDP during these years. A solidarity tax imposed on west Germans and increased borrowing of money on the part of the German government (the national debt more than doubled from 1989 to 1995) provided the main sources to fund the enormous enterprise—creating a wellspring of criticism and resentment in the western parts of the reunified country for years to come.[8]

To be sure, wages, pensions, and living standards for most in the new German states significantly increased in the 1990s, but they also stayed well below west German averages. The average income of employed workers in the former GDR increased from roughly 55 percent of the corresponding salary in western Germany in 1991 to about 75 percent by the mid-1990s. Retired people, one of the poorest groups in the former GDR, saw dramatic increases in their pensions as well. At the same time, young families and single women with children fared less well than they had during socialist times. And a population that was reared to identify themselves with their work experienced unemployment on a vast scale. By the mid-1990s, four million had lost their jobs. By 1994, roughly 20 percent of east Germans were unemployed, and many more chronically underemployed. One single figure captures the massive displacement particularly well: by the end of 1993, less than 30 percent of former GDR citizens still worked in the same enterprises as they had in November 1989. And even for these lucky few, enormous personal and societal transformations ensued. The familiarity and routines of their daily lives had vanished, leaving them with uncertainty, anxiety, and questions no one could answer.[9]

For a large portion of the east German population, a better life did not materialize nearly fast enough, and the future looked decidedly bleak and uncertain for many. The widespread social and economic trauma expressed itself in a number of ways. One of the most telling signs came through demographic indicators: The number of births in the former GDR, for example, fell from 200,000 in 1989 to 108,000 in 1991 to less than 80,000 in 1994. And a society that hardly knew homelessness saw its rapid spike in the early 1990s—in numbers that reached into the hundreds of thousands. In addition to these sweeping changes, immigration rates rapidly increased in the reunified Germany after 1990 just as former East Germans tried to transition into the tight labor market, fueled by the influx of German-speaking Russians, ethnic Germans from Eastern European countries, migrant workers, and laborers from within the European Union. In 1991 alone, 1.5 million immigrants sought a new home and employment in the reunified Germany, in addition to millions of east Germans who were desperately looking to start a new life as well. And these high levels of immigration continued throughout the 1990s. The accompanying heightened economic anxiety increased anti-foreign sentiments among Germans on both sides of the former Berlin Wall, but the xenophobic reverberations this produced were far more pronounced and widespread in the former GDR territory. Rising disparity of incomes and wealth, greater social rivalry, as well as the breakdown of cherished notions of solidarity and community in the former East Germany in the 1990s, as Milena Veenis demonstrated, only further amplified this sense of "shattered illusions" and the dissolution of east Germans' familiar and socially secure world. As the residents of

Figure 6.2. "Ossi," 1990. Reiner Schwalme prophetically anticipated the difficult transition ahead for most East Germans in this sympathetic portrayal of the *Ossi*, who could finally buy Western goods after 1989—though many also received their first pink slip (*Entlassung*) in the early 1990s. (Courtesy of Reiner Schwalme.)

Rudolfstadt, where Veenis did her fieldwork in the 1993 and 1994, told her repeatedly, they missed the camaraderie of the socialist days when, despite the deprivations and scarcity, at least "everyone was in the same boat."[10]

Similarly alienating and isolating was the exclusive west German focus on the GDR as "Stasiland" and the "second dictatorship" on German soil and the seemingly unanimous and exclusive excoriation of socialist East Germany as a tyrannical state (Unrechtsstaat), especially in the first decade after the fall of the Berlin Wall. East Germans were not blind to the ruthless system of surveillance and arbitrary criminalization as well as the many lives lost or ruined by the dictatorial control of the communist regime. But many also took exception to what felt like judicial retribution on the part of the west German authorities as they handed out over one thousand indictments to former SED and Stasi officials and created a special commission that adjudicated over 2.5 million controversial property claims in the former GDR over the course of the 1990s. To the majority of easterners, the west German condemnation of all things East German smacked of "victor's justice" and "victor's history," ignoring multiple and often contradictory dimensions of GDR history.[11] It also cut short the possibilities for more nuanced reflections of their personal lives and experiences as well as the numerous milieus that had existed under the socialist regime. Moreover, it ignored the pushback against the government's totalitarian demands and priorities, and not just by well-known dissidents, which altered the nature and character of the regime over the long run well in advance of the peaceful mass demonstrations of 1988 and 1989, as this book has emphasized.

In light of these dramatic changes and developments, the next cultural turn of the decidedly serpentine unification process may not be as surprising as it first appears. Starting in 1991, and maybe even a few months before that, the socialist GDR—in the form of its artefacts and material culture—was beginning to make a comeback in eastern Germany, a cultural renaissance that was ultimately termed *Ostalgie* (nostalgia for the East). It emerged not as a staged political movement, but rather as a spontaneous grassroots expression of reconnecting with a shared past. In late 1990 and early 1991, east Germans began to invite friends and neighbors to themed "*Ossi* parties," with decidedly playful and carnivalesque characteristics. Partygoers could sport their finest GDR-styled fashion while the hosts surprised them with almost forgotten treats and other GDR knickknacks. "*Ossi* discos" were not far behind in popularizing this cultural movement reclaiming a common past, where DJs mixed popular East German rock tunes as well as other familiar GDR oldies into the nightly music program. At about the same time, two entrepreneurial students in east Berlin saw their chance and developed the first of many GDR-themed card games that emerged in the 1990s, called "Kost the Ost." Translated as "Taste the East," it was a purposeful rejoinder to the West German cigarette slogan "Test the West," but it also playfully parodied a west German language that was littered with anglicized words—a trend that greatly accelerated as the digital age expanded its reign in the 1990s. Finally, it provided an ironic self-reflection as east Germans struggled to master and keep up with the heavily anglicized German lexicon. Playing "Kost the Ost" reassuringly displayed the cultural literacy of east Germans as consumers, even if it was that of a bygone era, placing the west German player in the role of newcomer and cultural neophyte. Similar east-themed card and board games followed as the 1990s progressed.[12]

Anyone familiar with popular grassroots developments could have guessed the next phase of the *Ostalgie* culture: the arrival of advertisers and marketers, or what Rainer Gries has called the "Product-*Wende*." Starting in 1991 and 1992, based on both a willingness on the part of consumers in eastern Germany to refocus on their local products and an eagerness on the part of businesses and advertisers to satiate this new appetite, the second phase of *Ostalgie* kicked into high gear. Soon east Germans rediscovered their own cola advertised as "Club Cola: Our Coke" in both the regular and diet version. For good measure, the west German company that had bought the business marketed the familiar drink with the slogan "Hurray, I'm still alive!" (Hurrah, ich lebe noch!), which invited the consumer to celebrate their mutual survival during the difficult post-socialist transition period. By early 1992, 65 percent of east Germans indicated that they frequently chose their "own" (east German) products, and only 3 percent indicated that they would rarely or never do so. Slogans for bread "baked locally," "Berlin Pilsener: the beer from here," or products advertised with the sticker "from our region" (Aus unserer Heimat) frequently encouraged consumers to choose "their own products" over Western brands. The former GDR cigarette brand Club enticed its potential customers with the dare "Rediscover the Good Taste" (Gutes neu erleben), while its east German rival Cabinet bet on the purity of its product: "Unadulterated and Unperfumed" (unverfälscht und unparfümiert). And in what can only be described as a Product-*Wende* miracle, twenty years after the 1977 coffee crisis, East German coffee brands came roaring back by 1997—improved and often under Western ownership, but with only slightly "renovated" packaging. The middle-priced east German Rondo made its way back into the hearts of consumers in the new states, who greeted it with endearing surprise and familiar recognition as one of their own: "good old Rondo" was back.[13]

What is even more surprising than the return of the reappropriated and upgraded east German products was the positioning of these brands in the competitive post-*Wende* consumer landscape. The advertising for Cabinet cigarettes points to this new direction. Having experienced what German author Roger Willemsen calls "the discrepancy between the desire for Western products and the disappointment upon their arrival," east Germans added a particularly unexpected twist to the serpentine unification of the 1990s. While in the 1970s and 1980s only Western culture and products deserved the exclusive designations "real," "genuine," or "authentic," it was local eastern products that frequently received this honor in the 1990s. As so often, advertising firms were some of the first ones to realize that they had to develop different marketing strategies for east German audiences. Having tasted the West, accompanied by the full-throttle incursions of capitalist entrepreneurs, both respectable and shady, who turned their lives upside down, many east Germans recoiled, and the West suddenly looked far less golden than it had during GDR days. Germans in the new states began to catch on to the overblown and deceptive marketing schemes of some Western entrepreneurs, as well as the artificial hype of a profit-driven, capitalist system. In response, many were ready to seek safety in familiar, unspoiled, and even ordinary local products. East Germans refocused on the merit and functionality of consumer items, wary of the hyperbole of Western advertising spin. As Rainer Gries put it pointedly, "Not 'light' [products] or 'lifestyle' are in demand, but rather east German earthiness—unadulterated and unperfumed. 'Perfumed' and 'adulterated' represents the other and the others; those are brands that designate Western products in eastern Germany, and they are attributes by which east Germans characterize their reunification experiences with west Germans."[14]

In connection with this study, the parallels of these developments are very intriguing. In the pre-1989 days, East Germans utilized a highly selective and appealing version of Western culture to push back against a dictatorial and suffocating GDR regime. The cultural appropriation of Western culture opened up spaces for cultural resistance and self-expression, as well as limited opportunities to create a distinct hybrid culture different from the prescribed socialist vision. *Ostalgie* filled a similar function during the post-socialist transition period: despite their own approval and support for the full-scale absorption of the GDR into capitalist West Germany, the new capitalist order soon proved disorienting, and its impact caused a general sense of displacement far beyond what east Germans had imagined. The growing resentment against *Ossis* in the west, moreover, convinced many Germans in the new states that they were only second-class citizens, looked down upon by their more prosperous and well-versed west German compatriots. One major strand of *Ostalgie*, thus, served as restorative therapy: east German products and brands became symbolic vehicles that expressed their resistance against the new domineering order as well as material objects designed to assert their distinct culture and identity within the reunified Germany. Similar to the idealized version of Western culture during socialist days, the re-creation of the GDR past in the 1990s was selective and idealizing. Yet *Ostalgie* allowed east Germans to inhabit secure terrain with a familiar material landscape where their cultural literacy and belonging were never questioned, but instead soothingly reaffirmed. *Ostalgie* was the most overt expression of an eastern German cultural and political distinctiveness, often explained by the term *Trotzidentität* (defiant counter-identity).[15]

On the other side of the collapsed Wall, Germans were wondering what was happening to their reunited neighbors. Were they ready to return to their socialist past? Had they already forgotten how miserable their lives had been, oppressed by a dictatorial regime and deprived of basic consumer goods? The concurrent rise of the Party of Democratic Socialism (Partei des Demokratischen Sozialismus [PDS]) in the early to mid-1990s, the successor party to the former SED, only added fuel to this growing resentment. In fact, the political utilization of the *Ostalgie* phenomenon on the part of the PDS created a second, and to some ominous, layer of this cultural development and led many in the old FRG to question if Germans in the new eastern states were backsliding. As many surveys confirmed, there was indeed a close correlation between those who expressed a more distinct east German identity and political support for the PDS. By verbalizing and at times manipulating the emerging eastern disillusionment with aspects of the promised Western paradise, the PDS was able to gain 20 percent of the vote in the 1994 election in eastern Germany. It emerged as the third-largest party in the new states during the 1990s, while receiving hardly any support in states of the old FRG.[16]

To be very clear, however, every survey of the dozens conducted in east and west Germany during the two decades after the fall of the Berlin Wall confirmed one notion in unanimous fashion: the vast majority of east Germans did not want to return to socialism or GDR days. Healthy majorities affirmed the benefits of reunification, and Germans in the new states in fact often expressed a greater commitment to a unified Germany than Germans living in the old western states. In addition, a majority of east Germans consistently expressed the view that their lives had improved since the fall of the Berlin Wall, with significant increases in their standard of living. In a 1995 public opinion survey, for example, despite continued high unemployment and ongoing displacement, a majority of residents in eastern Germany stated that their lives were either better or much better than before the *Mauerfall*. About 30 percent indicated that their standard of living had stayed about the same, and less than 20 percent stated that their personal situation had gotten worse or much worse. This general split in east German sentiment actually remained rather consistent in subsequent surveys in the early 2000s. In several polls between 2000 and 2010, only about 10 percent of former East Germans expressed a desire to return to GDR days. As in the 1995 survey, a strong majority stated that their lives had improved since reunification, while about 25 percent reported no significant difference in their personal well-being. Yet all of these surveys also confirmed one common sentiment shared by most Germans from the former GDR: they strongly believed that they were second-class citizens in a reunified Germany. In 1995, over 70 percent of eastern Germans expressed this view. In 2002 and 2008, roughly 60 percent of east Germans still shared this sentiment. Paradoxically, convergence and differentiation went hand in hand during the first two decades of the Berlin Republic.[17]

This lack of consensus and the vastly diverging perspectives on how to interpret and remember the experiences and history of the former East Germany have been insightfully captured by Martin Sabrow's analysis of three fairly distinct memories of GDR history. Prominent among west Germans and many east German dissidents and refugees, as well as dominant in most German media, is the "dictatorship memory" (Diktaturgedächtnis), which was particularly pronounced in the immediate post-*Wende* discussions and interpretations. As the term implies, it focuses heavily on the realities of the second German dictatorship, political oppression, lack of political freedom, and the omnipresent role of the Stasi. On the other end of the spectrum is what Sabrow calls the "progress memory" (Fortschrittsgedächtnis), which is representative of a rather small segment of followers especially in east Germany, particularly former SED officials, socialist supporters, and some current politicians who emphasize the overall advantages of the socialist model compared to its Western capitalist counterpart. Situated in between these two poles, and favored by a majority of former East German residents, is the "arrangement memory" (Arrangementgedächtnis), which remembers the political oppression and coercion of the GDR communist system, yet merges it with the parallel personal universe of lived experiences and memories. As Sabrow highlights, the "arrangement memory" combines the political and personal in an organic and natural way, but it should not be misunderstood for favoring the socialist model. Belonging to certain SED youth organizations in the pre-*Wende* days, for example, represented a tacit support for and strengthening of the communist system to be sure. Yet on a personal level it was equally or perhaps even more strongly connected to memories of enjoyable excursions and life-long friendships that grew out of such memberships.[18]

As this discussion highlights, there never was a uniform all-German or an agreed-upon east German perspective of the GDR history or the post-*Wende* period, and there probably will not be one for the foreseeable future. Overlapping with the different memories emphasized above, multiple factors further divided the former East German population. One of the most significant ones, as highlighted in the introduction, were age and generational belonging, which produced highly varied differences among former East Germans both in terms of their views of the GDR and their opinions about the post-socialist transformations. Following a broad-stroke approach, historians of East Germany have divided its population into several more or less well-defined generations: first, the founding generation of the GDR, primarily those born between the mid-1920s and mid-1930s ("the 1929er"); second came those "born into the GDR"—roughly those born in the 1940s and early 1950s; followed by the third generation, "the 1968er"—born in the mid-1960s and early 1970s; and finally, there was the youngest generation, born in East Germany between the mid-1970s and the late 1980s, who experienced only their childhood during socialist days.[19]

As one might predict, members of the "founding generation" were the most committed and "un-repenting" east Germans after the *Mauerfall*; they had stayed through the tough rebuilding years and did not move to West Germany in the 1950s when this was still possible. Their lives' work and meaning were deeply intertwined with the socialist past, and many stayed loyal to the communist enterprise. Most members of this generation were of retirement age or eligible for early retirement by the early 1990s. The generation who encountered the most significant difficulties especially after reunification was the one "born into the GDR"—those born in the 1940s and early 1950s. These east Germans generally came of age when the Berlin Wall was built in 1961 and soon thereafter lived through the traumatic dismantling of the Prague Spring in the late 1960s. Even more challenging was the fact that many of this generation were in their forties when the Wall collapsed, asked to restart their lives and careers at an awkward point in their life cycles and in a turbulent environment for which they were ill-prepared. The third generation, "the 1968er," by contrast, born between the mid-1960s and early 1970s, were in their twenties or early thirties during the early 1990s and, as my study highlights, had grown up in the 1970s and 1980s when the GDR society and culture attained a decidedly more Western, international, and hybrid character. Often unfettered and free to move after 1990, ready to study or in the early phases of their careers, many of them transitioned relatively easily into the reunified Berlin Republic and were frequently able to take full advantage of new opportunities the *Mauerfall* provided. This also applied, to an even greater degree, to the youngest generation born after the mid-1970s.[20]

Based on these insights, it is apparent that *Ostalgie* has different meanings and appeals for different groups and generations of east Germans. In light of the generational understanding of GDR history, it is obvious that the associations of *Ostalgie* for east Germans of the "1929er" and "1968er" differed drastically. For the first generation, GDR history encompassed the majority of their lives, including their lives' work and meaning in most cases. For members of the third GDR generation, by comparison, it largely entailed memories of their childhood, upbringing and socialization. This varied perspective is even further complicated by the divergent layers and purposes of the *Ostalgie* discourse in the 1990s and beyond: while the personal memories and a shared culture predominated in the appeal of the *Ostalgie* for most east Germans, marketers and business amplified this cultural distinctiveness for their own profit-driven purposes, as did political parties and politicians in order to enhance their voter appeal. The conversations around the *Ostalgie* discourse became even more charged as tentative attempts were made to memorialize GDR everyday history through museum exhibitions during the first two post-*Wende* decades, which often led to emotional and conflict-laden discussions and disagreements.[21]

In addition, the emergence of a unified perspective was further undermined by the division of Germans in the new states into what became known as "*Wende*-winners" (Wendegewinner) and "*Wende*-losers" (Wendeverlierer). Those "born into the GDR," in their forties and early fifties in 1990, as mentioned earlier, faced a very difficult road ahead, especially if they were low-skilled workers or employed in unproductive manufacturing jobs. Some researchers have gone so far as to call them the "lost generation" of the post-socialist transition. East German women—many of whom had been clustered in low-skilled and low-wage jobs despite the promise of socialist gender equality—also saw their chances reduced in the 1990s. Overall, their unemployment rates were significantly higher than those of men in the new states during the early unification period. Many east Germans became chronically unemployed or underemployed in the 1990s and saw themselves at times as "third-class citizens" in the new Berlin Republic. Single women with young children also fared worse after reunification because the relatively generous benefits of the west German welfare system simply did not provide the same safety net that the GDR had offered this particular segment of the population.[22]

On the other end of the spectrum, the material conditions for retired people—including vast numbers of early retirees—increased dramatically. Average monthly pension payments more than doubled from 1991 to 1994, for example, which included improved retirement conditions for the GDR founder generation. Widows and the disabled, too, received more attention and support from the Berlin Republic than they previously had during socialist times. Finally, there was also a strong regional dimension to those who gained and lost during post-Wall decades. Generally speaking, the new capital city of Berlin and the two southern states in the former GDR, Thuringia and Saxony, which already had more established industries and more attractive cities like Weimer and Erfurt as well as Dresden and Leipzig, received more funding and were quicker to capitalize on the new opportunities. The less industrialized, more remote, as well as more thinly populated northern states, such as Mecklenburg-Vorpommern and Saxony-Anhalt, often were last in line when it came to investments and the rebuilding of infrastructure.[23]

The divergent layers of the emerging *Ostalgie* culture and discourse as well as the rather different east German generational and regional perspectives on reunification were only poorly understood in the western states of the reunified Germany. As during the GDR days, there was a relatively muted interest in the former FRG to get to know the new states; only about half of west Germans had visited the former GDR ten years after reunification. And while easterners were lining up at the unemployment offices, west Germans frequently had to be enticed with pay incentives to move to the new states, which quickly became dubbed "bush" or "jungle supplements" (Busch- or Dschungelzulage) in popular west German parlance. Strained by the triple economic burden of the economic reunification, high immigration rates, and increasing budget deficits in the 1990s, stereotypes against *Ossis* hardened even further in the second half of the decade. The fact that the PDS, the successor party of the SED, received increasing voter support in the new states and achieved its best result in the 1998 election only further soured German-German relations and increased resentments in the former FRG states. By the end of the 1990s, on the ten-year anniversary of the fall of the Berlin Wall when Germans had jubilantly celebrated reunification with the chant "We are one people," a joke began to circulate that picked up on this mutual suspicion: "*Wessi* to *Ossi*: 'We are one people!' *Ossi* to *Wessi*: 'So are we.'" And in a countrywide survey in 2008, only one-third of German respondents believed that east and west had grown together as one people, highlighting the continued separation between the two regions. Removing or overcoming "the Wall in the heads of Germans" was clearly not an accomplished goal yet, even a decade or two after the removal of the physical Wall and the creation of the Berlin Republic. The portrayals of east Germans, likewise, remained negatively slanted in many national media in the late 1990s and early 2000s, while reporting on the new states and its residents declined nationwide, receding into the background of daily and weekly news reports as the twenty-first century progressed.[24]

Figure 6.3. "Menschen-Mauer" (People-Wall), 1996. As Henniger emphasizes in this cartoon, removing the wall in the minds of the German people after 1989 proved far harder than expected. (*Tour guide:* "There used to be a horrible wall right here that separated people.") (Courtesy of Barbara Henniger.)

While east Germany was receding in the news narrative, this decreasing interest was most certainly not reflected in the national German entertainment industry of the early twenty-first century. Quite to the contrary, what can be called the third phase of the *Ostalgie* phenomenon burst onto the national—and even international—stage by the first decade of the twenty-first century. Most notably initiated by the film *Good Bye Lenin!* (2003), which brought national and some international attention to what had largely been a regional *Ostalgie* movement in the 1990s, *Ostalgie* now went mainstream. In her analysis of *Ostalgie* as "nostalgic longing or counter-memory," Berdahl calls this third phase "the culmination of *Ostalgie* [as] a truly mass cultural phenomenon." Released in the summer of 2003 and produced by west German screenwriter and director Wolfgang Becker, *Good Bye Lenin*'s comedic portrayal of the GDR in the dramatic months before and after the fall of the Berlin Wall quickly attracted large audiences and won numerous European film prizes. The movie plot centers on Christiane, a strong SED loyalist, who has a heart attack and falls into a coma after she sees her adult son in one of the mass protests that took place during the dramatic months prior to the fall of the Berlin Wall. When she finally reawakens from her coma, the GDR has evaporated. But after being told by her doctor that his mother's heart is very weak and might fail if she experiences a major shock, her son Alex makes it his life's mission to protect her from the news of the historic transformation that transpired while she was comatose. He embarks on a frantic search for GDR-style household items and memorabilia to furnish the room and home to which she is restricted. In addition, he recruits friends and neighbors in order to celebrate socialist national holidays in traditional fashion and with familiar songs. He even goes so far as to produce soothing news reports, which reinterpret the scaling of the Berlin Wall as desperate attempts by West Germans who want to join their socialist paradise. Alex keeps up the ruse just long enough for his mother to pass away peacefully, confident that her life's work and vision lives on. But the experiences of restaging the GDR past for his mother's sake also prove therapeutic for Alex, allowing him to process the bewildering emotional highs and lows of the months surrounding this historic moment. In addition, similar to *Ostalgie* culture, he is able to re-create and reinvent GDR society and culture not as it was but as he would have liked it to be.[25]

In the fall of 2003, *Good Bye Lenin!* inspired a remarkable wave of German television programs focused on East German history and culture. Like so much of the *Ostalgie* discourse, it was a mixture of reminiscences and cultural expressions. As Paul Cooke has emphasized, the many *Ostalgie* television shows that aired in the span of a few months fluctuated between normalizing the former East Germany for a national audience, on the one hand, and what he calls "nostalgic condescension," on the other. As part of the latter trend, for example, a show televised on a private TV channel consisted largely of examining the common bathroom items found in a former GDR household and was largely aimed at drawing derisive laughter from the live studio audience and those watching at home, showcasing exotic and strange products that did not always seem to fit their intended purposes. At the other end of the spectrum, a television channel located in the new German states broadcast an entertainment program closely mirroring a popular GDR television show that reintroduced familiar entertainers and genres from years past. Its tone was sympathetic and leveling, allowing audiences to reminisce about their past without denigrating it.[26]

Considering the contradictory nature of the former GDR, which contained both dictatorial political structures exemplified by the Stasi surveillance state as well as everyday cultural and social milieus experienced by millions of its citizens, it is rather fitting that the *Ostalgie* craze at the beginning of the twenty-first century was succeeded and in a way capped off by the film *The Lives of Others* (*Das Leben der Andern*, 2006), directed by Florian Henckel von Donnersmarck. As several historians have highlighted, the simultaneous portrayals of the GDR as "Stasiland" and as the site for a nostalgic *Ostalgie* culture are rightfully seen as "the conjoined twins" of East German socialism. The movie *The Lives of Others* powerfully highlights the totalitarian aspects of GDR history, especially the dehumanizing and destructive impact of East German Stasi activities and abuses. Revolving around an uncharacteristically sympathetic Stasi officer, the film captures the realistic and ruthless nature of the regime in stark detail, a realism that was confirmed by both GDR politicians and former victims of the regime. Purposefully filmed as a corrective to the *Ostalgie* wave that preceded it, the movie singularly and effectively focuses on the world of GDR political dissidents and their Stasi tormenters set on destroying their lives. *The Lives of Others* was a huge box-office success and was screened to wide critical acclaim, winning an Academy Award for Best Foreign Film in 2006.[27]

***

In light of the larger study, it needs to be emphasized that the simultaneous, and often contradictory, emulation and rejection of Western media and consumer culture persisted through the post-socialist transition period in Eastern Europe. As a number of recent studies have highlighted, the prominent appeal of Western and especially American TV series combined with the dominance of Hollywood blockbuster films continued and temporarily even increased in the 1990s and early twenty-first century in several Eastern Bloc countries. At the same time, after coming face-to-face with long desired Western travel destinations or capitalist consumer goods, the other-worldly aura of the West gradually receded and led to a more sober reassessment of its glamour and desirability across Eastern European countries. Equally important, the direct encounter with Western economies and capitalist practices frequently proved shocking and disillusioning for large segments of the former Eastern Bloc populations, which encouraged nostalgic longings for certain aspects of the socialist past. And finally, just as the adoption and adaptation of imported Western culture prior to 1989 took greatly diverging directions, the individual paths of Eastern European countries after the end of the communist era were highly varied and uniquely shaped by different geographical locations, regional affinities, and the diverse political and cultural developments of specific countries.[28]

Directly related to this, there are several intriguing similarities and differences in the emergence and cultural significance of the *Ostalgie* discourse of the post-*Wende* period and the Western media and consumer culture of the GDR years as far as East Germany is concerned. As indicated earlier, both movements emerged as cultural expressions of resistance against dominant, alienating systems, neither of which had organically emerged over time in East Germany. Communism had been imposed in the postwar period and was endured rather than embraced. Especially in the 1970s and 1980s, as my analysis demonstrates, Western culture and consumer products emerged as a powerful antidote against its hegemonic demands, which provided a space of refuge as well as an arena for individual and group identity. Although Western capitalism had been voted in by East Germans in 1990, once it had fully arrived the promises of its capitalist marketers seemed just as overblown as those of the political salesmen of socialism. Capitalist practices and routines quickly dominated the lives of Germans in the new states and turned them upside down, which was both unexpected and shocking. *Ostalgie* provided a safe space to reminisce and to assert cultural competency, replete with familiar material artifacts recalling fond memories during less turbulent and disorienting times. As part of this curious reversal, labels like "real" and "genuine," which had been the exclusive preserve of Western articles before 1989, often became attached to local east German products after 1990. But just like the magical West of the pre-

Wende days, the imagined GDR projected by the *Ostalgie* discourse was a selective, purified version of the actual past. While they spawned two distinct cultural movements during different times and were motivated by divergent intentions and desires, then, *Eigen-Sinn* (gumption or dogged and creative self-reliance) of the socialist days and *Trotzidentität* (a defiant East German counter-identity) of the post-socialist transition were nevertheless cut from the same oppositional cloth.[29]

However, one significant difference between these two cultural movements and discourses, pre- and post-1989, is equally noteworthy. The yearning for Western culture and consumer products in the 1970s and 1980s was not a desire for the familiar. Very few East Germans had actually traveled to the West and seen the "real" thing. Instead it was a mere hypothesis, a projection based on media influences and consumerist desires, born in an oppressive, dictatorial system that tried to enforce strict, monotonous conformity and elicit confessions of consent. *Ostalgie*, by contrast, implied an imagined return to familiar, secure surroundings and a safe cultural mnemonic reservoir, spurred by the chaotic and turbulent transition period into a capitalist culture that was foreign and alienating to many. Both of these oppositional cultural movements—Western culture in the socialist GDR and *Ostalgie* in the reunified Germany—served similar functions by opening up spaces of refuge and arenas to assert one's individuality and unique cultural identity, but with very different ends. Western culture was a projection of the future in order to survive and escape from the present in the 1970s and 1980s, while *Ostalgie* reflected a nostalgic longing for a past in order to survive and transition into the present during the unification years. Both of them functioned as second cultures, which, in their own unique ways, added distinctive and distinguishing elements to hybrid east German cultures that emerged before and after 1989.

Another differentiating aspect of the *Ostalgie* discourse is similarly striking. *Ostalgie* culture and memory were more than mere crutches to transition into a new societal paradigm. In light of the ongoing privileging of west German models and narratives as well as the continued slighting of east German lives and shared past during the 1990s and beyond, *Ostalgie* was also tied to a desire for and insistence on cultural and societal validation. In order to recognize themselves in the new Berlin Republic, residents from the former East Germany insisted that their culture and their memories be taken seriously and integrated into the broader German history and culture—one that went beyond the master narrative of the GDR as the second dictatorship on German ground. *Ostalgie* expressed the insistence on the relevance and significance of one's own memories, a "counter-memory" reflective of competing values, sensibilities, and priorities that facilitated personal transitions into a novel political and cultural setting but also demanded a widening of the national imagination and consciousness.[30]

Even though it cannot be explored in depth in this epilogue, the expansion of post-Wall German culture and society can be observed in other areas as well, such as politics and east German literature. Parallel to the *Ostalgie* discourse, which burst onto the national stage in the early twenty-first century and reverberated through ensuing television shows in the following years, for example, the German political arena also widened at that time. The election of east German Angela Merkel as chancellor in 2005 and the emergence of the national Left Party as a successor to the regional PDS in 2007, although on opposing ends of the political spectrum and usually at odds with each other, reflect further examples of this normalizing and nationalizing trends of east-Germanness.[31]

Very similarly, post-Wall east German authors developed a strand of humorous and satirical literature with a politically charged edge that continued a strand of East German writing from GDR days. As writers such as Thomas Rosenlöcher, Reinhard Ulbrich, and Ingo Schulze attest, they viewed their satirical rendering of the transition years as a continuation of the ways that jokes and humor helped them and their compatriots endure and survive the GDR. The pleasurable and slightly conspiratorial nature of such humor seemed fitting for the sudden reversals and uncertainties after 1989, when east Germans had once again become "the objects of history" rather than masters of their own fate. To be sure, these writers initially found most of their readership in the former East, but like *Ostalgie* culture, their influence slowly expanded, making some of them well-known and best-selling authors in a reunified Germany. And like the *Ostalgie* discourse, this literature often served a dual purpose. It gave Germans in the new states a humorous arena for reflection as they transitioned into the Berlin Republic. Simultaneously, these writers widened the circle of national culture and strengthened a genre, humorous and satirical literature, which had not always been viewed as the forte of German authors in the past.[32]

Despite the many ongoing controversies and debates, there seems to be overwhelming agreement about two aspects of the state of the Berlin Republic several decades after the fall of the Berlin Wall: there is a near-unanimous consensus that Germany has made significant progress in terms of merging the former FRG and GDR, but there is equal unanimity that the unification of Germany is still a work in progress.[33]

The nationalizing moment of *Ostalgie* culture and GDR history in the first decade of the twenty-first century represented an important step on the path toward unification and the nationalization of east German history, memory, and priorities. While numerous differences and tensions remain between the east and west in the reunified Germany, then, biographies, cultures, and political priorities shaped by an east German identity continue to merge into the national dialogue and the maelstrom of mainstream politics and culture of an enlarged, more inclusive Berlin Republic.

Notes

1. This definition is based on Kerstin E. Reimann's usage of the term *Wende* or *Wendejahr* in *Schreiben nach der Wende—Wende im Schreiben? Literarische Reflexionen nach 1989/90* (Wiesbaden: Verlag Königshausen & Neumann, 2008), chapter 2.
2. For an excellent broad-based discussion of the history of both Germanys since the 1970s, which extends into the post-1989 period, see the essays in Frank Bösch, ed., *A History Shared and Divided: East and West Germany since the 1970s* (New York and Oxford: Berghahn Books, 2018).
3. Thomas Ahbe, *Ostalgie: Zum Umgang mit der DDR-Vergangenheit in den 1990er Jahren* (Erfurt: Landeszentrale für politische Bildung Thüringen, 2005), 6. For the rapid replacement of GDR products with Western brands, see pp. 15–18. See also Rainer Gries, *Produkte als Medien: Kulturgeschichte der Produktkommunikation in der Bundesrepublik und der DDR* (Leipzig: Leipziger Universitätsverlag, 2003), chapter 1 as well as pp. 135–47.
4. Daphne Berdahl, "Consumption Rites: The Politics of Consumption in a Unified Germany," in *On the Social Life of Postsocialism: Memory, Consumption, Germany*, ed. Matti Bunzl (Bloomington and Indianapolis: Indiana University Press, 2010), 38. See also Berdahl's book, *Where the World Ended: Re-unification and Identity in the German Borderland* (Berkeley: University of California Press, 1999), especially chapter 5.
5. To be fair, the terms *Ossi* and *Wessi* already circulated prior to the fall of the Berlin Wall but did not attain mainstream usage until after 1989; see, for example, Julia Franck, ed., *Grenzübergänge: Autoren aus Ost und West erinnern sich* (Frankfurt am Main: Fischer Verlag, 2009), introduction. The jokes are quoted in Berdahl, "'Go, Trabi, Go!': Reflections on a Car and Its Symbolization over Time," in *On the Social Life of Postsocialism*, ed. Bunzl, 63. The quote from the *Spiegel* article from September 1990 is referenced in Gries, *Produkte als Medien*, 27. On *Jammerossi* and *Besserwessi*, see Grix's introduction in *East German Distinctiveness in a Unified Germany*, ed. Jonathan Grix and Paul Cooke (Birmingham: University of Birmingham Press, 2002), 1–9.

6. See, among others, Konrad H. Jarausch, *The Rush to German Unity* (Oxford and New York: Oxford University Press, 1994); Charles Maier, *Dissolution: The Crisis of Communism and the End of East Germany* (Princeton, NJ: Princeton University Press, 1997); Patrick Major, *Behind the Berlin Wall: East Germany and the Frontiers of Power* (Oxford and New York: Oxford University Press, 2010); and Gerhard A. Ritter, *The Price of German Unity: Reunification and the Crisis of the Welfare State* (Oxford and New York: Oxford University Press, 2011), part 1.
7. In this epilogue, I generally use the capitalized versions of "West German" and "East German" when it refers to the pre-1990 period, when they were citizens of two different countries. The lowercase "west German" and "east German" designate their unified citizenship in the post-socialist transition period.
8. Ritter, *The Price of German Unity*, 74–75, 86–91.
9. Ibid., 76–85. See also Milena Veenis, *Material Fantasies: Expectations of the Western Consumer World among East Germans* (Amsterdam: Amsterdam University Press, 2012), for firsthand accounts of these dramatic transformations in one specific city in East Germany, as well as the reflections of everyday East Germans captured by Mary Fulbrook, *Dissonant Lives: Generations and Violence through the German Dictatorships* (Oxford and New York: Oxford University Press, 2011), especially chapter 11.
10. On the declining birth rates, see chapter 4 in Ritter, *The Price of German Unity*, 103–4. For the increase in homelessness as well as people living in emergency shelters, see Günter Manz, *Armut in der "DDR"-Bevölkerung: Lebensstandard und Konsumtionsniveau vor und nach der Wende* (Augsburg: MaroVerlag, 1992), 136–37. The increasing immigration, labor competition, and displacements are discussed in two articles of the anthology edited by Ruth A. Starkman, *Transformations of the New Germany* (New York: Palgrave Macmillan, 2006): Nora Räthzel, "Aussiedler und Ausländer: Transforming German National Identity," 157–79; and Hermann Kurthen, "Germany's Coming Out: Citizenship and Immigration Reform Since Unification," 181–97. See also Veenis, *Material Fantasies*, chapters 5 and 8.
11. For a detailed analysis of these highly controversial judicial issues, see A. James McAdams, *Judging the Past in Unified Germany* (Cambridge and New York: Cambridge University Press, 2001). For the number of indictments, see both the introduction and the conclusion. McAdams discusses the private property claims in chapter 5.
12. See Ahbe, *Ostalgie*, 42–45. For a discussion of the GDR-themed card and board games, see Berdahl, "(N)Ostalgie for the Present: Memory, Longing, and East German Things," in *On the Social Life of Postsocialism*, ed. Bunzl, 51–58.
13. Gries, *Produkte als Medien*, 28–47; several consumer responses to the resurrection of Rondo are printed on p. 47. See also Rüdiger Läzer, "'Schön, daß es das noch gibt': Werbetexte für Ostprodukte. Untersuchungen zur

Sprache einer ost-west-deutschen Textsorte," in *Von "Buschzulage" und "Ossinachweis,"* ed. Ruth Reiher and Rüdiger Läzer (Berlin: Aufbau Taschenbuch Verlag, 1996), 206–8; and Ahbe, *Ostalgie*, 45–51. For a particularly insightful analysis of the powerful intersections between *Heimat*, memory, and nostalgia as part of this *Ostalgie* discourse, see Nick Hodgin's excellent analysis of *Wende* films: *Screening the East: "Heimat," Memory and Nostalgia in German Films since 1989* (New York and Oxford: Berghahn Books, 2011).

14. Gries, *Produkte als Medien*, 27; see also Patricia Hogwood, "'Red is for Love . . .': Citizens as Consumers in East Germany," in *East German Distinctiveness in a Unified Germany*, ed. Grix and Cooke, 45–60. For Willemsen's quote, see his essay "Ein kleines Winken," in *Grenzübergänge*, ed. Franck, 163–64.

15. For a discussion of the term *Trotzidentität*, see Paul Cooke, *Representing East Germany since Unification: From Colonization to Nostalgia* (Oxford and New York: Berg, 2005), 7–9. In addition to the studies already cited previously, see also the excellent essays on memory, nostalgia, and *Ostalgie* published in Anna Saunders and Debbie Pinfold, eds., *Remembering and Rethinking the GDR: Multiple Perspectives and Plural Authenticities* (New York: Palgrave Macmillan, 2013), especially the introduction by the editors and three other introductory essays: Silke Arnold-de Simine and Susannah Radstone, "The GDR and the Memory Debate," 19–33; Patricia Hogwood, "Selective Memory: Channelling the Past in Post-GDR Society," 34–48; and Claire Hyland, "'*Ostalgie* Doesn't Fit!': Individual Interpretations of and Interactions with *Ostalgie*," 101–15. See also Grix's introduction in Grix and Cooke, *East German Distinctiveness in a Unified Germany*, as well as several other articles in that volume.

16. See Daniel Hough, "East German Identity and Party Politics," in *East German Distinctiveness in a Unified Germany*, ed. Grix and Cooke, 99–117; Ritter, *The Price of German Unity*, 47–53; and chapter 2 in Cooke, *Representing East Germany since Unification*, 46–53. For specific analyses of political election campaigns and rhetoric in east Germany, see Ruth Geier, "Die Welt der schönen Bilder: Wahlwerbung in Ostdeutschland—Wahlwerbung für Ostdeutsche?," and Johannes Volmert, "Wahlkampf-Rhetorik: Ludger Volmer und Gregor Gysi im 'Nachtduell' des ZDF," both *Von "Buschzulage" und "Ossinachweis,"* ed. Reiher and Läzer, 229–44 and 245–64, respectively.

17. For the 1995 survey, see Ahbe, *Ostalgie*, 37. Ahbe discusses the surveys from the early twenty-first century in his essay "Competing Master Narratives: *Geschichtspolitik* and Identity Discourse in Three German Societies," in *The GDR Remembered: Representations of the East German State since 1989*, ed. Nick Hodgin and Caroline Pearce (Rochester, NY: Camden House, 2011), 220–31.

18. For a brief elaboration of Sabrow's analysis of memory, see "Die DDR erinnern" in his collected anthology of essays *Zeitgeschichte schreiben: Von der Verständigung über die Vergangenheit in der Gegenwart* (Göttingen: Wallstein Verlag, 2014), 275–88. For a longer analysis and related discus-

sions, see Martin Sabrow, ed., *Erinnerungsorte der DDR* (Munich: C. H. Beck, 2009). Closely related to and expanding on this is Michael Meyen's intriguing study *"Wir haben freier gelebt": Die DDR im kollektiven Gedächtnis der Deutschen* (Bielefeld: Transcript, 2013), especially the last part "Die DDR im kommunikativen Gedächtnis der Deutschen," which is based on focus group discussions.

19. For an overview of the four-generation model during GDR history, see Bernd Lindner, "Die Generation der Unberatenen," in *Die DDR aus generationengeschichtlicher Perspektive: Eine Inventur*, ed. Annegret Schüle, Thomas Ahbe, and Rainer Gries (Leipzig: Leipziger Universitätsverlag, 2006), 96–97.

20. See Mary Fulbrook, "Living Through the GDR: History, Life Stories, and Generations in East Germany," in *The GDR Remembered*, ed. Hodgin and Pearce, 201–20. The significant generational differences are also powerfully illustrated in Martin Diewald, Anne Goedicke, and Karl Ulrich Mayer, eds., *After the Fall of the Wall: Life Courses and the Transformation of East Germany* (Stanford: Stanford University Press, 2006). As Rainer Gries's article in the same volume highlights, generational belonging also had a tremendous impact in terms of the *Ostalgie* discourse: "Waren und Produkte als Generationenmarker: Generationen der DDR im Spiegel ihrer Konsumhorizonte," 271–300. Finally, these different generational perspectives have also become the focal point of many *Wende*-novels, as Susanne Bach highlights in her study *Wende-Generationen/Generationen-Wende: Literarische Lebenswelten vor dem Horizont der Wiedervereinigung—Mit Autoreninterviews* (Heidelberg: Universitätsverlag Winter, 2017).

21. See Zsuzsa Gille's discussion of the concept of heteroglossia in connection with *Ostalgie* in the postscript of the volume edited by Maria Todorova and Zsuzsa Gille, *Post-Communist Nostalgia* (New York and Oxford: Berghahn Books, 2010), 278–89. On a discussion of the different layers of the *Ostalgie* discourse, see Thomas Ahbe, "Competing Master-Narratives: *Geschichtspolitik* and Identity Discourse in Three German Societies," in *The GDR Remembered*, ed. Hodgin and Pearce, 231–39. Martin Sabrow's edited volume *Wohin treibt die DDR-Erinnerung: Dokumentation einer Debatte* (Göttingen: Vandenhoeck & Ruprecht, 2007) also provides great insights into the continuing and deep divisions related to GDR historiography. The role of museum exhibits and memorials is discussed in Hodgin and Pearce, *The GDR Remembered*, part 2, as well as Chloe Paver's essay "Colour and Time in Museums of East German Everyday Life," in *Remembering and Rethinking the GDR*, ed. Saunders and Pinfold, 132–46; on this same theme, see Bill Niven and Chloe Paver, eds., *Memorialization in Germany since 1945* (New York: Palgrave Macmillan, 2010), part 4.

22. On the respective winners and losers during the *Wende* period, see Ritter, *The Price of German Unity*, 96–101, as well as chapter 11 and the conclusion. For the reference to "third-class citizens," see Daphne Berdahl, "The Spirit of Capitalism and the Boundaries of Citizenship in Post-Wall Germany," in *On*

the *Social Life of Postsocialism*," ed. Bunzl, 95. For the term "lost generation," see the conclusion in Diewald, Goedicke, and Mayer, *After the Fall of the Wall*, 304.

23. See several of the articles in the anthology edited by Hannes Bahrmann and Christoph Links, *Am Ziel Vorbei: Die deutsche Einheit—Eine Zwischenbilanz* (Berlin: Ch. Links Verlag, 2005), especially in the sections focusing on politics and the economy.

24. The pay incentive is mentioned in Veenis's study, *Material Fantasies*, 207–12, and the joke is referenced in Berdahl, "Go, Trabi, Go!," in *On the Social Life of Postsocialism*, ed. Bunzl, 67. For a discussion of the hardening and overall receding portrayal of East Germans in the media, see Thomas Ahbe, Rainer Gries, and Wolfgang Schmale, eds., *Die Ostdeutschen in den Medien: Das Bild von den "Anderen" nach 1990* (Leipzig: Leipziger Universitätsverlag, 2009); and Meyen, "Wir haben freier gelebt," chapter 4. The 2008 survey is cited in Christian Kolmer's essay, "Nachrichten aus einer Krisenregion. Das Bild Ostdeutschlands und der DDR in den Medien, 1994-2007," in *Die Ostdeutschen in den Medien*, ed. Ahbe, Gries, and Schmale, 182. Nick Hodgin states that only about 10 percent of West Germans had visited the GDR during its existence; see *Screening the East*, 18.

25. Berdahl's notion of *Ostalgie* as "counter-memory" is discussed in her essay "Expressions of Experience and Experiences of Expression: Museum Re-presentations of GDR History," and her excellent analysis of the film in "Goodbye Lenin, Auf Wiedersehen GDR: On the Social Life of Socialism," both in *On the Social Life of Postsocialism*, ed. Bunzl, 121–22, 123–33, respectively; see also Nick Hodgin's analysis in *Screening the East*, chapter 6. On the notion of *Ostalgie* as an imagined past, see the introduction to Hodgin and Caroline, *The GDR Remembered*. The editors also cite Christoph Dieckmann's telling definition of *Ostalgie*: "Ostalgie bezeichnet das Heimweh nach einer DDR, wie sie gewesen wäre, wenn sie nicht die DDR gewesen wäre" (p. 11).

26. Paul Cooke, "Ostalgie's Not What It Used to Be: The German Television Craze of 2003," *German Politics & Society* 22, no. 4 (2004): 134–50. See also Cooke's book *Representing East Germany since Unification*, especially chapters 4–5; Hodgin, *Screening the East*, chapter 6; and Mary-Elizabeth O'Brien, "The Afterlife of the GDR in Post-Wall German Cinema," in *Virtual Walls? Political Unification and Cultural Difference in Contemporary Germany*, ed. Franziska Lys and Michael Dreyer (Rochester, NY: Camden House, 2017), 72–95. For another analysis of GDR-themed TV shows in the late 2000s, see Patricia Feise-Mahnkopp, "'Wir sind das Volk'—auf der Couch zur Primetime?," in *Grenzenlos: Mauerfall und Wende in (Kinder- und Jugend-) Literatur und Medien*, ed. Ute Dettmar and Mareile Oetken (Heidelberg: Universitätsverlag Winter, 2010), 77–95.

27. The quote is by Peter Thompson and is cited in Karen Leeder, ed., *Rereading East Germany: The Literature and Film of the GDR* (Cambridge: Cambridge

University Press, 2015), introduction, 1–2. See also Hodgin, *Screening the East*, chapter 6, as well as his article "Screening the Stasi: The Politics of Representation in Postunification Film," in *The GDR Remembered*, ed. Hodgin and Pearce, chapter 4. Likewise, see Alke Vierck's essay "Der horchende Blick: Hören und Sehen in Donnersmarcks *Das Leben der Anderen* (2006)," in *NachBilder der Wende*, ed. Inge Stephan and Alexandra Tracke (Cologne: Böhlau Verlag, 2008), 215–36.

28. The overall increase of Western and especially American TV imports in Eastern European countries in the 1990s and early 2000s is highlighted in several articles of the anthology *Popular Television in Eastern Europe during and since Socialism*, ed. Anikó Imre, Timothy Havens, and Katalin Lustyik (New York and London: Routledge, 2013); see the introduction as well as chapters 7 and 9, on Hungary and Poland respectively. Similarly, for the full embrace of Hollywood in Serbia and the widespread appeal of American culture in Poland, see Vlastimir Sudar, "Belgrade as New York: The Voluntary Americanization of Serbian Cinema," in *Postcommunist Film—Russia, Eastern Europe and World Culture: Moving Images of Postcommunism*, ed. Lar Kristensen (London and New York: Routledge, 2012), 35–52; and Magdalena Ziólek, "American Smiles on Polish Faces: American Culture in the Discourse of Globalization from the Perspective of the Polish Young Generation," in *Ambivalent Americanizations: Popular and Consumer Culture in Central and Eastern Europe*, ed. Sebastian M. Herrmann et al. (Heidelberg: Universitätsverlag Winter, 2008), 211–32. On the sobering effects of direct contact with the West, by contrast, see among others Alexei Yurchak, *Everything Was Forever, Until It Was No More: The Last Soviet Generation* (Princeton, NJ, and Oxford: Princeton University Press, 2005), chapter 5; Sibelan Forrester, Magdalena J. Zaborowska, and Elena Gapova, *Over the Wall/After the Fall: Post-Communist Cultures through an East-West Gaze* (Bloomington and Indianapolis: Indiana University Press, 2004); and Todorova and Gille, *Post-Communist Nostalgia*.

29. I am utilizing here Eli Ruben's translation of *Eigensinn* based on his essay "Consumption, Eigen-Sinn, and Movement," *History Workshop Journal* 68, no. 3 (2009): 28; and a slightly altered version of Paul Cooke's translation of *Trotzidentität* from his book *Representing East Germany since Unification*, 8.

30. Based on Michel Foucault's concept of "contre-mémoire," Carsten Gansel uses this notion of "counter-memory" in his discussion of East German literature in his article "Atlantiseffekte in der Literatur? Zur Inszenierung von Erinnerung an die verschwundene DDR," in *Grenzenlos*, ed. Dettmar and Oetken, 17–49. Much like Berdahl highlighted, *Ostalgie* culture functioned and functions in a very similar fashion.

31. For a discussion of the political state of affairs in Germany on the twenty-year anniversary of reunification, see Konrad H. Jarausch, ed., *United Germany: Debating Processes and Prospects* (New York and Oxford: Berghahn Books, 2013), especially the introduction by Jarausch as well as the articles

in part 1. The continued trend of German television shows with a GDR or east German focus are discussed by Gabrielle Mueller, "Re-imagining the Niche: Visual Reconstructions of Private Spaces in the GDR," in *Remembering and Rethinking the GDR*, ed. Saunders and Pinfold, 205–11.

32. See Jill E. Twark's excellent study *Humor, Satire, and Identity: Eastern German Literature in the 1990s* (Berlin and New York: De Gruyter, 2007). Twark emphasizes both the criticism of the West as well as the humorous play with the language of capitalism as core elements of these authors. In her interviews, a number of writers make the connections between pre- and post-Wall humor as well as the liberating power of laughter; see, for example, the interviews with Thomas Rosenlöcher and Reinhard Ulbricht. The term of East Germans as "objects of history" is used by Rosenlöcher (p. 346). This prominent focus of east German writers is also highlighted by Kerstin Reimann in her study *Schreiben nach der Wende—Wende im Schreiben?*, especially chapter 5. See also Ingo Schulze, *Unsere schönen neuen Kleider: Gegen die marktkonforme Demokratie—für demokratiekonforme Märkte* (Munich: Carl Hanser Verlag, 2012). On his literary and political impact, see Heinz Ludwig Arnold, ed., *Ingo Schulze*, Text + Kritik: Zeitschrift für Literatur 193 (Munich: Richard Boorberg Verlag, January 2012).

33. For a 15-year-anniversary perspective, see Bahrmann and Links, *Am Ziel Vorbei*. For two 20-year-anniversary anthologies with different emphases, see Jarausch, *United Germany*; and Elisa Goudin-Steinmann and Carola Hähnel-Mesnard, eds., *Ostdeutsche Erinnerungsdiskurse nach 1989: Narrative kultureller Identität* (Berlin: Frank & Timme, 2013). A more limited 25-year-anniversary view on east Germany development and identity is provided by the anthology of essays edited by Leeder, *Rereading East Germany*.

Bibliography

Unpublished Sources

Archives

Archives at the University of Illinois, Urbana-Champaign (UCIC)

Avery Brundage Collection

Bibliothek der Hochschule für Film und Fernsehen "Konrad Wolf"
(HFF "Konrad Wolf"), Berlin

Pressedokumentation

Bundesarchiv-Filmarchiv, Berlin

DEFA-Aussenhandel Files

Bundesarchiv Koblenz (BAK)

Bundeskanzleramt (B 136)
Bundesnachrichtendienst (B 206)
Organisationskomitee für die Spiele der XX. Olympiade München 1972 (B 185)

Bundesbeauftragter für die Unterlagen des Staatssicherheitsdienstes
der ehemaligen DDR (BStU), Berlin

BStU Chemnitz
BV Berlin
BVfS Leipzig

Deutsches Rundfunkarchiv Babelsberg (DRA Babelsberg)

Historisches Archiv—*Die lieben Mitmenschen*, Sendeunterlagen, Einzelfolgen &
    Zuschauerpost
Historisches Archiv—Hörerpost
Historisches Archiv—*Rentner Haben Niemals Zeit*; Sendeunterlagen,
    Einzelfolgen & Zuschauerpost

Historisches Archiv—Serienproduktion, Presseabteilung
Historisches Archiv—*Treffpunkt Flughafen; Zahn um Zahn; Neues übern Gartenzaun*
Historisches Archiv—Unterhaltung

Friedrich-Ebert Stiftung Bonn (FES)—Archiv der sozialen Demokratie (AdsD), Bonn

Egon Bahr Papers
Pressedokumentation

Ministerium für Auswärtige Angelengenheiten der DDR (MfAA), Berlin

Abteilung USA

National Archives at College Park, Maryland

General Records of the Department of State
NSC Files, Nixon Papers
Records of the United States Information Agency, Office of Research (RG 306)
Tapes of Nixon White House Conversations

Stiftung Archiv der Parteien und Massenorganisationen der DDR im Bundesarchiv Berlin (SAPMO-BArch)

Hauptverwaltung Film (DR 1)
Institut für Marktforschung (DL 102)
Kommerzielle Koordinierung, KoKo (DL 226)
Ministerium für Handel und Versorgung (DL 1)
SED, Abteilung Kultur & Abteilung Agitation; Büro Erich Honecker; Büro Hager; Büro Adameck, Korrespondenz (DY 30)
Sekretariat des Ministerrats (DC 20)
Staatliches Komitee für Rundfunk (DR 6)
Staatliches Komitee für Fernsehen (DR 8)
Zentralinstitut für Jugendforschung (DC 4)

Dissertations and Habilitationsschriften

Bauhaus, Andreas. "Jugendpresse, -hörfunk und –fernsehen in der DDR. Ein Spagat zwischen FDJ-Interessen und Rezipientenbedürfnissen." Dissertation, Universität Münster, 1994.
Chalip, Laurence Hilmond. "The Framing of Policy: Explaining the Transformation of American Sport." PhD dissertation, University of Chicago, 1988.
Friedrich, Alexandra. "Awakenings: The Impact of the Vietnam War on West German–American Relations in the late 1960s." PhD dissertation, Temple University, 2000.

Garncarz, Joseph. "Populäres Kino in Deutschland: Internationalisierung einer Film Kultur, 1925–1990." Habilitationsschrift, 1996.
Yamac, Alva. "Jugendradio DT 64 zum Ende der DDR (1987–1991)." Diplomarbeit, Fachhochschule Mittweida, 2005.

Filmography

All the President's Men
Apocalypse Now
Aristocats
Blade Runner
Blutige Erdbeeren (*Strawberry Statement*)
Bound for Glory
Chinatown
Der grosse Bluff (*Destry Rides Again*)
Einer flog über das Kuckucksnest (*One Flew Over the Cuckoo's Nest*)
Funny Girl
In der Hitze der Nacht (*In the Heat of the Night*)
Little Big Man
Nur Pferden gibt man den Gnadenschuss (*They Shoot Horses—Don't They?*)
On the Waterfront
West Side Story

Periodicals

Baltimore Sun
Charleston Gazette
Christian Science Monitor
Eulenspiegel
Frankfurter Rundschau
Junge Welt (Berlin)
Montreal Gazette
Der Morgen (Berlin)
Neues Deutschland
Der Neue Weg (Halle)
Ostsee-Zeitung (Rostock)
Sächsisches Tageblatt
Sächsische Zeitung (Dresden)
San Francisco Examiner/Chronicle
Sonntag (Berlin)
Sports Illustrated
Thüringische Landzeitung (Weimar)

Time
Das Volk (Erfurt)
Volkswacht (Gera)

Secondary Literature

Ahbe, Thomas. *Ostalgie: Zum Umgang mit der DDR-Vergangenheit in den 1990er Jahren*. Erfurt: Landeszentrale für politische Bildung Thüringen, 2005.
———. "Competing Master Narratives: *Geschichtspolitik* and Identity Discourse in Three German Societies." In *The GDR Remembered*, edited by Hodgin and Pearce.
Ahbe, Thomas, Rainer Gries, and Wolfgang Schmale, eds. *Die Ostdeutschen in den Medien: Das Bild von den "Anderen" nach 1990*. Leipzig: Leipziger Universitätsverlag, 2009.
Ahrens, Ralf. "Debt, Cooperation and Collapse: East German Foreign Trade in the Honecker Years." In *The East German Economy, 1945–2010*, edited by Berghoff and Balbier.
Allan, Seán, and John Sandford, eds. *DEFA: East German Cinema, 1946–1992*. New York and Oxford: Berghahn Books, 1999.
Alter, Nora. *Projecting History: German Nonfiction Cinema, 1967–2000*. Ann Arbor: University of Michigan Press, 2002.
Antoszek, Andrzej, and Kate Delaney. "Poland: Transmissions and Translations." In *The Americanization of Europe: Culture, Diplomacy, and Anti-Americanism after 1945*, edited by Alexander Stephan. New York and Oxford: Berghahn Books, 2006.
Arendt, Joachim. *Johnson, Vietnam, und der Westen: Transatlantische Beziehungen, 1963–1969*. Munich: Olzog Verlag, 1994.
Arnaud, Pierre, and James Riordan, eds. *Sports and International Politics*. London and New York: E & FN Spon, 1998.
Arnold, Klaus, and Christoph Classen, eds. *Zwischen Pop und Propaganda: Radio in der DDR*. Berlin: Ch. Links Verlag, 2004.
Arnold, Klaus. "Musikbox mit Volkserziehungsauftrag: Radio in der DDR I. Radio zwischen Partei und Publikum." In *Wie im Westen, nur anders*, edited by Zahlmann.
Bach, Susanne. *Wende-Generationen/Generationen-Wende: Literarische Lebenswelten vor dem Horizont der Wiedervereinigung—Mit Autoreninterviews*. Heidelberg: Universitätsverlag Winter, 2017.
Bahrmann, Hannes, and Christoph Links, eds. *Am Ziel Vorbei: Die deutsche Einheit—Eine Zwischenbilanz*. Berlin: Ch. Links Verlag, 2005.
Balbier, Uta A. "'Der Welt das modern Deutschland vorstellen': Die Eröffnungsfeier der Spiele der XX. Olympiade in München 1972." In *Auswärtige Repräsentation: Deutsche Kulturpolitik nach 1945*, edited by Johannes Paulmann. Cologne, Weimar, and Vienna: Böhlau Verlag, 2005.

———. *Kalter Krieg auf der Aschenbahn: Der deutsch-deutsche Sport, 1952–1972: Eine politische Geschichte.* Paderborn: Ferdinand Schöningh, 2007.
Balbier, Uta A., and Christiane Rösch, eds. *Umworbener Klassenfeind: Das Verhältnis der DDR zu den USA.* Berlin: Ch. Links Verlag, 2006.
Bange, Oliver, and Gottfried Niedhart, eds. *Helsinki 1975 and the Transformation of Europe.* New York and Oxford: Berghahn Books, 2008.
Barck, Simone, Christoph Classen, and Thomas Heimann, "The Fettered Media." In *Dictatorship as Experience*, edited by Jarausch.
Berdahl, Daphne. *Where the World Ended: Re-unification and Identity in the German Borderland.* Berkeley: University of California Press, 1999.
———. "Consumption Rites: The Politics of Consumption in a Unified Germany." In *On the Social Life of Postsocialism*, edited by Bunzl.
———. "Expressions of Experience and Experiences of Expression: Museum Re-presentations of GDR History." In *On the Social Life of Postsocialism*, edited by Bunzl.
———. "'Go, Trabi, Go!': Reflections on a Car and Its Symbolization over Time." In *On the Social Life of Postsocialism*, edited by Bunzl.
———. "(N)Ostalgie for the Present: Memory, Longing, and East German Things." In *On the Social Life of Postsocialism*, edited by Bunzl.
———. "The Spirit of Capitalism and the Boundaries of Citizenship in Post-Wall Germany." In *On the Social Life of Postsocialism*," edited by Bunzl.
Berghahn, Daniela. *Hollywood behind the Wall: The Cinema of East Germany.* Manchester and New York: Manchester University Press, 2005.
Berghoff, Hartmut, and Uta Andrea Balbier, eds. *The East German Economy, 1945–2010: Falling Behind or Catching Up?* New York: German Historical Institute and Cambridge University Press, 2013.
Binas, Susanne. "Kassetten als Kassiber." In *Wir wollen immer artig sein . . .* , edited by Galenza and Havemeister.
Bisky, Lothar, and Dieter Wiedemann. *Der Spielfilm—Rezeption und Wirkung. Kultursoziologische Analysen.* Berlin: Henschelverlag, 1985.
Blasius, Tobias. *Olympische Bewegung, Kalter Krieg und Deutschlandpolitik, 1949–1972.* Frankfurt am Main: Peter Lang Verlag, 2001.
Bock, Siegfried, Ingrid Muth, and Hermann Schwiesau, eds. *DDR-Aussenpolitik im Rückspiegel: Diplomaten im Gespräch.* Münster: LIT Verlag, 2004.
Bösch, Frank, ed. *A History Shared and Divided: East and West Germany since the 1970s.* New York and Oxford: Berghahn Books, 2018.
Borejsza, Jerzy W., and Klaus Zimmer, eds. *Totalitarian and Authoritarian Regimes in Europe: Legacies and Lessons from the Twentieth Century.* New York and Oxford: Berghahn Books, 2006.
Boyer, Christoph. "Stabilisation of Power through Social and Consumer Policy in the GDR." In *Totalitarian and Authoritarian Regimes in Europe*, edited by Borejsza and Zimmer.
Braune, Thomas. "Gegen allerschärfste Anweisungen: *DT 64* Journalismus zwischen 1985 und 1989." In *DT64*, edited by Ulrich and Wagner.

Bren, Paulina. *The Greengrocer and His TV: The Culture of Communism after the 1968 Prague Spring*. Ithaca and London: Cornell University Press, 2010.
———. "Mirror, Mirror, on the Wall . . . Is the West the Fairest of Them All? Czechoslovakian Normalization and Its (Dis)Contents." In *Imagining the West in Eastern Europe and the Soviet Union*, edited by Péteri.
———. "Tuzex and the Hustler: Living It Up in Czechoslovakia." In *Communism Unwrapped*, edited by Bren and Neuburger.
Bren, Paulina, and Mary Neuburger, eds. *Communism Unwrapped: Consumption in Cold War Eastern Europe*. Oxford and New York: Oxford University Press, 2012.
Bunzl, Matti, ed. *On the Social Life of Postsocialism: Memory, Consumption, Germany*. Bloomington and Indianapolis: Indiana University Press, 2010.
Burdumy, Alexander. "Reconsidering the Role of the Welfare State within the German Democratic Republic's Political System." *Journal of Contemporary History* 48, no. 4 (October 2013): 872–89.
———. *Sozialpolitik und Repression in der DDR: Ost-Berlin, 1971–1989*. Essen: Klartext Verlag, 2013.
Childs, David. "East Germany: Towards the Twentieth Anniversary." *World Today* 23, no. 10 (October 1969).
Ciesla, Burghard. "Hinter den Zahlen: Zur Wirtschaftsstatistik und Wirtschaftsberichterstattung in der DDR." In *Akten. Eingaben. Schaufenster*, edited by Lüdtke and Becker.
Classen, Christoph. "Captive Audience? GDR Radio in the Mirror of Listeners' Mail." In *Cold War History* 13, no. 2 (2013), 239–254.
———. "'Um die Empfangsmöglichkeiten...des Senders RIAS völlig auszuschalten...' Störsender in der DDR 1952–1988." *Rundfunk und Geschichte* 40, no. 3–4 (2014): 25–40.
———. "Enemies, Spies, and the Bomb. Cold War Cinema in Comparison: Germany and the USA (1948–1970)." In *The Cold War. History, Memory, and Representation*, edited by Andreas Etges, Konrad H. Jarausch, and Christian Ostermann. Oldenbourg: De Gruyter 2017.
———. "Medialization in Opposing Systems: Approaching a Media History of Divided Germany." *German Historical Institute London Bulletin* 41, no. 1 (May 2019), 19–49.
Cook, David A. *Lost Illusions: American Cinema in the Shadow of Watergate and Vietnam, 1970–1979*. Berkeley and Los Angeles: University of California Press, 2000.
Cooke, Paul. "Ostalgie's Not What It Used to Be: The German Television Craze of 2003." *German Politics & Society* 22, no. 4 (Winter 2004): 134–50.
———. *Representing East Germany since Unification: From Colonization to Nostalgia*. Oxford and New York: Berg, 2005.
Crew, David F., ed. *Consuming Germany in the Cold War*. Oxford and New York: Berg, 2003.

Crowley, David, and Susan E. Reid, eds. *Pleasures in Socialism: Leisure and Luxury in the Eastern Bloc*. Evanston, IL: Northwestern University Press, 2010.
Csatári, Bence, and Béla Szilárd Jávorszky. "Omega: Red Star from Hungary." In *Popular Music in Eastern Europe*, edited by Mazierska.
Cunningham, John. *Hungarian Cinema: From Coffee House to Multiplex*. London and New York: Wallflower Press, 2004.
Daum, Andrew W., Lloyd C. Gardner, and Wilfried Mausbach, eds. *America, the Vietnam War, and the World: Comparative and International Perspectives*. Publications of the German Historical Institute. Washington, DC, and Cambridge: Cambridge University Press, 2003.
Dettmar, Ute, and Mareile Oetken, eds. *Grenzenlos: Mauerfall und Wende in (Kinder- und Jugend) Literatur und Medien*. Heidelberg: Universitätsverlag Winter, 2010.
Dieckmann, Christoph. "Küche, Kammer, Weite Welt: Mythen der Erinnerung." In *Bye Bye Lübben City*, edited by Rauhut and Kochan.
Diewald, Martin, Anne Goedicke, and Karl Ulrich Mayer, eds. *After the Fall of the Wall: Life Courses and the Transformation of East Germany*. Stanford: Stanford University Press, 2006.
Dittmar, Claudia. "GDR Television in Competition with West German Programming." *Historical Journal for Film, Radio and Television* 24, no. 3 (2004): 327–43.
———. *Feindliches Fernsehen: Das DDR-Fernsehen und seine Strategien im Umgang mit dem Westdeutschen Fernsehen*. Bielefeld: Transcript Verlag, 2010.
———. "Opfer ihrer eigenen Propaganda: Die Eliten des DDR-Fernsehens und ihre Auseinandersetzung mit dem 'Westfernsehen.'" In *Rhetorik der Selbsttäuschung*, edited by Bettina Radelski and Gerd Antos. Berlin: Frank und Timme, 2014.
Dombos, Tamas, and Lena Pellandini-Simanyi. "Kids, Cars, or Cashews? Debating and Remembering Consumption in Socialist Hungary." In *Communism Unwrapped*, edited by Bren and Neuburger.
Dussel, Konrad. *Hörfunk in Deutschland: Politik, Programm, Publikum (1923–1960)*. Potsdam: Verlag für Brandenburg, 2002.
———. "Rundfunk in der Bundesrepublik und der DDR: Überlegungen zum systematischen Vergleich." In *Zwischen Pop und Propoganda*, edited by Arnold and Classen.
Eichholz, Anita. *Der Vietnamkrieg im SPIEGEL: Eine inhaltsanalytische Untersuchung*. Berlin: Verlag Volker Spiess, 1979.
Elsaesser, Thomas. *European Cinema: Face to Face with Hollywood*. Amsterdam: Amsterdam University Press, 2005.
Feinstein, Joshua. *The Triumph of the Ordinary: Depictions of Daily Life in the East German Cinema, 1949–1989*. Chapel Hill and London: University of North Carolina Press, 2002.

Feise-Mahnkopp, Patricia. "'Wir sind das Volk'—auf der Couch zur Primetime?" In *Grenzenlos*, edited by Dettmar and Oetken.
Fensch, Eberhard. *So und nur noch besser: Wie Honecker das Fernsehen wollte*. Berlin: edition ost, 2003.
Fink, Carole, and Bernd Schaefer, eds. *Ostpolitik, 1969–1974: European and Global Responses*. New York: Cambridge University Press, 2009.
Forrester, Sibelan, Magdalena J. Zaborowska, and Elena Gapova. *Over the Wall/After the Fall: Post-Communist Cultures through an East-West Gaze*. Bloomington and Indianapolis: Indiana University Press, 2004.
Franck, Julia, ed. *Grenzübergänge: Autoren aus Ost und West erinnern sich*. Frankfurt am Main: Fischer Verlag, 2009.
Freedman, Paul. "Luxury Dining in the Later Years of the German Democratic Republic." In *Becoming East German*, edited by Fulbrook and Port.
Fricke, Karl-Wilhelm, Peter Steinbach, and Johannes Tuchel, eds. *Opposition und Widerstand in der DDR: Politische Lebensbilder*. Munich: C. H. Beck Verlag, 2002.
Fulbrook, Mary. *Anatomy of a Dictatorship: Inside the GDR, 1949–1989*. Oxford and New York: Oxford University Press, 1998.
———. *The People's State: East German Society from Hitler to Honecker*. New Haven and London: Yale University Press, 2005.
———. *Dissonant Lives: Generations and Violence through the German Dictatorships*. Oxford and New York: Oxford University Press, 2011.
———. "Living Through the GDR: History, Life Stories, and Generations in East Germany." In *The GDR Remembered*, edited by Hodgin and Pearce.
Fulbrook, Mary, and Andrew I. Port, eds. *Becoming East German: Socialist Structures and Sensibilities after Hitler*. New York and Oxford: Berghahn Books, 2013.
Fürst, Juliane, and Josie McLellan, eds. *Dropping Out of Socialism: The Creation of Alternative Spheres in the Soviet Bloc*. Lanham, MD, and London: Lexington Books, 2017.
Gaddis, John Lewis. *The Cold War: A New History*. New York: Penguin Books, 2007.
Gaiduk, Ilya V. *The Soviet Union and the Vietnam War*. Chicago: Ivan R. Dee, 1996.
Galenza, Ronald. "Glatzen & Bombenjacken: Skinheads in der DDR." In *Wir wollen immer artig sein . . .* , edited by Galenza and Havemeister.
Galenza, Roland, and Heinz Havemeister, eds. *Wir wollen immer artig sein . . . : Punk, New Wave, Hiphop, und Independent-Szene in der DDR von 1980 bis 1990*. Berlin: Schwarzkopf & Schwarzkopf, 2013.
Gansel, Carsten. "Atlantiseffekte in der Literatur? Zur Inszenierung von Erinnerung an die verschwundene DDR" In *Grenzenlos*, edited by Dettmar and Oetken.
Gardner, Lloyd C., and Ted Gittinger, eds. *International Perspectives on Vietnam*. College Station: Texas A&M University Press, 2000.

Geier, Ruth. "Die Welt der schönen Bilder: Wahlwerbung in Ostdeutschland—Wahlwerbung für Ostdeutsche?" In *Von "Buschzulage" und "Ossinachweis,"* edited by Reiher and Läzer.
Gemünden, Gerd. "Between Karl May and Karl Marx: The DEFA Indianerfilme (1965–1983)." *New German Critique* 82 (Winter 2001): 25–38.
Gerrard, Kate. "Punk and the State of Youth in the GDR." In *Youth and Rock in the Soviet Bloc*, edited by Risch.
Geyer, David C., and Bernd Schaefer, eds. *American Détente and German Ostpolitik, 1969–1972*. Washington, DC: German Historical Institute, 2004.
Geyer, Martin H. "Der Kampf um die nationale Repräsentation: Deutsch-deutsche Sportbeziehungen und die 'Hallstein-Doktrin'." *Vierteljahreshefte für Zeitgeschichte* 44, no. 1 (January 1996): 55–86.
———. "On the Road to a German 'Postnationalism'? Athletic Competition between the Two German States in the Era of Konrad Adenauer." *German Politics and Society* 25, no. 2 (Summer 2007): 140–67.
Glaeßner, Gert-Joachim, ed. *Die DDR in der Ära Honecker: Politik—Kultur—Gesellschaft*. Opladen: Westdeutscher Verlag, 1988.
Goddard, Peter, ed. *Popular Television in Authoritarian Europe*. Manchester and New York: Manchester University Press, 2013.
Goudin-Steinmann, Elisa, and Carola Hähnel-Mesnard, eds. *Ostdeutsche Erinnerungsdiskurse nach 1989: Narrative kultureller Identität*. Berlin: Frank & Timme, 2013.
Gries, Rainer. *Produkte als Medien: Kulturgeschichte der Produktkommunikation in der Bundesrepublik und der DDR*. Leipzig: Leipziger Universitätsverlag, 2003.
Grix, Jonathan. *The Role of the Masses in the Collapse of the GDR*. London and New York: Macmillan, 2000.
Grix, Jonathan, and Paul Cooke, eds. *East German Distinctiveness in a Unified Germany*. Birmingham: University of Birmingham Press, 2002.
Grossman, Victor. "Sauerstoff im stickigen Leipzig: Eindrücke eines US-Amerikaners von der Internationalen Dokumentarfilmwoche in Leipzig." In *Umworbener Klassenfeind*, edited by Balbier and Rösch.
Gumbert, Heather L. *Envisioning Socialism: Television and the Cold War in the German Democratic Republic*. Ann Arbor: University of Michigan Press, 2014.
Gutmann, Gernot, and Hannsjörg F. Buck. "Die Zentralplanwirtschaft der DDR—Funktionsweise, Funktionsschwächen und Konkursbilanz." In *Die wirtschaftliche und ökologische Situation der DDR in den 80er Jahren*, edited by Kuhrt.
Guttmann, Allen. *The Games Must Go On: Avery Brundage and the Olympic Movement*. New York: Columbia University Press, 1984.
Hake, Sabine. *German National Cinema*. London and New York: Routledge, 2002.
Hallenberg, Gerd, et al. "Programmstrukturen in BRD und DDR." In *Zwei Mal zur Wende*, edited by Mühl-Benninghaus.

Hanrieder, Wolfram F. *Germany, America, Europe: Forty Years of German Foreign Policy*. New Haven and London: Yale University Press, 1989.
Harsch, Donna. *Revenge of the Domestic: Women, the Family and Communism in the German Democratic Republic*. Princeton and Oxford: Princeton University Press, 2007.
Hartmann, Grit. *Goldkinder: Die DDR im Spiegel ihres Spitzensports*. Leipzig: Forum Verlag Leipzig, 1997.
Haslam, Jonathan. *Russia's Cold War: From the October Revolution to the Fall of the Wall*. New Haven and London: Yale University Press, 2011.
Hayton, Jeff. "Ignoring Dictatorship? Punk Rock, Subculture, and Entanglement in the GDR." In *Dropping Out of Socialism*, edited by Fürst and McLellan.
Heinze, Helmut, and Doris Rosenstein, eds. *Zum Fernsehspiel und zur Fernsehserie in der DDR*. Siegen: Bildschirmhefte 71, 1997.
Heldmann, Philipp. *Herrschaft, Wirtschaft, Anoraks: Konsumpolitik in der DDR der Sechzigerjahre*. Göttingen: Vandenhoeck & Ruprecht, 2004.
Henke, Klaus-Dietmar, Peter Steinbach, and Johannes Tuchel, eds. *Widerstand und Opposition in der DDR*. Cologne, Weimar, and Vienna: Böhlau Verlag, 1999.
Hepp, Andreas. *Cultures of Mediatization*. Cambridge and Malden, MA: Polity Press, 2013.
Herrmann, Sebastian M., et al., eds. *Ambivalent Americanizations: Popular and Consumer Culture in Central and Eastern Europe*. Heidelberg: Universitätsverlag Winter, 2008.
Hertle, Hans Hermann. "Die DDR an die Sowjetunion verkaufen? Stasi-Analysen zum ökonomischen Niedergang der DDR." *Deutschland Archiv* 42, no. 3 (2009): 476–95.
Hesse, Kurt R. *Westmedien in der DDR. Nutzung, Image und Auswirkungen bundesrepublikanischen Hörfunks und Fernsehens*. Cologne: Böhlau Verlag, 1988.
Hickethier, Knut. *Geschichte des deutschen Fernsehens*. Stuttgart and Weimar: Verlag J. B. Metzler, 1998.
Historische Kommission der ARD, ed. *Die Ideologiepolizei: Die rundfunkbezogenen Aktivitäten des Ministeriums für Staatssicherheit der ehemaligen DDR in der DDR sowie in der Bundesrepublik Deutschland*. Frankfurt am Main: Redaktion ARD Jahrbuch im Deutschen Rundfunkarchiv, 2008.
Hjarvard, Stig. *The Mediatization of Culture and Society*. London and New York: Routledge, 2013.
Hodgin, Nick. *Screening the East: "Heimat," Memory and Nostalgia in German Films since 1989*. New York and Oxford: Berghahn Books, 2011.
———. "Screening the Stasi: The Politics of Representation in Postunification Film." In *The GDR Remembered*, edited by Hodgin and Pearce.
Hodgin, Nick, and Caroline Pearce, eds. *The GDR Remembered: Representations of the East German State since 1989*. Rochester, NY: Camden House, 2011.

Hoff, Peter. "Wettbewerbspartner oder Konkurrent? Zum Verhältnis von Film, Kino und Fernsehen in der DDR." *Rundfunk und Fernsehen* 33, no. 3/4 (1985): 437–55.

Hogwood, Patricia. "'Red is for Love . . .': Citizens as Consumers in East Germany." In *East German Distinctiveness in a Unified Germany*, edited by Grix and Cooke.

Holtmann, Everhard, and Anne Köhler. *Wiedervereinigung vor dem Mauerfall: Einstellungen der Bevölkerung der DDR im Spiegel geheimer westlicher Meinungsumfragen*. Frankfurt and New York: Campus Verlag, 2015.

Holzweissig, Gunter. *Diplomatie im Trainingsanzug: Sport als politisches Instrument der DDR in den innerdeutschen und internationalen Beziehungen*. Munich and Vienna: R. Oldenbourg Verlag, 1981.

Horschig, Michael. "In der DDR hat es nie Punks gegeben." In *Wir wollen immer artig sein . . .* , edited by Galenza and Havemeister.

Horten, Gerd. "The Mediatization of War: A Comparison of the American and German Media Coverage of the Vietnam and Iraq Wars." *American Journalism: A Journal of Media History* 28, no. 4 (Fall 2011): 29–54.

———. "Sailing in the Shadow of the Vietnam War: The GDR Government and the 'Vietnam Bonus' of the Early 1970s." *German Studies Review* 36, no. 3 (2013): 557–78.

———. "The Impact of Hollywood Film Imports in East Germany and the Cultural Surrender of the GDR Film Control in the 1970s and 1980s." *German History* 34, no. 1 (2016): 70–87.

Hough, Daniel. "East German Identity and Party Politics." In *East German Distinctiveness in a Unified Germany*, edited by Grix and Cooke.

Howarth, Marianne. "Die Westpolitik der DDR zwischen internationaler Aufwertung und ideologischer Offensive (1966–1989)." In *Die DDR und der Westen*, edited by Pfeil.

Hunt, Thomas M. *Drug Games: The International Olympic Committee and the Politics of Doping, 1960–2008*. Austin: University of Texas Press, 2011.

Imre, Anikó, ed. *East European Cinemas*. New York and London: Routledge, 2005.

———. *TV Socialism*. Durham and London: Duke University Press, 2016.

Imre, Anikó, Timothy Havens, and Katalin Lustyik, eds. *Popular Television in Eastern Europe during and since Socialism*. New York and London: Routledge, 2013.

Jarausch, Konrad H. *The Rush to German Unity*. Oxford and New York: Oxford University Press, 1994.

———, ed. *Dictatorship as Experience: Towards a Socio-Cultural History of the GDR*. New York and Oxford: Berghahn Books, 2004.

———. "Beyond the National Narrative: Implications of Reunification for Recent German History." In "Contemporary History as Transatlantic Project: The German Problem, 1960–2000," supplement, *Historical Social Research/Historische Sozialforschung* 24 (2012).

———, ed. *United Germany: Debating Processes and Prospects*. New York and Oxford: Berghahn Books, 2013.
Jarausch, Konrad H., and Martin Sabrow, eds. *Weg in den Untergang: Der innere Zerfall der DDR*. Göttingen: Vandenhoeck & Ruprecht, 1999.
Judt, Matthias. "Periodisierung der Wirtschaft der DDR." In *Die Wirtschaft im geteilten und vereinten Deutschland*, edited by Karl Eckart and Jörg Roesler. Berlin: Duncker & Humblot, 1999.
———. *Koko—Mythos und Realität: Das Imperium des Alexander Schalck-Golodkowski*. Berlin: Edition Berolina, 2015.
Junes, Tom. "Facing the Music: How the Foundations of Socialism Were Rocked in Communist Poland." In *Youth and Rock in the Soviet Bloc*, edited by Risch.
Kaiser, Paul. "Heckenscheren gegen Feindfrisuren: Das Vokabular der Macht. Asozialität, Dekadenz und Untergrund." In *Bye Bye Lübben City*, edited by Rauhut and Kochan.
Kaminsky, Annette. "Ungleichheiten in der SBZ/DDR am Beispiel des Konsums: Versandhandel, Intershop und Delikat." In *Soziale Ungleichheit in der DDR*, edited by Mertens.
Kilian, Werner. *Die Hallstein-Doktrin: Der diplomatische Krieg zwischen der BRD und der DDR, 1955–1973*. Berlin: Duncker & Humblot, 2001.
Kirshner, Jonathan. *Hollywood's Last Golden Age: Politics, Society, and the Seventies Film in America*. Ithaca and London: Cornell University Press, 2012.
Kleßmann, Christoph. "Die Opposition in der DDR vom Beginn der Ära Honecker bis zur polnischen Revolution 1980/81." In *Möglichkeiten und Formen abweichenden und widerständigen Verhaltens und oppositionellen Handels, die friedliche Revoltuion im Herbst 1989, die Wiedervereinigung Deutschlands und das Fortwirken von Strukturen und Mechanismen der Diktatur*, edited by Enquette-Kommission. Frankfurt am Main: Suhrkamp Verlag, 1995.
———. *The Divided Past: Rewriting Post-War German History*. New York and Oxford: Berghahn Books, 2001.
Knabe, Hubertus. *Der Diskrete Charme der DDR: Stasi und Westmedien*. Berlin: Propyläen, 2001.
Knecht, Willi Ph. *Das Medaillenkollektiv: Fakten, Dokumente und Kommentare zum Sport in der DDR*. Berlin: Verlag Gebr. Holzapfel, 1978.
Kochan, Thomas. "Da hilft kein Jammern: Zwischen Resignation und Aufbegehren. Die Szene lebt den Blues." In *Bye Bye Lübben City*, edited by Rauhut and Kochan.
Kolmer, Christian. "Nachrichten aus einer Krisenregion. Das Bild Ostdeutschlands und der DDR in den Medien, 1994–2007." In *Die Ostdeutschen in den Medien*, edited by Ahbe, Gries, and Schmale.
Krewer, Peter. *Geschäfte mit dem Klassenfeind: Die DDR im innerdeutschen Handel, 1949–1989*. Trier: Kliomedia, 2007.
Kristensen, Lars, ed. *Postcommunist Film—Russia, Eastern Europe and World Culture: Moving Images of Postcommunism*. London and New York: Routledge, 2012.

Krüger, Stefan, and Wolfgang Mühl-Benninghaus, "'Fragments of Freedom': Fernsehunterhaltung und das Unterhaltungsverständnis für Jugendliche in Ost und West (1965–1990)." In *Zwei Mal zur Wende*, edited by Mühl-Benninghaus.

Küchler, Falk. *Die Wirtschaft der DDR: Wirtschaftspolitik und die industrielle Rahmenbedingungen 1949 bis 1989*. Berlin: FIDES Verlag, 1997.

Kuhrt, Eberhard, ed. *Die wirtschaftliche und ökologische Situation der DDR in den 80er Jahren*. Opladen: Leske + Budrich, 1996.

Kuhrt, Eberhard, et al., eds. *Die Endzeit der DDR-Wirtschaft—Analysen zur Wirtschafts-, Sozial- und Umweltpolitik*. Opladen: Leske + Budrich, 1999.

Kuschel, Franziska. *Schwarzhörer, Schwarzseher und heimliche Leser: Die DDR und die Westmedien*. Göttingen: Wallstein Verlag, 2016.

Landsman, Mark. *Dictatorship and Demand: The Politics of Consumerism in East Germany*. Cambridge, MA, and London: Harvard University Press, 2005.

Larkey, Edward. "GDR Rock Goes West: Finding a Voice in the West German Market." *German Politics & Society* 23, no. 4 (Winter 2005): 45–68.

———. *Rotes Rockradio: Populäre Musik und die Kommerzialisierung des DDR-Rundfunks*. Berlin: LITVerlag, 2007.

———. "Radio Reform in the 1980s: RIAS and DT-64 Respond to Private Radio." In *Cold War Cultures: Perspectives on Eastern and Western European Societies*, edited by Annette Vowinckel, Marcus M. Payk, and Thomas Lindenberger. New York and Oxford: Berghahn Books, 2012.

Lawrence, Mark Atwood. *The Vietnam War: A Concise International History*. Oxford and New York: Oxford University Press, 2008.

Läzer, Rüdiger. "'Schön, daß es das noch gibt': Werbetexte für Ostprodukte. Untersuchungen zur Sprache einer ost-west-deutschen Textsorte." In *Von "Buschzulage" und "Ossinachweis,"* edited by Reiher and Läzer.

Lee, Woo-Seung. *Das Fernsehen im geteilten Deutschland (1952–1989): Ideologische Konkurrenz und programmliche Kooperation*. Potsdam: Verlag für Berlin-Brandenburg, 2003.

Leeder, Karen, ed. *Rereading East Germany: The Literature and Film of the GDR*. Cambridge and New York: Cambridge University Press, 2015.

Leffler, Melvyn P., and Odd Arne Westad, eds. *The Cambridge History of the Cold War*. Vol. 2, *Crises and Détente*. Cambridge and New York: Cambridge University Press, 2010.

Lindenberger, Thomas, ed. *Herrschaft und Eigensinn in der Diktatur: Studien zur Gesellschaftsgeschichte der DDR*. Cologne: Böhlau Verlag, 1999.

Lindenberger, Thomas, and Martin Sabrow, eds. *German Zeitgeschichte: Konturen eines Forschungsfeldes*. Göttingen: Wallstein, 2016.

Lindner, Bernd. "Die Generation der Unberatenen." In *Die DDR aus generationengeschichtlicher Perspektive*, edited by Schüle, Ahbe, and Gries.

Loth, Wilfried, and George Soutou, eds. *The Making of Détente: Eastern Europe and Western Europe in the Cold War, 1965–1975*. London: Routledge, 2010.

Lüdtke, Alf. "'Helden der Arbeit'—Mühen beim Arbeiten. Zur missmutigen Loyalität von Industriearbeitern in der DDR." In *Sozialgeschichte der DDR*, edited by Hartmut Kaeble, Jürgen Kocka, and Hartmut Zwahr. Stuttgart: Klett-Cotta, 1994.

Lüdtke, Alf, and Peter Becker, eds. *Akten. Eingaben. Schaufenster. Die DDR und ihre Texte: Erkundungen zu Herrschaft und Alltag*. Berlin: Akademie-Verlag, 1997.

Lys, Franziska, and Michael Dreyer, eds. *Virtual Walls? Political Unification and Cultural Difference in Contemporary Germany*. Rochester, NY: Camden House, 2017.

Maas, Georg, and Hartmut Reszel. "Whatever Happened to . . . : The Decline and Renaissance of Rock in the Former GDR." *Popular Music* 17, no. 3 (October 1998): 267–77.

Maase, Kaspar. *BRAVO Amerika: Erkundungen zur Jugendkultur der Bundesrepublik in den fünfziger Jahren*. Hamburg: Junius Verlag, 1992.

Madarász, Jeannette Z. *Conflict and Stability in East Germany, 1971–1989: A Precarious Stability*. New York: Palgrave Macmillan, 2003.

Maier, Charles. *Dissolution: The Crisis of Communism and the End of East Germany*. Princeton, NJ: Princeton University Press, 1997.

Major, Patrick. *Behind the Berlin Wall: East Germany and the Frontiers of Power*. Oxford and New York: Oxford University Press, 2010.

Malycha, Andreas. "Ungeschminkte Wahrheiten: Honeckers Wirtschafts- und Sozialpolitik—ein zentrales Konfliktfeld im SED-Politbüro. Ein vertrauliches Gespräch von Gerhard Schürer, Chefplaner der DDR, mit der Stasi über die Wirtschaftslage der SED im April 1978." *Vierteljahrshefte für Zeitgeschichte* 59, no. 2 (2011): 283–305.

———. *Die SED in der Ära Honecker: Machtstrukturen, Entscheidungsmechanismen und Konfliktfelder in der Staatspartei 1971 bis 1989*. Oldenburg: De Gruyter, 2014.

Mandell, Richard D. *The Olympics of 1972: A Munich Diary*. Chapel Hill and London: University of North Carolina Press, 1991.

Manz, Günter. *Armut in der "DDR"-Bevölkerung: Lebensstandard und Konsumtionsniveau vor und nach der Wende*. Augsburg: MaroVerlag, 1992.

Matthes, Philip. "David and Goliath: Der Anerkennungslobbyismus der DDR in den USA von 1964 bis 1974." In *Umworbener Klassenfeind*, edited Balbier and Rösch.

Mausbach, Wilfried. "Auschwitz and Vietnam: West German Protest against America's War during the 1960s." In *America, the Vietnam War, and the World*, edited by Daum, Gardner, and Mausbach.

Mazierska, Ewa, ed. *Popular Music in Eastern Europe: Breaking the Cold War Paradigm*. London: Palgrave Macmillan, 2016.

Mazierska, Ewa, and Zsolt Győri, eds. *Popular Music and the Moving Image in Eastern Europe*. New York: Bloomsbury Academic, 2019.

McAdams, A. James. *Judging the Past in Unified Germany*. Cambridge and New York: Cambridge University Press, 2001.

McLellan, Josie. *Love in the Time of Communism: Intimacy and Sexuality in the GDR*. Cambridge and New York: Cambridge University Press, 2011.

Megas, Achilleas. *Soviet Foreign Policy towards East Germany*. London: Springer, 2015.

Menzel, Rebecca. *Jeans in der DDR: Vom tieferen Sinn einer Freizeithose*. Berlin: Ch. Links Verlag, 2004.

Merkel, Ina, ed. *"Wir sind doch nicht die Mecker-Ecke der Nation": Briefe an das DDR Fernsehen*. Cologne: Böhlau Verlag, 1998.

———. *Utopie und Bedürfnis: Die Geschichte der Konsumkultur in der DDR*. Cologne: Böhlau Verlag, 1999.

———. "Alternative Rationalities, Strange Dreams, Absurd Utopias: On Social Advertising and Market Research." In *Socialist Modern*, edited by Pence and Betts.

Merseburger, Peter. *Willy Brandt, 1913–1992: Visionär und Realist*. Munich: Deutsche Verlags-Anstalt, 2006.

Mertens, Lothar, ed. *Soziale Ungleichheit in der DDR: Zu einem tabuisierten Strukturmerkmal der SED-Diktatur*. Berlin: Duncker & Humblot, 2002.

———. "'Was die Partei wusste, aber nicht sagte . . .' Empirische Befunde sozialer Ungleichheit in der DDR-Gesellschaft." In *Soziale Ungleichheit in der DDR*, edited by Mertens.

Meurer, Hans Joachim. *Cinema and National Identity in a Divided Germany, 1979–1989: The Split Screen*. Lewiston, NY: Edwin Mellon Press, 2000.

Meyen, Michael. *Einschalten, Umschalten, Ausschalten? Das Fernsehen im DDR-Alltag*. Leipzig: Leipziger Universitätsverlag, 2003.

———. *"Wir haben freier gelebt": Die DDR im kollektiven Gedächtnis der Deutschen*. Bielefeld: Transcript, 2013.

Meyen, Michael, and Anke Fiedler, eds. *Die Grenze im Kopf: Journalisten in der DDR*. Berlin: Berlin: Panama Verlag, 2010.

Michael, Klaus. "Macht aus dem Staat Gurkensalat: Punk und die Exerzitien der Macht." In *Wir wollen immer artig sein . . .*, edited by Galenza and Havemeister.

Michalski, Jens. *. . . und nächstes Jahr—wie jedes Jahr: Kinogeschichte Kreis Döbeln, 1945–1990. Das Beispiel für das Lichtspielwesen der SBZ und der DDR*. Berlin: topfilm, 2003.

Morgan, Michael Cotey. *The Final Act: The Helsinki Accords and the Transformation of the Cold War*. Princeton and Oxford: Princeton University Press, 2018.

Mueller, Gabrielle. "Re-imagining the Niche: Visual Reconstructions of Private Spaces in the GDR." In *Remembering and Rethinking the GDR*, edited by Saunders and Pinfold.

Mühl-Benninghaus, Wolfgang, ed. *Zwei Mal zur Wende: Fernsehunterhaltung in Deutschland*. Berlin: Avinus-Verlag, 2008.

———. *Unterhaltung als Eigensinn: Eine ostdeutsche Mediengeschichte*. Frankfurt and New York: Campus Verlag, 2012.

Muth, Ingrid. *Die DDR-Aussenpolitik: Inhalte, Strukturen, Mechanismen.* Berlin: Ch. Links Verlag, 2000.
Neubert, Ehrhart. *Geschichte der Opposition in der DDR, 1949–1989.* Bonn: Bundeszentrale für politische Bildung, 2012.
Niedhart, Gottfried. "The Federal Republic's Ostpolitik and the United States: Initiatives and Constraints." In *The United States and the European Alliance since 1945*, edited by Kathleen Burk and Melvyn Stokes. New York and Oxford: Berghahn Books, 1999.
Niemann, Heinz. *Meinungsumfragen in der DDR: Die geheimen Berichte des Instituts für Meinungsforschung an das Politbüro der SED.* Cologne: Bund-Verlag, 1993.
Niven, Bill, and Chloe Paver, eds. *Memorialization in Germany since 1945.* New York: Palgrave Macmillan, 2010.
O'Brien, Mary-Elizabeth. "The Afterlife of the GDR in Post-Wall German Cinema." In *Virtual Walls? Political Unification and Cultural Difference in Contemporary Germany*, edited by Franziska Lys and Michael Dreyer. Rochester, NY: Camden House, 2017.
Oehmig, Richard. *"Besorgt mal Filme!" Der internationale Programmhandel des DDR Fernsehens.* Göttingen: Wallstein Verlag, 2017.
Ohse, Marc-Dietrich. *Jugend nach dem Mauerbau: Anpassung, Protest und Eigensinn (DDR 1961–1974).* Berlin: Ch. Links, 2003.
Ostermann, Christian M. "Die USA und die DDR." In *Die DDR und der Westen*, edited by Pfeil.
Paleczny, Gerhard, et al., eds. *Punk und Rock in der DDR: Musik als Rebellion einer überwachten Generation.* Norderstedt, Germany: Books on Demand GmbH, 2014.
Parks, Jennifer. "Verbal Gymnastics: Sports, Bureaucracy, and the Soviet Union Entrance into the Olympic Games, 1946–1952." In *East Plays West*, edited by Wagg and Andrews.
Patterson, Patrick Hyder. "Risky Business: What Was Really Being Sold in the Department Stores of Socialist Eastern Europe?" In *Communism Unwrapped*, edited by Bren and Neuburger.
Pence, Katherine, and Paul Betts, eds. *Socialist Modern: East German Everyday Culture and Politics.* Ann Arbor: University of Michigan Press, 2008.
Pence, Katherine. "Grounds for Discontent? Coffee from the Black Market to the Kaffeeklatsch in the GDR." In *Communism Unwrapped*, edited by Bren and Neuburger.
Péteri, György, ed. *Imagining the West in Eastern Europe and the Soviet Union.* Pittsburgh: University of Pittsburgh Press, 2010.
Pfau, Sebastian. *Vom Seriellen zur Serie—Wandlungen im DDR-Fernsehen: Die Entwicklung der fiktionalen Serie im DDR-Fernsehen mit dem Schwerpunkt auf Familienserien.* Leipzig: Leipziger Universitätsverlag, 2009.
Pfeil, Ulrich, ed. *Die DDR und der Westen: Transnationale Beziehungen, 1949–1989.* Berlin: Ch. Links Verlag, 2001.

Pfister, Gertrud. "Cold War Diplomats in Tracksuits: Die *Fräuleinwunder* of East German Sport." *European Sports History Review* 5 (2003).
Port, Andrew. *Conflict and Stability in the German Democratic Republic*. Cambridge and New York: Cambridge University Press, 2007.
Preuss, Torsten. "Stasi, Spass und E-Gitarren: Die Geschichte der Berliner Punkband *Namenlos*." In *Wir wollen immer artig sein . . .* , edited by Galenza and Havemeister.
Prommer, Elizabeth. *Kinobesuch im Lebenslauf: Eine historische und medienbiographische Studie*. Konstanz: UVK Medien, 1999.
Ramet, Sabrina Petra, ed. *Rocking the State: Rock Music and Politics in Eastern Europe and Russia*. Boulder: Westview Press, 1994.
Rauhut, Michael. *Beat in der Grauzone: DDR-Rock 1964–1972: Politik und Alltag*. Berlin: BasisDruck, 1993.
——. *Schalmei und Lederjacke: Udo Lindenberg, BAP, Underground. Rock und Politik in den achziger Jahren*. Berlin: Schwarzkopf & Schwarzkopf, 1996.
Rauhut, Michael, and Thomas Kochan, eds. *Bye Bye Lübben City: Bluesfreaks, Tramps und Hippies in der DDR*. Berlin: Schwarzkopf & Schwarzkopf, 2013.
Reiher, Ruth, and Rüdiger Läzer, eds. *Von "Buschzulage" und "Ossinachweis."* Berlin: Aufbau Taschenbuch Verlag, 1996.
Reimann, Kerstin E. *Schreiben nach der Wende—Wende im Schreiben? Literarische Reflexionen nach 1989/90*. Wiesbaden: Verlag Königshausen & Neumann, 2008.
Rennhack, Horst. *BRD-Imperialismus: Komplice der USA-Agressoren in Indochina*. Berlin: Staatsverlag der Deutschen Demokratischen Republik, 1973.
Riordan, James. *Sports, Politics and Communism*. Manchester and New York: Manchester University Press, 1991.
Risch, William Jay, ed. *Youth and Rock in the Soviet Bloc: Youth Cultures, Music, and the State in Russia and Eastern Europe*. Lanham, MD: Lexington Books, 2015.
Ritter, Andreas. *Wandlungen in der Steuerung des DDR-Hochleistungssports in den 1960er und 1970er Jahren*. Potsdam: Universitätsverlag Potsdam, 2003.
Ritter, Gerhard A. *The Price of German Unity: Reunification and the Crisis of the Welfare State*. Oxford and New York: Oxford University Press, 2011.
Ross, Corey. *The East German Dictatorship: Problems and Perspectives in the Interpretation of the GDR*. Oxford and New York: Oxford University Press, 2002.
Roth-Ey, Kristin. *Moscow Prime Time: How the Soviet Union Built the Media Empire That Lost the Cultural Cold War*. Ithaca and London: Cornell University Press, 2011.
Rubin, Eli. *Synthetic Socialism: Plastics and Dictatorship in the German Democratic Republic*. Chapel Hill: North Carolina Press, 2008.
——. "The Trabant: Consumption, Eigen-Sinn, and Movement." *History Workshop Journal* 68, no. 3 (2009): 27–44.

Rukov, Mogens. "Respekt vor der Autorität der Tatsachen: Zur Rezeption der H&S-Filme in Westeuropa." In *Dokument und Kunst: Vietnam bei H&S. Eine Werkstatt-Ein Thema-Elf Jahre-Dreizehn Filme*. Berlin: Akademie der Künste der Deutschen Demokratischen Republik, 1977.

Ryback, Timothy W. *Rock around the Bloc: A History of Rock Music in Eastern Europe and the Soviet Union*. New York and Oxford: Oxford University Press, 1990.

Sabrow, Martin, ed. *Wohin treibt die DDR-Erinnerung: Dokumentation einer Debatte*. Göttingen: Vandenhoeck & Ruprecht, 2007.

———, ed. *Erinnerungsorte der DDR*. Munich: C. H. Beck, 2009.

———. *Zeitgeschichte schreiben: Von der Verständigung über die Vergangenheit in der Gegenwart*. Göttingen: Wallstein, 2014.

Sabrow, Martin, and Peter Ulrich Weiss, eds. *Das 20. Jahrhundert vermessen: Signaturen eines vergangenen Zeitalters*. Göttingen: Wallstein, 2017.

Sarantakes, Nicholas Evan. *Dropping the Torch: Jimmy Carter, the Olympic Boycott, and the Cold War*. Cambridge and New York: Cambridge University Press, 2011.

Sarotte, M. E. *Dealing with the Devil: East Germany, Détente, & Ostpolitik, 1969–1973*. Chapel Hill and London: University of North Carolina Press, 2001.

Saunders, Anna, and Debbie Pinfold, eds. *Remembering and Rethinking the GDR: Multiple Perspectives and Plural Authenticities*. New York: Palgrave Macmillan, 2013.

Schiller, Kay, and Christopher Young. *The 1972 Munich Olympics and the Making of Modern Germany*. Berkeley and Los Angeles: University of California Press, 2010.

Schittly, Dagmar. *Zwischen Regie und Regime: Die Filmpolitik der SED im Spiegel der DEFA Produktionen*. Berlin: Ch. Links, 2002.

Schmidt, Michael. "Fernsehen—aus der Nähe betrachtet." *UTOPIE kreativ*, Sonderheft 2000.

Schneider, Irmela. "Ein Weg zur Alltäglichkeit: Spielfilme im Fernsehprogramm." In *Das Fernsehen und die Künste*, edited by Helmut Schanze und Bernhard Zimmermann. Geschichte des Fernsehens in der Bundesrepublik Deutschland 2. Munich: Fink Verlag, 1994.

Schneider, Irmela, and Christian W. Thomsen, eds. *Lexikon der britischen und amerikanischen Spielfilme in den Fernsehprogrammen der Bundesrepublik Deutschland, 1954–1985*. Berlin: Wissenschaftsverlag Volker Spiess GmbH, 1989.

Schöbel, Heinz. *The Four Dimensions of Avery Brundage*. Leipzig, 1968.

Scholtyseck, Joachim. *Die Aussenpolitik der DDR*. Munich: R. Oldenbourg Verlag, 2003.

Schramm, Lutz. "Sonderstufe mit Konzertberechtigung: Die DT64-Indie-Nische." In *DT64*, edited by Ulrich and Wagner.

Schüle, Annegret, Thomas Ahbe, and Rainer Gries, eds. *Die DDR aus generationengeschichtlicher Perspektive: Eine Inventur*. Leipzig: Leipziger Universitätsverlag, 2006.

Schürer, Gerhard. "Planung und Lenkung der Volkswirtschaft—Ein Zeitzeugenbericht aus dem Zentrum der DDR-Wirtschaftslenkung." In *Die Endzeit der DDR-Wirtschaft*, edited by Kuhrt et al.

Schulze, Ingo. *Unsere schönen neuen Kleider: Gegen die marktkonforme Demokratie—für demokratiekonforme Märkte*. Munich: Carl Hanser Verlag, 2012.

Senn, Alfred E. *Power, Politics, and the Olympic Games: A History of the Power Brokers, Events, and Controversies that Shaped the Games*. Champaign, IL: Human Kinetics, 1999.

Siegelbaum, Lewis H., ed. *The Socialist Car: Automobility in the Eastern Bloc*. Ithaca and London: Cornell University Press, 2011.

Slobodian, Quinn, ed. *Comrades of Color: East Germany in the Cold War*. New York and Oxford: Berghahn Books, 2015.

Stahl, Heiner. "Agit-Pop: Das Jugendstudio DT 64 in den swingenden 60er Jahren." in *Zwischen Pop und Propaganda*, edited by Arnold and Classen.

Starkman, Ruth A., ed. *Transformations of the New Germany*. New York: Palgrave Macmillan, 2006.

Steiner, André. *The Plans That Failed: An Economic History of the GDR*. New York and Oxford: Berghahn Books, 2010.

Steinmetz, Rüdiger. "Heynowski & Scheumann: The GDR's Leading Documentary Team." *Historical Journal of Film, Radio and Television* 24, no. 3 (2004): 365–79.

Steinmetz, Rüdiger, and Reinhold Viehoff, eds. *Deutsches Fernsehen Ost: Eine Programmgeschichte des DDR-Fernsehens*. Berlin: Verlag für Berlin-Brandenburg, 2008.

Stephan, Inge, and Alexandra Tacke, eds. *NachBilder der Wende*. Cologne: Böhlau Verlag, 2008.

Stiehler, Hans-Jörg. "Disappearing Reality: The End of East German Television." *Historical Journal of Film, Radio and Television* 24, no. 3 (2004): 483–89.

Stitziel, Judd. *Fashioning Socialism: Clothing, Politics, and Consumer Culture in East Germany*. Oxford and New York: Berghahn Books, 2005.

Stokes, Ray. "From Schadenfreude to Going-Out-of-Business Sale: East Germany and the Oil Crises of the 1970s." In *The East German Economy, 1945–2010*, edited Berghoff and Balbier.

Štoll, Martin. *Television and Totalitarianism in Czechoslovakia*. New York: Bloomsbury Academic, 2019.

Stott, Rosemary. *Crossing the Wall: The Western Feature Film Import in East Germany*. Oxford and Bern: Peter Lang, 2012.

Stöver, Bernd. "Radio mit kalkuliertem Risiko: Der RIAS als US-Sender für die DDR, 1946–1961." In *Zwischen Pop und Propaganda*, edited by Arnold and Classen.

Sudar, Vlastimir. "Belgrade as New York: The Voluntary Americanization of Serbian Cinema." In *Postcommunist Film*, edited by Kristensen.
Thomas, Nick. *Protest Movements in 1960s West Germany: A Social History of Dissent and Democracy*. Oxford and New York: Berg, 2003.
Thomsen, Christian W., ed. *Cultural Transfer or Electronic Imperialism? The Impact of American Television Programs on European Television*. Heidelberg: Winter Universitätsverlag, 1989.
Thrum, Alexander. "DDR Punker. Gefahr für Bürger und Staat? Analyse einer Jugendkultur, ihres Selbstverständnisses und ihrer Musik." In *Punk und Rock in der DDR*, edited by Paleczny et al.
Todorova, Maria, and Zsuzsa Gille, eds. *Post-Communist Nolstalgia*. New York and Oxford: Berghahn Books, 2010.
Trültzsch, Sascha, and Reinhold Vierhoff, "Undercover: How the East German Political System Presented Itself in Television Series." In *Popular Television in Authoritarian Europe*, edited by Goddard.
Twark, Jill E. *Humor, Satire, and Identity: Eastern German Literature in the 1990s*. Berlin and New York: De Gruyter, 2007.
Ulrich, Andreas, and Jörg Wagner, eds. *DT64: Das Buch zum Jugendradio, 1964–1993*. Leipzig: Thom Verlag, 1993.
Ulrich, Andreas, and Kalle Neumann. "Der Anfang: Andreas Ulrich im Gespräch mit Kalle Neumann, dem ersten Moderator von DT 64." In *DT64*, edited by Ulrich and Wagner.
Ungerleider, Steven. *Faust's Gold: Inside the East German Doping Machine*. New York: St. Martin's Press, 2001.
Van Huong, Nguyen. "Die Politik der DDR gegenüber Vietnam und den Vertragsarbeitern aus Vietnam sowie die Situation der Vietnamesen in Deutschland heute." In *Materialien der Enquete-Kommission "Überwindung der Folgen der SED-Diktatur im Prozess der deutschen Einheit,"* edited by Deutscher Bundestag, vol. 8, 2. Baden-Baden: Nomos Verlagsgesellschaft, 1995.
Veenis, Milena. *Material Fantasies: Expectations of the Western Consumer World among East Germans*. Amsterdam: Amsterdam University Press, 2012.
Ventsel, Aimar. "Estonian Invasion as Western Ersatz-Pop." In *Popular Music in Eastern Europe*, edited by Mazierska.
Viehoff, Reinhold, ed. *"Die Liebenswürdigkeit des Alltags": Die Familienserie "Rentner haben niemals Zeit."* Leipzig: Universitätsverlag Leipzig, 2004.
Vierck, Alke. "Der horchende Blick: Hören und Sehen in Donnersmarcks *Das Leben der Anderen* (2006)." In *NachBilder der Wende*, edited by Stephan and Tracke.
Voigt, Jutta. *Der Geschmack des Ostens: Vom Essen, Trinken und Leben in der DDR*. Berlin: Gustav Keipenheuer Verlag, 2006.
Volmert, Johannes. "Wahlkampf-Rhetorik: Ludger Volmer und Gregor Gysi im 'Nachtduell' des ZDF." In *Von "Buschzulage" und "Ossinachweis,"* edited by Reiher and Läzer.

Volze, Armin. "Zur Devisenverschuldung der DDR—Entstehung, Bewältigung und Folgen." In *Die Endzeit der DDR-Wirtschaft*, edited by Kuhrt et al.
von Dirke, Sabine. "An Analysis of the Development of German Rock Music." *German Politics & Society* 18, no. 3 (Fall 1989): 64–81.
von Richthofen, Esther. *Bringing Culture to the Masses: Control, Compromise and Participation in the GDR*. New York and Oxford: Berghahn Books, 2009.
Vowinckel, Annette, Marcus M. Payk, and Thomas Lindenberger, eds. *Cold War Cultures: Perspectives on Eastern and Western European Societies*. New York and Oxford: Berghahn Books, 2012.
Wagg, Stephen, and David L. Andrews, eds. *East Plays West: Sport and the Cold War*. London and New York: Routledge, 2007.
Ward, Christopher J. "Rockin' Down the Mainline: Rock Music during the Construction of the Baikal-Amur Mainline Railway (BAM), 1974." In *Youth and Rock in the Soviet Bloc*, edited by Risch.
Wentker, Hermann. *Aussenpolitik in engen Grenzen: Die DDR im internationalen System, 1949 1989*. Munich: Oldenburg Verlag, 2007.
Wenzel, Rebecca. "Wittstock vs. Woodstock: Hippies Ost und Hippies West." In *Bye Bye Lübben City*, edited by Rauhut and Kochan.
Wernicke, Günter. *"Solidarität hilft siegen!" Zur Solidaritätsbewegung mit Vietnam in beiden deutschen Staaten: Mitte der 60er bis Anfang der 70er Jahre*. Hefte zur DDR-Geschichte 72. Berlin, 2001.
Wicke, Peter, and Lothar Müller, eds. *Rockmusik und Politik: Analysen, Interviews und Dokumente*. Berlin: Ch. Links Verlag, 1996.
Wiedemann, Dieter. "Wo Bleiben die Kinobesucher? Daten und Hypothesen zum Kinobesuch in der neuen deutschen Republik." In *Medien der Ex-DDR in der Wende*, edited by Peter Hoff and Dieter Wiedemann. Berlin: VISTAS, 1991.
———. "Der DEFA-Jugendfilm und seine empirische Erforschung." In *Zwischen Bluejeans und Blauhemden: Jugendfilm in Ost und West*, edited by Ingelore König, Dieter Wiedemann, and Lothar Wolf. Berlin: Henschel Verlag, 1995.
Wierling, Dorothee. "Amerikabilder in der DDR." In *Umworbener Klassenfeind*, edited by Balbier and Rösch.
———. "Der Duft der Angela Davis: Politische Jugendkultur in der DDR der frühen 1970er Jahre." In *German Zeitgeschichte*, edited by Lindenberger and Sabrow.
Wilke, Manfred. "Ulbricht, East Germany, and the Prague Spring." In *The Prague Spring and the Warsaw Pact Invasion of Czechoslovakia in 1968*, edited by Günter Bischof, Stefan Karner, and Peter Ruggenthaler. Plymouth, UK: Lexington Books, 2010.
Willemsen, Roger. "Ein kleines Winken." In *Grenzübergänge*, edited by Franck.
Winrow, Gareth M. *The Foreign Policy of the GDR in Africa*. Cambridge and New York: Cambridge University Press, 1990.
Wissentz, Katrin. "Unabhängige Kulturszene ab Ende der 1970er Jahre: Die Punkbewegung in der DDR." In *Dropping out of Socialism*, edited by Fürst and McLellan.

Wolff, Franca. *Glasnost erst kurz vor Sendeschluss: Die letzten Jahre des DDR-Fernsehens (1985–1989/90)*. Cologne: Böhlau Verlag, 2002.

Wolle, Stefan. *Die heile Welt der Diktatur: Alltag und Herrschaft in der DDR, 1971–1989*. 3rd ed. Berlin: Ch. Links Verlag, 2009.

Young, Christopher. "Munich 1972: Re-presenting the Nation." In *National Identity and Global Sports Events: Culture, Politics and Spectacle in the Olympics and the Football World Cup*, edited by Alan Tomlinson and Christopher Young. Albany: State University of New York Press, 2006.

Yurchak, Alexei. *Everything Was Forever, Until It Was No More: The Last Soviet Generation*. Princeton and Oxford: Princeton University Press, 2005.

Zahlmann, Stefan, ed. *Wie im Westen, nur anders: Medien in der DDR*. Berlin: Panama Verlag, 2010.

Zatlin, Jonathan. *The Currency of Socialism: Money and Political Culture in East Germany*. Washington, DC: Cambridge University Press, 2007.

Ziółek, Magdalena. "American Smiles on Polish Faces: American Culture in the Discourse of Globalization from the Perspective of the Polish Young Generation." In *Ambivalent Americanizations*, edited by Herrmann et al.

Index

AC/DC, 142, 143
Adameck, Heinz, 102, 105, 116
Alice's Restaurant, 69
All the President's Men, 71, 72
Amphibian Man, 60
Apocalypse Now, 73
Aristocats, 74
"arrangement memory," 212–13

Bardot, Brigitte, 61
Barry Lyndon, 74
Baryshnikov, Mikhail, 70
Basic Treaty (Grundlagenvertrag, 1972), 76
Berlin Republic, 13, 216, 221–22
Berlin Wall, 2, 3, 6, 7, 19, 32, 80, 123, 167, 199, 215–16
   fall of the Berlin Wall (*Mauerfall*), 199–203, 204, 220–21
Beverly Hills Cops, 80
Biermann, Wolf, 70, 75, 164, 200
Black Sabbath, 142
Black Stallion (*Der schwarze Hengst*), 74
Blade Runner, 69
Bollywood, 61
Bonnie and Clyde, 69
Bound for Glory, 70
Brando, Marlon, 68
Brandt, Willy, 25, 200
Brundage, Avery, 34–38. *See also* Olympics

Cabaret, 78
Cabinet cigarettes, 210
Capitol Movie Theater in Leipzig, 58, 64. *See also* East German cinema
Ceaușescu, Nicolae, 111
Chicago, 142
Chinatown, 71

Circus World (*Zirkuswelt*), 68
City, 127, 128–29, 134. *See also* East German youth culture; East German rock music
Cold War competition, 1, 8–9, 19–21, 22–24, 28–29, 39–42, 88–89, 92–94, 103–104, 107, 110, 123, 144–45, 160–61
   cooperation between GDR and FRG, 105
Commercial Coordination (Kommerzielle Koordinierung [KoKo]), 161, 171
Comtourist, 162
consumer culture in East Germany, 2–3, 8–10, 12–13, 89, 150, 160–91, 202–203
   backlash against Western consumer culture, 209–210, 219–20. *See also* Ostalgie
   criticism by East German shoppers, 165, 180–81
   depoliticization of GDR socialist vision, 69–70, 76–77, 79–81, 91, 112–13
"consumer socialism," 1, 4–5, 12–13, 16n6, 94–95, 102–103, 160–63, 164, 168–69, 201
Coppola, Francis Ford, 73
Corecom, 162
Crosby, Stills, Nash & Young, 129

Damm-Wendler, Ursula, 96–97
Daume, Willi, 34–36. *See also* Olympics
Davis, Angela, 45
Delikat, 162–63, 168–71, 172–75, 184–87, 201. *See also* Exquisit
   Delikat-butter, 186–87
   expansion of Delikat stores, 173–75

Democratic Republic of Vietnam (DRV), 22, 23, 30–31
Destry Rides Again (Der grosse Bluff), 67
Deutsche Film-Aktiengesellschaft (DEFA), 54–55, 61–62. See also East German cinema
　DEFA Export (DEFA Aussenhandel), 62, 64, 66, 68–69, 74–75, 78
　DEFA Indianerfilme, 68, 74
Deutschmark, 163, 165, 175–76, 202–203. See also consumer culture in East Germany
　superiority of Deutschmark, 176–77, 202
Diamond, Neil, 142
dictatorship, 2, 39, 200–201. See also Ministry for State Security (Stasi)
　censorship, 62–73, 132–34, 135–38, 143–44
　disempowerment of dictatorship, 1–4, 9–10, 150–51, 169–70, 190–91, 200–202
　limits of dictatorship, 2–3, 4–5, 9, 143–44, 171–72, 190–91. See also economic crises in the GDR
　"second dictatorship," 15n3, 208
"dictatorship memory," 212
Dietl, Jaroslav, 100
Dietrich, Marlene, 67
Diller, Helmut, 62
Dirty Dancing, 80
DT 64, 141, 142, 143–44. See also East German youth radio
Duett: Music for the Cassette Recorder (Duett: Musik für den Rekorder), 142
Dylan, Bob, 135

Eastern European countries and popular cultures, 8–9, 56, 60–61, 75–76, 78–79, 89–90, 91, 100, 111, 124–25, 131–32, 138, 140–41, 162, 170, 200, 218–19. See also Soviet Union
East German cinema, 11, 54–81, 160. See also Capitol Movie Theater in Leipzig; Deutsche Film Aktiengesellschaft (DEFA)
　Central Film Administration (Hauptverwaltung Film), 57–58, 59
　decrease in film audiences, 55–56, 57
　Film Week in United States, 1975, 54–55, 80
　Progress Filmverleih, 62, 64, 66
　State Film Licensing Committee (Staatliche Filmabnahmekommission), 62
East German television, 9, 11–12, 41–42, 76–78, 88–116, 160, 172, 199
　alternative program structure, 106–107, 108, 201
　crisis of GDR television, 91–92, 106–107, 114
　popularity and rise of TV as mainstream medium, 56, 89–90, 95–98, 109
　TV family series, 94–101
　viewer responses, 42, 95–96
East German youth culture, 123–53. See also Institute for Youth Research
　conflicts over jeans and long hair, 129–30, 144
　criminalization of non-conformity, 131–32, 138–40, 152
　decline of GDR rock music, 133–35, 140, 150
　de-territorialized youth culture, 139–40
　East German rock music, 12, 123–40
　jeans and Levi's jeans, 165, 171–72
　punk music and movement, 135–40
East German youth radio, 12, 123–26, 172. See also Radio in the American Sector (RIAS)
　Jugendradio DT 64, 144–49, 201
　listener responses, 143–44
Easy Rider, 69
economic crises in the GDR, 10–11, 73–75, 101–102, 152, 163, 177–78, 190, 200. See also technological deficits of the GDR
　"appeasement through consumption," 172–73, 190
　black market exchanges, 166, 175
　"coffee crisis, 1977," 164, 168
　complaints, petitions, jokes and protests, 165, 178–81, 186–87, 189–90. See also dictatorship: limits of dictatorship
　debt and indebtedness, 5–6, 74–75, 101–102, 150, 161, 171–73, 176, 177–78
Eigen-Sinn, 2, 6, 15n4, 220

Index • 253

Electra, 133
E.T., 80
Ewald, Manfred, 21, 43
The Exorcist, 68
Exquisit, 162–63, 168–71, 172–75, 184–87, 201. *See also* Delikat
  expansion of Exquisit stores, 173–75

Federal Republic of Germany (FRG), 3, 6, 19
  anti-West German propaganda, 23–24, 25–27, 28, 40
  Bundeswehr, 23
Films of Your Choice, 108
Fonda, Jane, 63, 65
For the Movie and TV Friend, 108
Ford, Harrison, 70
Forman, Miloš, 72, 73
Forschungsinstitut für Körperkultur und Sport (FKS), 39–40. *See also* Olympics
Forum-checks, 175
Forum, Inc., 161
Franklin, Aretha, 142
Free German Youth (Freie Deutsche Jugend [FDJ]), 141, 145
Funny Girl, 65–66

generational divide in GDR, 7–8, 17n10, 213–14
  "distanced generation" ("distanzierte Generation"), 7, 214
  "founder generation" ("Aufbaugeneration") or "1929er," 7, 213
  "integrated generation" ("integrierte Generation"), 7, 213
  "unintegrated generation" ("Nicht-Mehr-Eingestiegenen") or "1968er," 7, 214
Genex (Geschenkdienst und Kleinexport GmbH), 167
German Sports Association (Deutscher Turn- und Sportbund [DTSB], 36–37
Godunov, Alexander, 70
Good Bye Lenin!, 217–18
Gorbachev, Mikhail, 75, 132
Göring, Helga, 97, 99
"goulash communism," 8

The Graduate, 69, 127
"guilt-by-association" (Mitschuld), 26
Gulf of Tonkin Resolution, 22
Guthrie, Woody, 70

Hagen, Nina, 135, 143
Hallstein Doctrine, 35
Harkenthal, Wolfgang, 62
Harris, Emmylou, 142
Henniger, Barbara, 216
Herrmann, Joachim, 102, 104
HO (Handelsorganization) stores, 163, 166, 170, 173, 175, 185–88
Hoffman, Dustin, 63, 67
Hoffmann, Hans-Joachim, 58
Hollywood movies, 11, 62–73, 78–79, 21920. *See also* Western films
  dislike of traditional western movies, 67–68
  Hollywood blockbuster movies (Millionenfilme), 11, 56, 60, 78–79, 80–81, 219
  New Hollywood, 63, 67–68, 71–73, 129
Honecker, Erich, 4–6, 21, 33, 43, 55, 89, 105, 116, 160. *See also* "consumer socialism" and economic crises in the GDR
  Honecker era, 10, 58–59, 90–91, 160–63, 200
  "Honecker's Crowning," 163
  "Main Task," 5, 58–59, 190–91, 200
hybrid media culture in GDR, 1, 8–9, 11–14, 98–100, 108–110, 123–24, 183–84, 200. *See also* East German cinema; East German television; East German youth culture; East German youth radio; mediatization

"Imaginary West," 8, 181. *See also* consumer culture in the GDR and Western films
Indiana Jones, 70
inequality in East Germany, 164–65, 168, 171, 181–84, 185–87, 190–91
Institute for Youth Research (Jugendforschungsinstitut Leipzig), 61–62, 126. *See also* East German youth culture

In the Heat of the Night (*In der Hitze der Nacht*), 64–65
International Leipzig Book Fair, 2
Intershops, 12–13, 160–61, 165–70, 175–76, 181–84, 200. *See also* consumer culture in East Germany; economic crises in the GDR
history of Intershops, 166–67
Intertourist, 162

Jackson, Michael, 135
Jacob the Liar (*Jakob der Lügner*), 59
Jaws, 69
Jethro Tull, 127, 142
Jewison, Norman, 64

Karat, 127, 128–29, 136. *See also* East German youth culture: East German rock music
Kazan, Elia, 68
Kirch, Leo, 63
KISS, 143
Klaus-Renft-Combo, 143
Köfer, Herbert, 97, 99
Krahl, Toni, 127
Kunen, James Simon, 65

late socialist era, 7, 9, 13, 163, 177–79. *See also* Honecker, Erich: Honecker era
L'attentat, 136
The Laughing Man: Confessions of a Murderer (*Der lachende Mann: Bekenntnisse eines Mörderers*), 28
The Legend of Paul and Paula (*Die Legende von Paul and Paula*), 59, 127
Lindenberg, Udo, 135, 142
Little Big Man, 67
The Lives of Others, 218

MacLaine, Shirley, 63
Maiak, 141
A Man Called Horse (*Der Mann, den man Pferd nannte*), 74
Marx, Karl, 178
Meckerkultur, 2, 6, 177–81
mediatization, 124–25, 126–27, 150–51. *See also* hybrid media culture in GDR
cable and satellite technology, 104, 116
convergence of media in East and West, 78–81, 89–90, 99–100, 150
Meeting Place Airport (*Treffpunkt Flughafen*), 100–101
Mey, Reinhard, 142
Midnight Cowboy, 69
Ministry for State Security (Ministerium für Staatssicherheit [MfS or Stasi]), 2, 31–32, 129–31, 137–38. *See also* dictatorship
Paragraph 249 of GDR Penal Code, 130
Ministry of Culture (Ministerium für Kultur), 57–58, 59, 75, 88, 102–103, 133–34, 139, 150
Ministry of Trade and Commerce, 180
Missing, 78
Mitic, Goyko, 68
Mittag, Günter, 102, 176
Morning Rock (*Morgenrock*), 146
Museum of Modern Art, 54

Namenlos, 136
Neues Deutschland, 22, 26, 160. *See also* Socialist Unity Party of Germany
New German Wave (Neue Deutsche Welle), 134–35
The New Sorrows of Young W. (*Die neuen Leiden des jungen W.*), 59
New Stories over the Garden Fence (*Neues übern Gartenzaun*), 113
Nicholson, Jack, 63, 72–73
Nowak, Friedel, 94, 95

Olympics, 10, 20–21, 34–44, 88, 200. *See also* Daume, Willi; Schöbel, Heinz
1936 Olympics, 36
1972 Olympics (Munich), 10, 21, 34–37, 40–41
1976 Olympics (Montreal), 10, 43–44
International Olympic Committee (IOC), 34–38. *See also* Brundage, Avery
Omega, 132
On the Waterfront, 68
One Flew Over the Cuckoo's Nest, 71, 72–73
Our Dear Fellow Men (*Die Lieben Mitmenschen*), 94–97, 98. *See also* East German television

Ossi, 13, 204, 207, 215–16
  Jammerossi, 204
  Ossi jokes, 204
Ostalgie. 13, 199, 208–211, 215–18, 220–21. *See also* consumer culture in East Germany
Ostmark (Mark der DDR), 32–33, 163, 168, 175, 189. *See also* economic crises in the GDR
Ostpolitik, 5, 26, 45

Pakula, Alan, 71
Parocktikum, 146–47
Party of Democratic Socialism (Partei des Demokratischen Sozialismus [PDS]), 211, 221
"Peaceful Revolution" (1989), 6, 202
Pehnert, Horst, 57, 63
Pewex, 162
Pilots in Pajamas (*Piloten im Pyjama*), 28
Pink Floyd, 135, 142
Poitier, Sidney, 63, 64
Polanski, Roman, 71
Polish protests and Solidarity movement, 169, 178
post-socialist transition, 13, 203–216, 218–19
  difficulties of economic integration, 205–206, 211–12
  job competition and unemployment, 206–207, 212, 215
  "lost generation," 214
  "victor's justice," 208
Prague Spring, 7, 8, 19, 73
"progress memory," 212
Puhdys, 127–28, 134, 136. *See also* East German youth culture: East German rock music

Queen, 142

Radio Free Europe, 12, 40, 123. *See also* Cold War competition
Radio in the American Sector (RIAS), 12, 123, 145, 147
Radio Liberty, 40. *See also* Cold War competition
Radio Luxembourg, 124

Rain Man, 79
Rambo, 70
Redford, Robert, 63
Retired People are Always Busy (*Rentner haben niemals Zeit*), 97–99, 113. *See also* East German television
Rocky, 70
Rolling Stones, 142, 143
Rondo coffee, 209–210
Rosenlöcher, Thomas, 221
Round (*Rund*), 115

The Sanatorium (*Das Kurheim*), 114
Schalk-Golodkowski, Alexander, 161
Schenk, Frank-Otto, 94, 95
Schöbel, Heinz, 37–38. *See also* Olympics
Schoenfeld, Heinz, 202
Schramm, Lutz, 146–47
Schulze, Ingo, 221
Schwalme, Reiner, 207
Sender Freies Berlin (SFB), 145
Sex Pistols, 142
Socialist German Student Union (Sozialistischer Deutscher Studentenbund [SDS]), 27
Socialist Unity Party of Germany (Sozialistische Einheitspartei Deutschlands [SED]), 1, 3, 4, 6, 12, 19, 22, 55, 102, 114–15, 124, 201–202. *See also* dictatorship; *Neues Deutschland*
  crisis of legitimacy, 6, 19–20, 44–46, 89–90, 96–97
Solidarity Committee of the GDR (Solidaritätskomitee der DDR), 25, 27–29, 30–32, 33. *See also* Vietnam War
Soviet Union, 6, 19–20, 34, 41, 44, 56, 60–61, 75, 78, 89, 131, 140–41, 170, 200, 205. *See also* Eastern European countries and popular cultures
Springsteen, Bruce, 135, 149
Starke, Johannes, 57
Steinbeck, John, 68
Stevens, Cat, 142
Stewart, James, 67
Stockholm Vietnam Conferences, 28, 29–30
The Strawberry Statement (*Blutige Erdbeeren*), 65, 71–72

Streisand, Barbra, 63, 65–66
Studio Heynowski and Scheumann (Studio H&S), 28–29, 49n24

technological deficits of the GDR, 93–94, 101–103, 105–106, 140, 145–46, 150–52, 153, 177, 188–89, 201. *See also* economic crises in the GDR
They Shoot Horses—Don't They? (*Nur Pferden gibt man den Gnadenschuss*), 65
Tom Petty and the Heartbreakers, 135
Tooth for Tooth (*Zahn um Zahn*), 109, 113
Trabant, 173
Train Station Leipzig (*Hier Leipzig Bahnhof*), 114
Trotzidentität, 211, 220
The Turning Point, 70
Tuzex, 162

Ulbricht, Reinhard, 221
Ulbricht, Walter, 169
United Nations, 45
United States, 20–22. *See also* Vietnam War
 anti-American propaganda, 20–22, 23–24, 65
 "the other America," 129
 recognition of GDR, 54
 United States Information Agency (USIA), 20, 24
Uprising of 1953, 3, 169

Valutamark, 75, 86n52, 102, 103, 171, 183

Vietnam War, 5, 10, 19–20, 21–34, 67, 200. *See also* Solidarity Committee of the GDR; United States
 invasions of Laos and Cambodia, 22, 24
 My Lai Massacre, 67
Viva Zapata, 68
Voice of America, 12, 123. *See also* Cold War competition
Voice of the GDR (Stimme der DDR), 141, 150

Wader, Hannes, 142
Watergate, 71, 200
Wayne, John, 67, 68
Wende, 13, 199, 203–205, 213
 "Product-Wende" ("Produkt-Wende"), 209–210
 "*Wende*-winners" and "*Wende*-losers," 214–15
Wendler, Horst Ulrich, 96–97, 98
Wessi, 13, 204, 215–16
 Besserwessi, 204
West German Federal Intelligence Agency (Bundesnachrichtendienst), 178
Western films, 9, 11, 54–84, 160, 199. *See also* Hollywood movies
 popularity of Western films, 59–60, 63, 69, 71–73, 76–78, 108–109, 110–11, 116, 218–19
 Western film revenue, 57, 76
West Side Story, 66–67
Who's Afraid of Virginia Wolff? 69
Wicke, Peter, 126, 148–49
Wonder, Stevie, 142
World Youth Festival (Weltfestspiele, 1973), 45, 66

www.ingramcontent.com/pod-product-compliance
Lightning Source LLC
Chambersburg PA
CBHW071336080526
44587CB00017B/2862